The Practice of

ADAPTIVE LEADERSHIP

TOOLS AND TACTICS

for Changing Your Organization and the World

RONALD HEIFETZ | ALEXANDER GRASHOW | MARTY LINSKY

HARVARD BUSINESS PRESS

BOSTON, MASSACHUSETTS

Printed in the United States of America
13 12 11 10   10 9 8

ISBN 978-1-4221-0576-4

Library of Congress Cataloging information available

The paper used in this publication meets the requirements of the American National
Standard for Permanence of Paper for Publications and Documents in Libraries and
Archives Z39.48-1992.

To our parents, Betsy and Milton Heifetz, Sheri Saltzberg and Mark Grashow, and Ruth and the late Harold Linsky, whose fingerprints, teachings, and values permeate this book and everything we do.

CONTENTS

Preface   xi

Acknowledgments   xv

Part One: Introduction: Purpose and Possibility

1. How to Use This Book   5
    Overview   8
    Adaptive Challenges and Adaptive Capacity   10

2. The Theory Behind the Practice   13
    The Illusion of the Broken System   17
    Distinguishing Technical Problems from Adaptive Challenges   19
    Distinguishing Leadership from Authority   23
    Living in the Disequilibrium   28
    Observe, Interpret, Intervene   32
    Experiment and Take Smart Risks Smartly   36
    Engage Above and Below the Neck   37
    Connect to Purpose   38

3. Before You Begin   41
    Don't Do It Alone   41
    Live Life as a Leadership Laboratory   42
    Resist the Leap to Action   44
    Discover the Joy of Making Hard Choices   45

Part Two: Diagnose the System

4. Diagnose the System   49
    The Elegance and Tenacity of the Status Quo   49
    Discover Structural Implications   54

Surface Cultural Norms and Forces   57

Recognize Default Interpretations and Behavior   63

5.   Diagnose the Adaptive Challenge   69

Determine the Technical and Adaptive Elements   70

Listen to the Song Beneath the Words   76

Four Adaptive Challenge Archetypes   77

6.   Diagnose the Political Landscape   89

Uncover Values Driving Behavior   91

Acknowledge Loyalties   93

Name the Losses at Risk   96

Realize Hidden Alliances   97

7.   Qualities of an Adaptive Organization   101

Name the Elephants in the Room   102

Share Responsibility for the Organization's Future   103

Value Independent Judgment   103

Build Leadership Capacity   104

Institutionalize Reflection and Continuous Learning   105

Part Three: Mobilize the System

8.   Make Interpretations   113

Notice When People Are Moving Toward the Left Side
of the Chart   116

Reframe the Group's Default Interpretations   118

Generate Multiple Interpretations   120

Audition Your Ideas   122

Generate a Diversity of Interpretations   122

9.   Design Effective Interventions   125

Step 1: Get on the Balcony   126

Step 2: Determine the Ripeness of the Issue in the System   126

Step 3: Ask, Who Am I in This Picture?   128

Step 4: Think Hard About Your Framing   128

Step 5: Hold Steady   129

Step 6: Analyze the Factions That Begin to Emerge   130

Step 7: Keep the Work at the Center of People's Attention   130

10. Act Politically   133
     Expand Your Informal Authority   133
     Find Allies   136
     Stay Connected to the Opposition   138
     Manage Authority Figures   142
     Take Responsibility for Casualties   144
     Protect and Engage the Voices of Dissent   145

11. Orchestrate Conflict   149
     Create a Holding Environment   155
     Select Participants   158
     Regulate the Heat   159
     Give the Work Back   161

12. Build an Adaptive Culture   165
     Make Naming Elephants the Norm   166
     Nurture Shared Responsibility for the Organization   168
     Encourage Independent Judgment   169
     Develop Leadership Capacity   170
     Institutionalize Reflection and Continuous Learning   171

Part Four: See Yourself as a System

13. See Yourself as a System   181
     Your Many Identities   182

14. Identify Your Loyalties   187
     Prioritize Your Loyalties   189
     Name Your Unspeakable Loyalties   191

15. Know Your Tuning   195
     Know Your Triggers   200
     Hungers and Carrying Water   201

16. Broaden Your Bandwidth   205
     Discover Your Tolerances   206

17. Understand Your Roles   209
     What Roles Do You Play?   210
     Identify Your Scope of Authority   215

18.   Articulate Your Purposes   221
    Prioritize Your Purposes   225
    The Story You Tell Yourself   228

Part Five: Deploy Yourself

19.   Stay Connected to Your Purposes   233
    Negotiate the Ethics of Leadership and Purpose   233
    Keep Purposes Alive   236
    Negotiate Your Purposes   239
    Integrate Your Ambitions and Aspirations   242
    Avoid Common Traps   244

20.   Engage Courageously   247
    Get Past the Past   247
    Lean Into Your Incompetence   252
    Fall in Love with Tough Decisions   255
    Get Permission to Fail   258
    Build the Stomach for the Journey   260

21.   Inspire People   263
    Be with Your Audience   264
    Speak from the Heart   269

22.   Run Experiments   277
    Take More Risks   280
    Exceed Your Authority   282
    Turn Up the Heat   284
    Name Your Piece of the Mess   286
    Display Your Own Incompetence   287

23.   Thrive   289
    Grow Your Personal Support Network   289
    Create a Personal Holding Environment   292
    Renew Yourself   295

Notes   299
Glossary   303
Index   309
About the Authors   325

On a beautiful spring evening in 2006, the three of us (two Boston Red Sox fans and a New York Mets fan) were watching a Red Sox baseball game on television at Ron's house. The Red Sox were well ahead. The conversation began to drift to reflecting on the insights we had gleaned from the clients and students with whom we had worked over the past quarter century as they tried to apply the frameworks we have offered to their own challenges of leadership on important and tough issues. This book grew out of our conversation that evening.

Our previously published work had been focused on developing the conceptual framework and practical basis for adaptive leadership, but as we talked together that night, we realized that we knew a lot more about the operational nitty-gritty, how to actually do adaptive leadership, than we had written before. The efforts of people with whom we had worked across all three sectors and all over the globe had created a real-time virtual learning laboratory for translating leadership into practical tools and techniques for leading adaptive change. By the end of that evening, we understood that together we had enough of a track record of real experience that we had the opportunity, perhaps even the responsibility, to share these insights and emerging best practices with a wider audience. The tools and tactics for leading adaptive change should be treated, we believe, in the same spirit as open source technology, made broadly available, so that people who lead adaptive change can learn from each other and improve their skills, and all of us improve our insights into practice.

During that evening, we talked about several people with whom we had recently worked. Gail went well beyond her job description to help people in her firm deal with persistently troubling external and internal pressures. Drew deliberately gave up a role he enjoyed enormously and performed with unique competence, defining his professional identity, and stepped into discomfort and incompetence by taking on new responsibilities to enable his firm to reach higher aspirations. Ed walked away from a secure career he loved with its promising personal trajectory to build an institution committed to helping the people of his state tackle the big questions, knowing he was going to have to raise the heat carefully in the system to have an impact. Clive and Brian took significant risks within each of their governments to develop the leadership capacity of senior officials to operate more creatively, courageously, and wisely in mobilizing collaboration and innovation across sectors in their countries. And Debbie believed so deeply in the need for leadership in her religious community that she put her own job on the line to change the way her organization thought about the qualities needed in its senior people.

Each of them faced what we call an adaptive challenge for themselves and for the communities in which they took action. In order to exercise leadership on that challenge, they had to go beyond what people expected of them, risk testing some relationships, and move themselves and their organizations into unfamiliar territory. They had to be coolly realistic and skilled at diagnosing their own resources and constraints, and make some necessary adaptations in their own preferred behaviors. And they needed to do the same coolheaded diagnosis for the situation: understand the underlying value conflicts embedded in the strategy of the organization or community, what and whose interests benefited from the status quo, and the political dynamics that both kept their organizations in their current equilibrium and offered some potential for catalyzing change. They each learned in the midst of action, made some mistakes and midcourse corrections, and stayed the course.

Their journeys are close-to-home sagas of leading adaptive change, with all the dangers, ambiguity, setbacks, and improvisations that leadership journeys involve. As of this writing, none of their journeys are over. The work of leadership continues.

In this book, we have tried to capture their experiences and those of many others (usually appropriately disguised) with whom we have worked in the classroom or the field, at the tactical level, teasing out lessons and then creating straightforward, practical, accessible resources and tools in the hope that doing so will be useful to you as you take on the issues you consider most important. Everything in this book comes from the field and has been tested there by our clients and students.

They have been out on the edge, trying techniques and honing their skills, and we are no more than the vehicles for transmitting their insights to you.

In a very real sense, this field book is a tribute them, our clients and students, who have taught us more than they can imagine.

| ACKNOWLEDGMENTS |

This book could not have been written without the generosity of our clients, program participants, students, and friends in sharing their challenges, stories, and learning with us over the past quarter century, particularly during the years after the publication of *Leadership Without Easy Answers* and *Leadership on the Line* and the formation of Cambridge Leadership Associates (CLA). This book is theirs as much as it is ours.

As we have noted in the text, this book has many intellectual and practitioner progenitors. These ideas and tools have lineage that goes back centuries, as well as a distinctly twentieth-century context. Starting more than thirty years ago, Riley Sinder, collaborating with Ron Heifetz, created much of the intellectual bedrock on which adaptive leadership rests. Sousan Abadian deepened this work and enriched its articulation in countless ways for over two decades as colleague, practitioner, and Ron's former wife.

We thank many of our current colleagues at CLA, including Jeff Lawrence, Karen Lehman, Eric Martin, JoAnn Martin, Hugh O'Doherty, Lee Teitel, and Kristin von Donop, for their wisdom and input, for their significant additions to the ideas and tools in this book, for their willingness to road test so much of this material, and for their forbearance while we took much more time away from CLA core activities than we had planned in order to see this field book through to publication. And we recognize the contributions of Liz Nill, our founding managing director, who believed in this project from the outset and without whom CLA would likely not exist.

Ron and Marty appreciate the colleagueship of our friends at the Harvard Kennedy School, the succession of deans under whom we have worked, and particularly our faculty colleagues in the management, leadership, and politics areas of the school, and the team at Executive Education under Pete Zimmerman and now Chris Letts, all of whom have supported our work in their own ways. Alexander is grateful to the friends, family, and colleagues from across the globe who have shaped his experience of the world and shared many long, animated meals. Gil Skillman, Peggy Dulany, the Blue Unit, Imraan Jamal, and Rachel Grashow, in particular, expanded Alexander's ideas and experience and encouraged his dreams.

Our families and loved ones put up with last-minute trips out of town and innumerable phone-call interruptions of our time with them so that we could work together and make this book a real collaboration instead of parallel play. David Abadian Heifetz improved the quality of this book by offering the wonderful strength of his encouragement and editorial suggestions. Ariana Shirin Abadian-Heifetz helped test these ideas in the field by giving articulate feedback and ongoing perspective as only she can. Kathryn Ann Herring sustained, embraced, and provided a wonderful ear for words. Yasuko Tamaki, Alexander's wife, was extraordinarily generous during this process: bringing her strength and grace to taking care of one baby and having another during the writing of this book. Marty's wife, Lynn Staley, who has somehow adapted to his stubbornness, irrationality, and self-absorption for the past thirty years, was once again a tower of tolerance and a superb informal design consultant, as this project's deadline kept slipping. Thank you.

We thank Britt Ayler, who helped us on the glossary, and Lauren Keller Johnson, who provided much needed clarity as an outside editor. Jeff Kehoe, our editor at Harvard Business Press, provided his usual skilled performance, artfully employing both the carrot and the stick to bring this project from a one-line idea to a finished project.

Finally, we acknowledge each other, for hanging together trying to write a book with three authors and one voice, testing our relationship and our commitment to coming through this journey more closely bonded, knowing that such collaborations have sometimes ended professional and personal relationships rather than strengthened them.

PART ONE

INTRODUCTION

Purpose and Possibility

I F YOU WANT TO HELP your organization, your community, and your society thrive in a changing world, this book is for you.

If you want to mobilize greater progress on the issues most important to you, this book is for you.

If you want to strengthen your practice of leadership no matter where you sit in your society or organization, this book is for you.

If you want to help others strengthen their capacity for change, as a trainer, coach, consultant, facilitator, or friend, this book is for you.

This book is about possibility. Not daydreaming, wishful-thinking possibility, but rather a roll-up-your-sleeves, optimistic, realistic, courage-generating, and make-significant-progress kind of possibility. Leadership for change demands inspiration *and* perspiration. We present tools and tactics to lead and stay alive, to build up a sweat by inspiring others, to mobilize people to tackle tough problems while reaching high. This book comes out of our experience in working with people in organizations around the world, across sectors, cultures, and countries in positions high and low, helping them tackle their most pressing challenges. We have had the blessing and have taken no greater delight than helping people get more traction on moving their organizations, communities, and societies forward.

These are extraordinary times. The turn of the millennium brought the pressing realization that every human being, as a member of a globalizing set of nations, cultures, and economies, must find better ways to compete and collaborate. To build a sustainable world in an era of profound economic and environmental interdependence, each person, each country, each organization is challenged to sift through the wisdom and know-how of their heritage, to take the best from their histories, leave behind lessons that no longer serve them, and innovate, not for change's sake, but for the sake of conserving and preserving the values and competence they find most essential and precious.

This is a tall order, requiring people to look backward and forward at the same time. Looking backward, the challenge is to discover new ways to more quickly put to rest the traumas of the past in order to build a post-empire, post-Crusades, and post-colonial world. Looking forward, human beings have the ability to realize ancient dreams of civility, curiosity, and care as we tackle the pressing issues that surround us. These times call for new ways of doing the business of our daily lives as we take on these purposes with new, more adaptive solutions.

Between the time we wrote the bulk of our last book, *Leadership on the Line,* and its publication date, we experienced 9/11. Between the time we wrote the bulk of this book and its publication date, we saw Barack Obama elected President of the United States and the world economy go into crisis. The challenges posed by 9/11 and the international economic meltdown are in part the unresolved dilemmas of old ways and in part they are new. They are not amenable to authoritative expertise, although people might hope that if the right subject matter expert could only be found, these problems would be solved. These are what we call adaptive challenges, gaps generated by bold aspirations amid challenging realities. For these the world needs to build new ways of being and responding beyond the current repertoires of available know-how. What is needed from a leadership perspective are new forms of improvisational expertise, a kind of process expertise that knows prudently how to experiment with never-been-tried-before relationships, means of communication, and ways of interacting that will help people develop solutions that build upon and surpass the wisdom of today's experts. That is the aim of this book: to provide an understanding of the processes and practices of leadership so that you can address the adaptive pressures that challenge anyone's current individual and collective competence.

The answers cannot come only from on high. The world needs distributed leadership because the solutions to our collective challenges must come from many places, with people developing micro-adaptations to all the different micro-environments of families, neighborhoods and organizations around the globe.

Adaptive leadership is an approach to making progress on the most important challenges you face in your piece and part of the world, presumably in your professional life but perhaps in your personal life as well. Our concepts, tools, and tactics aim to help you mobilize people toward some collective purpose, a purpose that exists beyond your own individual ambition.

For some people, the hardest part of this work might be finding the courage to identify and claim what is most important to you, those goals and challenges for which it is worth taking on the pains and risks of leadership. Our work begins with the assumption that there is no reason to exercise leadership, to have a courageous conversation with a boss or a spouse, for example, or to take a risk on a new idea, unless you care about something deeply. What outcome would make the effort and the risk worthwhile? What purpose would sustain you to stay in the game when it gets rough? For other people, figuring out their purposes is not as daunting as grasping the practices required for making progress, stepping out into the unknown skillfully. We try to address both parts in this field book: purpose and skill.

Our goal is to provide practical steps you can take to act further on behalf of your deepest values, to maximize the chances of success and minimize the chances of your being taken out of action. We hope to enrich your personal and professional capacity to accomplish what you care most deeply about.

CHAPTER 1

How to Use This Book

THE PRACTICE OF *Adaptive Leadership* is a field book for two reasons: first, we have written it *from* the field, drawing on our experiences with thousands of people who are trying to create something better from the current reality.

Second, we have designed it *for* the field, to be of day-to-day utility in your own leadership efforts. As we wrote this book, we imagined you coming home after a particularly frustrating day at work trying to move an important initiative forward. We envisioned you using one of the balcony reflections to understand better why events did not go as well as you had hoped, or using one of the leadership exercises to develop your next plan of action.

Perhaps you have picked up this book to figure out how to organize a six-month program to reverse a problem of high turnover among your company's most talented employees. Or maybe you are using it to prepare for a particularly important meeting with key constituencies that resist wrestling with the perspective you offer. Perhaps you will copy a resonant section of the book or a particularly useful graphic for your team to create a shared understanding of a challenge you face together. You might even find it helpful for making progress on a tough problem at home.

We have designed this book with that flexibility in mind: you can read it from start to finish, or browse to find the concepts and tools most useful for understanding and dealing with a particular adaptive challenge you are facing. The book has a beginning, middle, and end, with a story line and an organizing frame. But we have also constructed it with self-contained elements and a detailed index so you can go directly to the ideas and activities that speak to the specific challenges before you.

To these ends, the book is organized into five parts: an introductory part and four content parts, displayed in the matrix in figure 1-1, which captures the four essential practices of adaptive leadership. While the four practice parts of the book come after one another in linear sequence, the matrix is meant to highlight that you need not read or use the book that way. How did we get to this matrix? We find it's often best to start with what's salient to you.

The practice of leadership, like the practice of medicine, involves two core processes: diagnosis first and then action. And those two processes unfold in two dimensions: toward the organizational or social system you are operating in and toward yourself. That is, you diagnose what is happening in your organization or community and take action to address the problems you have identified. But to lead effectively, you also have to examine and take action toward yourself in the context of the challenge. In the midst of action, you have to be able to reflect on your own attitudes and behavior to better calibrate your interventions into the complex dynamics of organizations and communities. You need perspective on yourself as well as on the systemic context in which you operate.

The *process* of diagnosis and action begins with data collection and problem identification (the *what*), moves through an interpretive stage (the *why*) and on to potential approaches to action as a series of interventions into the organization, community, or society (the *what next*).

FIGURE 1-1

Two-by-two diagnosis matrix

(Part II) Diagnosis/system	(Part III) Action/system
(Part IV) Diagnosis/self	(Part V) Action/self

Typically, the problem-solving process is iterative, moving back and forth among data collection, interpretation, and action.

There is a logic to the sequencing of the four parts, even though we have written them so that you can dive into any of the four, depending on where you locate yourself in your leadership challenge. We ordered the four sections in figure 1-1 to counteract two tendencies that often stymie progress.

First, in most organizations, people feel pressure to solve problems quickly, to move to action. So they minimize the time spent in diagnosis, collecting data, exploring multiple possible interpretations of the situation and alternative potential interventions. To counteract this drive toward a quick-fix response based on a too swift assessment of the situation, we spend a lot of time in this book on diagnosis ("What is *really* going on here?") for both the system-level and the self-level sections of the adaptive leadership process.

The single most important skill and most undervalued capacity for exercising adaptive leadership is diagnosis. In most companies and societies, those who have moved up the hierarchy into senior positions of authority are naturally socialized and trained to be good at taking action and decisively solving problems. There is no incentive to wade knee-deep into the murky waters of diagnosis, especially if some of the deeper diagnostic possibilities will be unsettling to people who look to you for clarity and certainty. Moreover, when you are caught up in the action, it is hard to do the diagnostic work of seeing the larger patterns in the organization or community. People who look to you for solutions have a stake in keeping you focused on what is right in front of your eyes: the phone calls and e-mails to be answered, the deadlines to be met, the tasks to be completed.

To diagnose a system or yourself while in the midst of action requires the ability to achieve some distance from those on-the-ground events. We use the metaphor of "getting on the balcony" above the "dance floor" to depict what it means to gain the distanced perspective you need to see what is really happening. If you stay moving on the dance floor, all you will see will be the people dancing with you and around you. Swept up in the music, it may be a great party! But when you get on the balcony, you may see a very different picture. From that vantage point, you might notice that the band is playing so loudly that everyone is dancing on the far side of the room, that when the music changes from fast to slow (or back again), different groups of people decide to dance, and that many people hang back near the exit doors and do not dance, whatever the music. Not such a great party after all. If someone asked you later to describe the dance, you would paint a very different picture if you had seen it from the balcony rather than only from the dance floor.

When you move back and forth between balcony and dance floor, you can continually assess what is happening in your organization and take corrective midcourse action. If you perfect this skill, you might even be able to do both simultaneously: keeping one eye on the events happening immediately around you and the other eye on the larger patterns and dynamics.

Second, too often in organizational life, people begin analyzing problems by personalizing them ("If only Joe was a leader . . .") or attributing the situation to interpersonal conflict ("Sally and Bill don't collaborate very well because their work styles are so at odds"). This tendency often obscures a deeper, more systemic (and perhaps more threatening) understanding of the situation. For example, "Sally and Bill represent conflicting perspectives on the tough strategic trade-offs that need to be made in our harsh economic climate, and each is protecting the functions and jobs of their own people. The conflict is structural, not personal, even if it's taken on a personal tone." To counteract the personalization of problems, start with diagnosing and acting on the system ("moving outside in") and then do the same for the self ("moving inside out").

Nevertheless, in our view, systemic and personal realities always play out simultaneously. Thus adaptive leadership is an iterative activity, an ongoing engagement between you and groups of people. But to strengthen your ability to practice this kind of leadership, you have to start somewhere. The good news is that you can do so at any point in the process: diagnosis of the system or yourself, or action on the system or yourself.

Overview

In this book, you will find ideas, resources, practices, and examples meant to help you lead adaptive work in whatever context you work. In each chapter, you will find framing ideas and illustrative stories followed by reflections, which we have called "On the Balcony," and exercises, which we have called "On the Practice Field." The On the Balcony reflections are designed to provide you with a focused and structured way to think about the ideas and stories you have just read in light of your own experience. And the On the Practice Field exercises are designed as low-risk experiments you might run as a way to try out some of those ideas in your leadership practice. You can do the reflections alone. The exercises involve engaging with others.

The *ideas* build directly on two previous books in which we developed the adaptive leadership framework: *Leadership Without Easy Answers* and *Leadership on the Line*.[1] You do not need to have read them to get value from *The Practice of Adaptive Leadership*. But it would help you to have some familiarity with the overall framework. To give you a quick review if you are familiar with these ideas, or to provide a concise introduction if you are not, we have provided a chapter called "The Theory Behind the Practice" that distills some basic concepts we think you will find most useful in your work. In the rest of this book, the theory fades into the background in favor of practical application.

The *resources* in this book—all the tools, lists, diagrams, reflections, exercises, and charts—were developed primarily for our engagements with client organizations, big and small, on every continent (except Antarctica), across public, private, and nonprofit sectors. We designed these resources to help you make significant progress on real challenges and opportunities. Each has been widely road tested. We hope they constitute a useful smorgasbord from which to choose as you tackle the issues that move you or keep you awake at night.

The book's resources are also designed to be used across teams and organizations. *Shared language* is important in leading adaptive change. When people begin to use the same words with the same meaning, they communicate more effectively, minimize misunderstandings, and gain the sense of being on the same page, even while grappling with significant differences on the issues. The language we have developed for adaptive leadership seems to fuel productive change much more powerfully than the languages that commonly swirl throughout organizations. That does not mean that our language is perfect; just that after more than twenty-five years of using it, we know it generates new and successful options for both diagnosis and action. To help you utilize this language, we have included a glossary.

The *practices* provided in this book are concrete steps you can take to move a change initiative forward. However, they are best understood as vehicles for disciplined experiments. We think of adaptive leadership as an art, not a science, an art that requires an experimental mindset. Each practice presented in this book has been successful alone or in combination with others, but none is foolproof. Each depends to some degree on the situation in which you use it. We include them all here because so much of adaptive leadership work is iterative: you try something, see how it goes, learn from what happened, and then try something else. You tailor your interventions to the individuals involved and to the unique (and shifting) characteristics of the situation facing you.

The *examples* we offer are drawn from the stories of people like you, individuals in organizations, communities, and societies who face difficult challenges and strive to create positive, enduring change. These stories come from three sources: our consulting and teaching experience; our own personal and professional challenges; and material in other books, case studies, and popular culture where our usage is derivative but seems to us nevertheless to illuminate a particular aspect of leadership practice.

Adaptive Challenges and Adaptive Capacity

In our work, people often come to us for assistance with a specific adaptive challenge. For example, a young but rapidly growing design and advertising business geared to the entertainment industry was stuck because the founder/CEO and the senior management team were colluding to keep the founder tied down in day-to-day operations so that he was unable to spend his time focusing on the strategic issues involved in exploding growth. They enjoyed their dependence on him, and he enjoyed continuing to do what he knew how to do well. The CEO came to us because he saw that the way he and his team were currently dealing with each other was unsustainable as the business grew. They faced adaptive challenges in building more widespread operating capacity, reducing the team's dependence, and developing the CEO's own leadership ability to take the organization to scale.

Sometimes people come to us when they see big changes on the horizon in the external environment that will catch up with them soon, and they worry that the organization does not have the wherewithal to adapt and thrive in those new realities. So we start there with a larger frame for tackling the situation: building adaptive capacity. As an example, we were engaged by a recently globalized financial services firm coming off of highly profitable years where most people were quite self-satisfied. But several senior executives realized that not too far down the road the firm's future growth potential would be at risk by a combination of factors: more nimble competitors in new markets; awkward postmerger conflicts between the parent and a large, newly acquired organization; the difficulty of creating shared objectives within an organization spread in small pockets across the face of the globe; and a people pipeline not robust enough to produce the next generation of corporate leadership because it had never needed to be. They understood that tackling any one of those problems alone would avoid the deeper, broader issue, namely, that the organization itself had to develop the capacity to adapt as a way of life to changing circumstances, had to learn how to live in a less predictable, more ambiguous competitive environment. Not surprisingly, in the process of helping them build the adaptive capacity to face an ongoing stream of adaptive challenges over time, we had to work with them on most of the discrete and immediate challenges they faced, too.

The resources in these pages are intended to be equally applicable whether you are starting with a singular vexing adaptive challenge in your organization or trying to create a more adaptive culture in the organization overall. The two situations are obviously intimately connected. Successfully moving through a particular adaptive challenge will enhance the capacity of the organization to deal with adaptive change more broadly. And addressing the deep cultural value-laden constraints in an organization's capacity to adapt and thrive over time will make it easier to identify and address the challenges currently on the table.

| CHAPTER 2 |

The Theory Behind the Practice

SINCE 1994, ADAPTIVE leadership has been advanced and explored in a series of other books in addition to *Leadership Without Easy Answers* and *Leadership on the Line*.[1] The burgeoning literature in this emerging field includes the work of our colleagues Sharon Daloz Parks, in *Leadership Can Be Taught*, and Dean Williams, in *Real Leadership*.[2] Other books have applied the adaptive leadership framework to the challenges in specific professional contexts. These include Richard Foster and Sarah Kaplan's *Creative Destruction* and Donald L. Laurie's *The Real Work of Leaders* on applications to big businesses; Gary De Carolis's *A View from the Balcony* on systems of care; Stacie Goffin and Valora Washington's *Ready or Not* on early childhood education; Shifra Bronznick, Didi Goldenhar, and Marty Linsky's *Leveling the Playing Field* on women in Jewish organizational life; and Kevin Ford's *Transforming Church: Bringing Out the Good to Get to Great* on the challenges facing American churches.[3]

This work grows from efforts to understand in practical ways the relationship among leadership, adaptation, systems, and change, but also has deep roots in scientific efforts to explain the evolution of human life, and before us, the evolution of all life going back to the beginning of the earth.

For nearly 4 million years, our early ancestors lived in small bands that foraged for food. They developed ever-increasing sophistication in the design of tools and strategies for hunting and movement; and their physical capacity grew as they developed ways, through evolutionary change, to increase their range. Drawing on what anthropologists and psychologists have identified as our capacity to internalize the wisdom of elders, the first humans went on to form cultures with self-sustaining norms that required minimal reinforcement by authorities. Cultural norms gave human beings remarkable adaptability and scalability when, quite recently, about twelve thousand years ago, people learned to domesticate plants and animals, and their new ability to store food allowed and required sustained settlements. Large numbers of people living together brought new needs for governing large organizations and communities.

Our early ancestors' process of adaptation to new possibilities and challenges has continued over the course of written history with the growth and variation in scope, structure, governance, strategy, and coordination of political and commercial enterprise. So has the evolution in understanding the practice of managing those processes, including in our lifetimes what we call adaptive leadership.

Adaptive leadership is the practice of mobilizing people to tackle tough challenges and thrive. The concept of *thriving* is drawn from evolutionary biology, in which a successful adaptation has three characteristics: (1) it preserves the DNA essential for the species' continued survival; (2) it discards (reregulates or rearranges) the DNA that no longer serves the species' current needs; and (3) it creates DNA arrangements that give the species' the ability to flourish in new ways and in more challenging environments. Successful adaptations enable a living system to take the best from its history into the future.

What does this suggest as an analogy for adaptive leadership?

- *Adaptive leadership is specifically about change that enables the capacity to thrive.* New environments and new dreams demand new strategies and abilities, as well as the leadership to mobilize them. As in evolution, these new combinations and variations help organizations thrive under challenging circumstances rather than perish, regress, or contract. Leadership, then, must wrestle with normative questions of value, purpose, and process. What does *thriving* mean for organizations operating in any particular context?

In biology, thriving means propagating. But in business, for example, signs of thriving include increases in short- and long-term shareholder value, exceptional customer service, high workforce morale, and positive social and environmental impact. Thus adaptive success in an organizational sense requires leadership that can orchestrate multiple stakeholder priorities to define thriving and then realize it.

- *Successful adaptive changes build on the past rather than jettison it.* In biological adaptations, though DNA changes may radically expand the species' capacity to thrive, the actual *amount* of DNA that changes is minuscule. More than 98 percent of our current DNA is the same as that of a chimpanzee: it took less than a 2 percent change of our evolutionary predecessors' genetic blueprint to give humans extraordinary range and ability. A challenge for adaptive leadership, then, is to engage people in distinguishing what is essential to preserve from their organization's heritage from what is expendable. Successful adaptations are thus both conservative *and* progressive. They make the best possible use of previous wisdom and know-how. The most effective leadership anchors change in the values, competencies, and strategic orientations that should endure in the organization.

- *Organizational adaptation occurs through experimentation.* In biology, sexual reproduction is an experiment: it rapidly produces variations—along with high failure rates. As many as one-third of all pregnancies spontaneously miscarry, usually within the first weeks of conception, because the embryo's genetic variation is too radical to support life. In organizations, the process appears similar. Global pharmaceutical giants must be willing to lose money in failures to find the next profitable medicine. Those seeking to lead adaptive change need an experimental mind-set. They must learn to improvise as they go, buying time and resources along the way for the next set of experiments.

- *Adaptation relies on diversity.* In evolutionary biology, nature acts as a fund manager, diversifying risk. Each conception is a variant, a new experiment, producing an organism with capacities somewhat different from the rest of the population.

By diversifying the gene pool, nature markedly increases the odds that *some* members of the species will have the ability to survive in a changing ecosystem. In contrast, cloning, the original mode of reproduction, is extraordinarily efficient in generating high rates of propagation, but the degrees of variation are far less than for those in sexual reproduction. Cloning, therefore, is far less likely to generate innovations for finding and thriving in new environments. The secret of evolution is variation, which in organizational terms could be called distributed or collective intelligence. Likewise, adaptive leadership on economic policy would want to diversify an economy so that people are less dependent on one company or industry for sustenance. For an organization, adaptive leadership would build a culture that values diverse views and relies less on central planning and the genius of the few at the top, where the odds of adaptive success go down. This is especially true for global businesses operating in many local microenvironments.

- *New adaptations significantly displace, reregulate, and rearrange some old DNA.* By analogy, leadership on adaptive challenges generates loss. Learning is often painful. One person's innovation can cause another person to feel incompetent, betrayed, or irrelevant. Not many people like to be "rearranged." Leadership therefore requires the diagnostic ability to recognize those losses and the predictable defensive patterns of response that operate at the individual and systemic level. It also requires knowing how to counteract these patterns.

- *Adaptation takes time.* Most biological adaptations that greatly enhance a species' capacity to thrive unfold over thousands, even millions, of years. Progress is radical over time yet incremental in time. It seems to work this way: a variant in the current population has the adaptive capacity in its time to venture a bit beyond the normal ecological niche for its kind, stressing itself near the margins of the range that it and its offspring can tolerate. For example, an unusual human being moves to colder or higher terrain and finds it can live there. By doing so, it "invites" the environment to place selective pressure over the next generations, favoring variants among its offspring that are stronger in that new environment. In that way, over time, new adaptive capacity consolidates; the progeny are no longer operating at the margins of their capacity, but in the midrange. Among their adaptations, the distribution of insulating fat and warming capillaries has changed. The process of evolution continues as some of their off-spring venture forth. Although organizational and political adaptations seem lightning fast by comparison, they also take time to consolidate into new sets of norms and processes. Adaptive leadership thus requires persistence. Significant change is the product of incremental experiments that build up over time. And cultures change slowly. Those who practice this form of leadership need to stay in the game, even while taking the heat along the way.

Mobilizing people to meet their immediate adaptive challenges lies at the heart of leadership in the short term. Over time, these and other culture-shaping efforts build an organization's adaptive capacity, fostering processes that will generate new norms that enable the organization to meet the ongoing stream of adaptive challenges posed by a world ever ready to offer new realities, opportunities, and pressures.

The Illusion of the Broken System

There is a myth that drives many change initiatives into the ground: that the organization needs to change because it is broken. The reality is that any social system (including an organization or a country or a family) is the way it is because the people in that system (at least those individuals and factions with the most leverage) want it that way. In that sense, on the whole, on balance, the system is working fine, even though it may appear to be "dysfunctional" in some respects to some members and outside observers, and even though it faces danger just over the horizon. As our colleague Jeff Lawrence poignantly says, "There is no such thing as a dysfunctional organization, because every organization is perfectly aligned to achieve the results it currently gets."

No one who tries to name or address the dysfunction in an organization will be popular. Enough important people like the situation exactly as it is, whatever they may say about it, or it would not be the way it is.

Suppose you take it upon yourself to regularly point out the gap between the company's stated value of transparency and the reality that most people in the organization tightly control the flow of information. You are not likely to be rewarded or greeted with applause for identifying this disconnect, particularly by those who benefit from controlling information. Clearly, the system as a whole has decided to live with the gap between the espoused value and the current reality, the value-in-practice. Closing that gap would be more painful to the dominant coalition than living with it.

The importance of this idea lies in the impact it has on the techniques for trying to address the problem. Embarrassing or not, the organization prefers the current situation to trying something new where the consequences are unpredictable and likely to involve losses for key parties. Taking that into account will lead to different strategic options for closing the gap. When you realize that what you see as dysfunctional works for others in the system, you begin focusing on how to mobilize and sustain people through the period of risk that often comes with adaptive change, rather trying to convince them of the rightness of your cause.

Here is an example. We have worked with a large U.S. not-for-profit organization struggling with high turnover in its workforce. Talented young people are coming to work there, staying a few years, and then leaving for a job in a similar field. Nearly everyone in the organization pays lip service to the idea that, owing to high turnover, the talent pipeline is too narrow to ensure that the organization will have enough strong, qualified, experienced senior managers in the future. Panel discussions on retention have abounded. Task forces on retention have proliferated. New incentive programs have emerged. But nothing much has changed. Why? Middle and senior managers do not want talented young people to stick around for a long time, nipping at their heels, pushing them up or out, or questioning and changing the organization's orientation and purpose. The organization is the way it is because the people in authority and longtime employees want it that way. They prefer a world where they can perpetuate the revolving door *and* wring their hands about it.

The American automobile industry is perhaps the most dramatic example of an extremely well-functioning, highly complex set of organizations "aligned perfectly to get the results it currently gets" as it crashed headlong into adaptive pressures about which it had been warned for decades, since the first oil shocks in the late 1970s and the growing awareness of global warming in the 1980s and 1990s. The adaptive failures, resplendent by late 2008, can only be diagnosed in the context of the highly distributed, entrenched stakes of so many: from boards of directors, executives, middle managers, union members, to vendors and their organizations, a wide swath of investors, and millions of buyers with a taste for big and powerful cars, trucks, and SUVs "way more cool" than minivans.

Distinguishing Technical Problems from Adaptive Challenges

The most common cause of failure in leadership is produced by treating adaptive challenges as if they were technical problems. What's the difference? While technical problems may be very complex and critically important (like replacing a faulty heart valve during cardiac surgery), they have known solutions that can be implemented by current know-how. They can be resolved through the application of authoritative expertise and through the organization's current structures, procedures, and ways of doing things. Adaptive challenges can only be addressed through changes in people's priorities, beliefs, habits, and loyalties. Making progress requires going beyond any authoritative expertise to mobilize discovery, shedding certain entrenched ways, tolerating losses, and generating the new capacity to thrive anew. Figure 2-1, adapted from *Leadership Without Easy Answers*, lays out some distinctions between technical problems and adaptive challenges.

As figure 2-1 implies, problems do not always come neatly packaged as either "technical" or "adaptive." When you take on a new challenge at work, it does not arrive with a big *T* or *A* stamped on it. Most problems come mixed, with the technical and adaptive elements intertwined.

Here's a homey example. As of this writing, Marty's mother, Ruth, is in good health at age ninety-five. Not a gray hair on her head (although she has dyed a highlight in her hair so that people will know that the black is natural). She lives alone and still drives, even at night. When Marty goes from his home in New York City up to Cambridge, Massachusetts, to do his teaching at the Kennedy School at Harvard, Ruth

FIGURE 2-1

Distinguishing technical problems and adaptive challenges

Kind of challenge	Problem definition	Solution	Locus of work
Technical	Clear	Clear	Authority
Technical and adaptive	Clear	Requires learning	Authority and stakeholders
Adaptive	Requires learning	Requires learning	Stakeholders

often drives from her apartment in nearby Chestnut Hill to have dinner with him.

Some time ago, Marty began noticing new scrapes on her car each time she arrived for their dinner date. Now one way to look at the issue is: the car should be taken to the body shop for repair. In that sense, this situation has a technical component: the scrapes can be solved by the application of the authoritative expertise found at the body shop. But an adaptive challenge is also lurking below the surface. Ruth is the only one of her contemporaries who still drives at all, never mind at night. Doing so is a source of enormous pride (and convenience) for her, as is living alone, not being in a retirement community, and still functioning more or less as an independent person. To stop driving, even just to stop driving at night, would require a momentous adjustment from her, an adaptation. The technical part is that she would have to pay for cabs, ask friends to drive her places, and so forth. The adaptive part can been found in the loss this change would represent, a loss of an important part of the story she tells herself about who she is as a human being, namely, that she is the only ninety-five-year-old person she knows who still drives at night. It would rip out a part of her heart, and take away a central element of her identity as an independent woman. Addressing the issue solely as a technical problem would fix the car (although only temporarily, since the trips to the body shop would likely come with increasing frequency), but it would not get at the underlying adaptive challenge: refashioning an identity and finding ways to thrive within new constraints.

In the corporate world, we have seen adaptive challenges that have significant technical aspects when companies merge or make significant acquisitions. There are huge technical issues, such as merging IT systems and offices. But it is the adaptive elements that threaten success. Each of the previously independent entities must give up some elements of their own cultural DNA, their dearly held habits, jobs, and values, in order to create a single firm and enable the new arrangement to survive and thrive. We were called in to help address that phenomenon in an international financial services firm where, several years after the merger, the remnants of each of the legacy companies are still doing business their own way, creating barriers to collaboration, global client servicing, and cost efficiencies. Whenever they get close to changing something important to reflect their one-firmness, the side that feels it is losing something precious in the bargain successfully resists. The implicit deal is pretty clear: you let us keep our entire DNA, and we will let you keep all of yours. They have been able to merge only some of the basic technology and communications systems, which made life easier for everyone without threatening any dearly held values or ways of doing business. In a similar client case, a large U.S. engineering firm functions like a franchise operation. Each of its offices, most of which were acquired, not homegrown, goes its own way, although the firm's primary product line has become commoditized, and the autonomy that has worked for these smaller offices in the past, and is very much at the heart of how they see themselves, will not enable them to compete on price for large contracts going forward.

We have seen the same commoditization of previously highly profitable distinctive services also affecting segments of the professional services world such as law firms, where relationship building has been an orienting value and core strategy and where competing primarily on price is a gut-wrenching reworking of how they see themselves. Yet as previously relationship-based professions are coping with the adaptive challenge of commoditization of some of their work, the reverse process is simultaneously going on in many businesses that have been built on a product sales model and mentality.

In an increasingly flat, globalized third-millenium world, where innovation occurs so quickly, just having the best product at any moment in time is not a sustainable plan. So, like one of our clients, a leading global technology products company, these companies are trying to adapt, as they struggle to move from a transaction-based environment, where products are sold, to a relationship-based environment, where solutions are offered based on trust and mutual understanding.

The need to make this transformation is stressing many firms, from professional services to insurance to digital hardware. These companies have had great success with an evolving product line, talented salespeople, and brilliant marketing strategies. Now they are finding that the skills required are more interpersonal than technical, both in their relationship with each other within the organization and in connecting with their customers. A workforce that has been trained and has succeeded in a sales framework is not prepared by experience or skill set to succeed when relationship building and response is the primary lever for growth. Successful people in the middle third or latter half of their careers are being asked to move away from what they know how to do well and risk moving beyond their frontier of competence as they try to respond adaptively to new demands from the client environment.

Like Marty and his mother, systems, organizations, families, and communities resist dealing with adaptive challenges because doing so requires changes that partly involve an experience of loss. Ruth is no different in principle from the legacy elements of the newly merged company that do not want to give up what they each experience as their distinctiveness.

Sometimes, of course, an adaptive challenge is way beyond our capacity, and we simply cannot do anything about it, hard as we might try. Vesuvius erupts. But even when we might have it within our capacity to respond successfully, we often squander the opportunity, as with the American automobile industry in the past decades.

You know the adage "People resist change." It is not really true. People are not stupid. People love change when they know it is a good thing. No one gives back a winning lottery ticket. What people resist is not change per se, but loss. When change involves real or potential loss, people hold on to what they have and resist the change. We suggest that the common factor generating adaptive failure is resistance to loss. A key to leadership, then, is the diagnostic capacity to find out the kinds of losses at stake in a changing situation, from life and loved ones to jobs, wealth, status, relevance, community, loyalty, identity, and competence. Adaptive leadership almost always puts you in the business of assessing, managing, distributing, and providing contexts for losses that move people through those losses to a new place.

At the same time, adaptation is a process of conservation as well as loss. Although the losses of change are the hard part, adaptive change is mostly not about change at all. The question is not only, "Of all that we care about, what must be given up to survive and thrive going forward?" but also, "Of all that we care about, what elements are essential and must be preserved into the future, or we will lose precious values, core competencies, and lose who we are?" As in nature, a successful adaptation enables an organization or community to take the best from its traditions, identity, and history into the future.

However you ask the questions about adaptive change and the losses they involve, answering them is difficult because the answers require tough choices, trade-offs, and the uncertainty of ongoing, experimental trial and error. That is hard work not only because it is intellectually difficult, but also because it challenges individuals' and organizations' investments in relationships, competence, and identity. It requires a modification of the stories they have been telling themselves and the rest of the world about what they believe in, stand for, and represent.

Helping individuals, organizations, and communities deal with those tough questions, distinguishing the DNA that is essential to conserve from the DNA that must be discarded, and then innovating to create the organizational adaptability to thrive in changing environments is the work of adaptive leadership.

Distinguishing Leadership from Authority

Exercising adaptive leadership is radically different from doing your job really, really well. It is different from authoritative expertise, and different from holding a high position in a political or organizational hierarchy. It is also different from having enormous informal power in the forms of credibility, trust, respect, admiration, and moral authority. As you have undoubtedly seen, many people occupy positions of senior authority without ever leading their organizations through difficult but needed adaptive change. Others with or without significant formal authority but with a large admiring group of "followers" also frequently fail to mobilize those followers to address their toughest challenges. To protect and increase their informal authority, they often pander to their constituents, minimizing the costly adjustments the followers will need to make and pointing elsewhere at "the others who must change, or be changed," as they deny and delay the days of reckoning.

People have long confused the notion of leadership with authority, power, and influence. We find it extremely useful to see leadership as a practice, an activity that some people do some of the time. We view leadership as a verb, not a job. Authority, power, and influence are critical tools, but they do not define leadership. That is because the resources of authority, power, and influence can be used for all sorts of purposes and tasks that have little or nothing to do with leadership, like performing surgery or running an organization that has long been successful in a stable market.

The powers and influence that come from formal and informal authority relationships have the same basic structure. The social contract is identical: Party A entrusts Party B with power in exchange for services. Sometimes this contract is formalized in a job description or an authorization establishing a task force, organizational unit, government agency, or organizational mission. Sometimes the contract is left implicit, as it is with charismatic authorities and their constituents, or with your subordinates and lateral colleagues, who may to varying degrees trust, respect, and admire you, and therefore give you the key power resource of their attention. However, all authority relationships, both formal and informal, appear to fit the same basic definitional pattern: power entrusted for service—"I look to you to serve a set of goals I hold dear."

Authority, then, is granted by one or more people on the assumption that you will then do what they want you to do: centrally in organizational life to promptly provide solutions to problems. People will confer authority or volunteer to follow you because they are looking to you to provide a service, to be a champion, a representative, an expert, a doer who can provide solutions *within the terms that they understand the situation.* And if life presented exclusively technical problems, people would get what they need looking routinely to authorities for solutions to problems.

Take a closer look at the difference between authority and adaptive leadership. In your organizational life, your authorizers (those who grant you authority) include bosses, peers, subordinates, and even people outside your organization, such as clients or customers and possibly the media. An authorizer is anyone who gives you attention and support to do your job of providing solutions to problems.

In any of your roles, whether parent or CEO or doctor or consultant, you have a specific *scope* of authority (see figure 2-2) that derives from your authorizers' expectations and that defines the limits of what you are expected to do. As long as you do what is expected of you, your authorizers are happy. If you do what you are supposed to do *really* well, you will be rewarded in the coin of the realm, whatever it is: a pay raise, a bonus, a bigger job, a plaque, a more impressive title, a better office.

And one of the most seductive ways your organization rewards you for doing exactly what it wants—to provide operational excellence in executing directions set by others—is to call you a "leader." Because you, like most people, aspire to have that label, conferring it on you is a brilliant way of keeping you right where the organization wants you, in the middle of your scope of authority and far away from taking on adaptive leadership work.

Twenty years ago, Ron taught in a Harvard executive program for senior officers in the U.S. military. Six weeks into the program, an Air Force colonel came into the seminar room looking crestfallen. Ron asked him, "What happened?" The colonel responded, "When I was commissioned an officer many years ago, they told me that I was a leader. Now I

FIGURE 2-2

Formal and informal authority

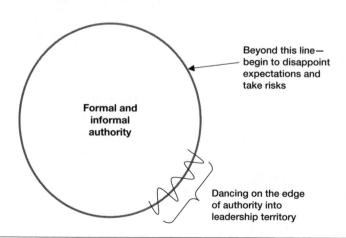

Beyond this line— begin to disappoint expectations and take risks

Formal and informal authority

Dancing on the edge of authority into leadership territory

realize I've been an authority figure, and I'm not sure I've exercised any leadership at all." The following week, he came to the same seminar room having reflected on this disturbing idea, but he looked energetic. "Now I see options for leadership that I never saw before."

When your organization calls you a leader, it is rewarding you for doing what your authorizers want you to do. Of course, meeting authorizers' expectations is important. In medicine, doctors and nurses save lives every day fulfilling the hopes of patients who entrust them to provide trustworthy service. But doing an excellent job usually has nothing to do with helping your organization deal with adaptive challenges. To do that, you have to possess the will and skill to dance on the edges of that circle shown in figure 2-2, on behalf of a purpose you care deeply about. Adaptive leadership is not about meeting or exceeding your authorizers' expectations; it is about *challenging* some of those expectations, finding a way to disappoint people without pushing them completely over the edge. And it requires managing the resistance you will inevitably trigger. When you exercise adaptive leadership, your authorizers will push back, understandably. They hired you, or voted for you, or authorized you to do one thing, and now you are doing something else: you are challenging the status quo, raising a taboo issue, pointing out contradictions between what people *say* they value and what they *actually* value. You are scaring people. They may want to get rid of you and find someone else who will do their bidding.

Imagine a cardiac surgeon, for example, telling patients that he will refuse to do the operation unless the patients do their part of the work: quit smoking and put an exercise regime and a healthy diet into their daily routines after the surgery. Moreover, to ensure compliance, the surgeon insists that patients place 50 percent of all their assets in an escrow account controlled by a third party for six months. It's likely that most patients will find another surgeon, someone who will do the operation and let them off the hook. And the cardiac surgeon who was eager to mobilize adaptive work among his patients will lose his business.

No wonder there is so little adaptive leadership going on in daily organizational life. Exercising adaptive leadership is dangerous. The word *leader* comes from the Indo-European root word *leit*, the name for the person who carried the flag in front of an army going into battle and usually died in the first enemy attack. His sacrifice would alert the rest of the army to the location of the danger ahead.

The dangers reside in the need to challenge the expectations of the very people who give you formal and informal authority. Yet very often, leadership challenges are about managing conflicts within your authorizing environment. For example, elements of the multiple-faction and overlapping-faction authorizing environments that politicians cobble together to win elections are sometimes not only conflicting but mutually exclusive. That may be true for you at times as well. If you have been or are now a middle manager, you probably have had moments when you were squeezed between the expectations of your subordinates that you would protect them and advocate for them, and those of your senior authorities that you would control costs on salaries, expenses, and year-end bonuses, or even fire some of your subordinates. As a parent, you might have been caught between your spouse or partner and your children, or worse, between your spouse or partner and your own mother!

A friend of ours was recently hired by a large Web design firm to be the first manager of its design studio. She was hired by the executive team to bring discipline, professionalism, and a business orientation to the group of young, talented Web designers. But the Web designers, whose confidence she needed in order to accomplish the task, saw her coming as their opportunity to have an advocate in the upper reaches of the company. She could not satisfy both groups. Then the question became, which people in her authorizing environment was she going to disappoint, and how could she do that at a rate they could absorb? Timing and sequencing become critical to success and survival. For example, it is easier generally for you initially to honor your authorization from the senior authority than to challenge it on behalf of subordinates.

Conflating leadership and authority is an old and understandable habit. We all want to believe that we can exercise leadership just by doing really, really well at the job we are expected to carry out. But the distinction between exercising leadership and exercising authority is crucial. By practicing adaptive leadership beyond authoritative management, you risk telling people what they need to hear rather than what they want to hear, but you can also help your organization, community, or society make progress on its most difficult challenges.

Whether you are the president of a country or company, a hospital administrator or the head of an advocacy organization, or simply (simply?) a parent, your functions in your authority role are largely the

FIGURE 2-3

Leadership from a position of authority

Task	Technical	Adaptive
Direction	Provide problem definition & solution	Identify the adaptive challenge; frame key questions & issues
Protection	Protect from external threats	Disclose external threats
Order Orientation	Orient people to current roles	Disorient current roles; resist orienting poeple to new roles too quickly
Conflict	Restore order	Expose conflict or let it emerge
Norms	Maintain norms	Challenge norms or let them be challenged

same. You have three core responsibilities, to provide: (1) direction, (2) protection, and (3) order. That is, you are expected to clarify roles and offer a vision (direction), make sure that the group, organization, or society is not vulnerable and can survive external threat (protection), and maintain stability (order). Because addressing adaptive challenges requires stepping into unknown space and disturbing the equilibrium, it is an activity that is inherently uncertain, risky for the organization as well as for the individual, and, for these reasons, often disruptive and disorienting. (See figure 2-3.)

Living in the Disequilibrium

To practice adaptive leadership, you have to help people navigate through a period of disturbance as they sift through what is essential and what is expendable, and as they experiment with solutions to the adaptive challenges at hand. This disequilibrium can catalyze everything from conflict, frustration, and panic to confusion, disorientation, and fear of losing something dear. That is not what you are paid to do and will certainly not be as well received as when you are mobilizing people to address a technical issue that is within their competence or requires expertise that can be readily obtained. Consequently, when you are practicing adaptive leadership, distinctive skills and insights are necessary to deal with this swirling mass of energies. You need to be able to do two things: (1) manage yourself in that environment and (2) help people tolerate the discomfort they are experiencing. You need to live into the disequilibrium.

Honoring the reality that adaptive processes will be accompanied by distress means having compassion for the pain that comes with deep change. Distress may come with the territory of change, but from a strategic perspective, disturbing people is not the point or the purpose, but a consequence. The purpose is to make progress on a tough collective challenge. When you drive a car, heat is a natural byproduct of the engine, which then needs to be managed and kept within a productive temperature range. You do not drive a car to generate heat (except sometimes to get warm in winter); you drive a car to get somewhere. But every so often you have to look at the temperature gauge to make sure that the engine cooling systems are working properly.

Collective and individual disequilibrium is a byproduct generated when you call attention to tough questions and draw people's sense of responsibility beyond current norms and job descriptions. Of course, organizations and individuals like to stay in their comfort zone. When you raise a difficult issue or surface a deep value conflict, you take people out of their comfort zone and raise a lot of heat. That is tricky business. You have to continually fiddle with the flame to see how much heat the system can tolerate. Your goal should be to keep the temperature within what we call the *productive zone of disequilibrium* (PZD): enough heat generated by your intervention to gain attention, engagement, and forward motion, but not so much that the organization (or your part of it) explodes. (See figure 2-4.)

It is like a pressure cooker: set the temperature and pressure too low, and you stand no chance of transforming the ingredients in the cooker into a good meal. Set the temperature and pressure too high, and the cover will blow off the cooker's top, releasing the ingredients of your meal across the room. It helps to think of yourself as keeping your hand on the thermostat, carefully controlling how much heat and pressure is applied. This is much easier to do if you hold a senior authority position than if you are a junior person in the organization. People in authority are expected to have a hand on the thermostat (although they are usually expected to lower the temperature rather than raise it).

Examine figure 2-4 more closely. The technical problem line represents the changes in disequilibrium as an organization deals with a technical problem. The adaptive challenge line shows changes in disequilibrium as the organization deals with an adaptive challenge. The horizontal bar constitutes the productive zone of disequilibrium. Below the PZD, people are comfortable and satisfied. Above the PZD, the disequilibrium is so high, things are so hot, that tensions within the organization reach disabling proportions. Within the productive zone, the stress level is high enough that people can be mobilized to focus on and engage with the problem they would rather avoid. The dotted work avoidance line represents the easing of disequilibrium as the organization avoids dealing with hard issues.

Look again at the technical problem line. To illustrate how disequilibrium changes with a technical problem, say you break your leg skiing. At that moment, the disequilibrium is at its peak, virtually intolerable. You

FIGURE 2-4

The productive zone of disequilibrium

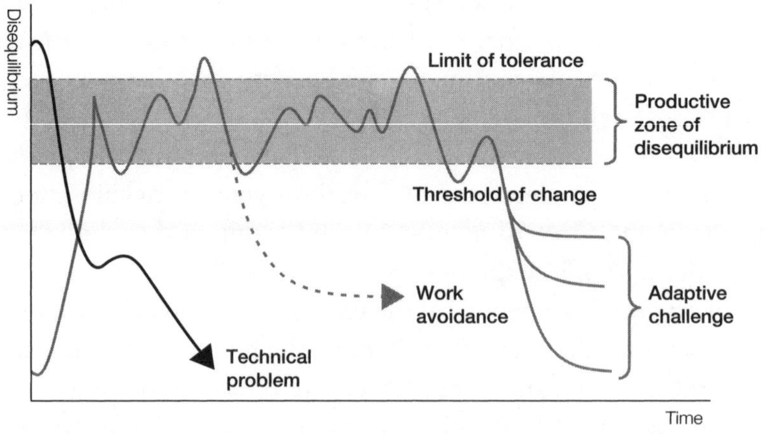

Source: Adapted from Ronald A. Heifetz and Donald L. Laurie, "Mobilizing Adaptive Work: Beyond Visionary Leadership," in *The Leader's Change Handbook,* eds. Jay A. Conger, Gretchen M. Spreitzer, and Edward E. Lawler III (San Francisco: Jossey-Bass, 1998).

are lying in the snow, freezing and in awful pain, and people are skiing by you. Then those nice folks from the ski patrol come by with a stretcher, a blanket, sympathy, and even a shot of whiskey if you want it. The disequilibrium lessens to a more tolerable level. It may go up again while you're waiting for the doctor in the emergency room, and again when you have to endure a few months of painful rehabilitation exercises. But overall, it decreases, finally disappearing once you are healed.

The disequilibrium pattern for an adaptive challenge is very different. At the beginning, disequilibrium is low. You have identified an adaptive problem that you know the company should address, but most people around you either do not see it or see it but do not want to deal with it. You need to raise the heat to the point where the discomfort of not dealing with the problem is the same as or more than the discomfort that would come from any nasty consequences of not addressing the problem. That is, you need to get the group into the PZD.

Things soon become a lot less linear when you are dealing with an adaptive challenge. The intensity of the disequilibrium rises and falls as you push your intervention forward. Sometimes it will seem that you are taking one step back for every two steps forward. Clearly, you need patience and persistence to lead adaptive change. You also have to anticipate and counteract tactics that people will use to lower the heat to more comfortable levels. This work avoidance can take numerous forms, such as creating a new committee with no authority or finding a scapegoat. Unlike with a technical problem, there is no clear, linear path to the resolution of an adaptive challenge. You need a plan, but you also need freedom to deviate from the plan as new discoveries emerge, as conditions change, and as new forms of resistance arise. Once you help unleash the energy to deal with an adaptive issue, you cannot control the outcome. That is why there are several possible outcomes at the end of the adaptive challenge line. Doing this work requires flexibility and openness even in defining success. The pathway is not a straight line, and because working through an adaptive challenge will always involve distributing some losses, albeit in the service of an important purpose, the systemic dynamics that ensue, the politics of change, will have many unpredictable elements. The pathway for getting to an adaptive resolution will look a bit like the flight of a bumblebee, so that at times you will feel as if you are not even heading in the right direction. And the resolution might be quite different from what you first imagined.

Observe, Interpret, Intervene

Adaptive leadership is an iterative process involving three key activities: (1) observing events and patterns around you; (2) interpreting what you are observing (developing multiple hypotheses about what is really going on); and (3) designing interventions based on the observations and interpretations to address the adaptive challenge you have identified. Each of these activities builds on the ones that come before it; and the process overall is iterative: you repeatedly refine your observations, interpretations, and interventions. (See figure 2-5.) Take a closer look at each of these activities.

Observations

Marty's wife, Lynn, has an art background. When she brings (uh, drags) him to a museum and they gaze at a painting on the wall, Marty sees about 25 percent of what Lynn sees. She urges him closer to the masterpiece, points out some elements, and, on a good day, she might get him up to 50 percent.

Two people observing the same event or situation see different things, depending on their previous experiences and unique perspectives. Observing is a highly subjective activity. But in exercising adaptive leadership, the goal is to make observing as objective as possible. Getting off the dance floor and onto the balcony is a powerful way to do this. It

FIGURE 2-5

The adaptive leadership process

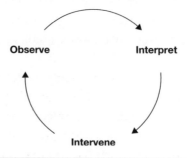

enables you to gain some distance, to watch yourself as well as others while you are in the action, and to see patterns in what is happening that are hard to observe if you are stuck at the ground-floor level.

Bill Russell, a member of the professional basketball Hall of Fame and star player and then player-coach for the Boston Celtics during their great championship runs of the late 1950s and 1960s, wrote a book called *Second Wind: The Memoirs of an Opinionated Man* and described how he was somehow able to see the whole court, the patterns and relationships among all ten players, including himself, and anticipate where people were going to be, in deciding where to make the next pass or cut.[4] He won two NBA championships as a player-coach, where the capacity to be in and out of the game at the same time was invaluable.

Collecting all the data that is out there to see, find, and discover is a critical first step. It is not that easy to watch what is going on. It is hard to observe objectively while you are in the middle of the action in an organization. The questions are endless: "Who's talking with whom? Who responds to whom? What are the alliances and relationships beyond the organizational chart? What is the history of the problem we're facing? What are the different views of it? What are the patterns of behavior relevant to the problem that are not visible unless you're looking for them? How are the organization's culture and structure affecting people's behavior?"

In our client work, we often ask someone to act as a "balcony person" in a meeting or workshop. This person's role is to sit in the back of the room and take notes on what happens, recapitulating participants' various comments and behaviors. It is remarkable how much more you can see when you momentarily take yourself out of the action and simply watch and record. We typically ask the balcony person to tell the group initially what he or she observed, just the facts, without any interpretation, as if the group were watching a videotape of a soccer game without any commentary.

Interpretations

Interpreting is more challenging than observing. When you hypothesize out loud and disclose the sense you are getting from your observations, you risk raising the ire of people who have formed different interpretations. They will want you to embrace whatever "truth" they favor. For example, suppose you and a peer manager both saw the same thing happen during a meeting: a soft-spoken member of the group, the only African American woman, was repeatedly interrupted when she spoke. You interpret what you saw as the group marginalizing the substance of her viewpoint on the tasks at hand, done more easily because the group's prejudices diminish her credibility. But your colleague interprets it as a consequence of her speaking softly. Owing to these clashing interpretations, your peer suggests hiring a performance coach for her, while you suggest that the team needs to focus on her perspectives on the work issues, however difficult they might be, and perhaps engage in some diversity counseling, too.

However provocative the practice may be, you cannot avoid making interpretations. Your brain is designed to make meaning out of what you see, and will look for patterns out of whatever information you take in through your senses. Most interpretative patterns are fashioned unconsciously and with lightning speed, throwing us into immediate action before we can ask ourselves, "Is my explanation for what is happening correct? What are some alternative hypotheses?" To practice adaptive leadership, you have to take time to think through your interpretation of what you observe, *before* jumping into action.

The activity of interpreting might be understood as listening for the "song beneath the words." The idea is to make your interpretations as accurate as possible by considering the widest possible array of sensory information. In addition to noticing what people are saying and doing explicitly, watch for body language and emotion, and notice what is *not* being said. Ask yourself, "What underlying values and loyalties are at stake?" "To what extent are people around me interpreting our situation as a technical problem rather than an adaptive challenge?" If you do not question your own and the group's preferred interpretation, you and your organization may end up colluding in avoiding the difficult work of addressing the more important issues.

That said, even the most carefully thought out interpretation will still be no more than a good guess. You can never have all the data needed to form a complete picture. And no one has the mental capacity to form and evaluate all the *possible* interpretations that could be made from a single set of observations.

However, if you are skilled at adaptive leadership, you might find yourself actively holding more than one interpretation about a particular observation open at any moment, even mutually exclusive ones, like your and your colleague's interpretation of the soft-spoken woman's difficulty getting heard in the conversation in the example above. Holding multiple interpretations in your head simultaneously is taxing, because our natural tendency is to always search for the one "right" answer. This mental balancing act requires the ability to view the same set of data from several different perspectives.

An interpretation is only a guess, although the more you practice this activity, the better your guesses will be. Making your interpretation public is itself an intervention and often a provocative one. Making it tentatively, experimentally, and then watching (and then interpreting) the reaction can help you gauge how close to the mark you came.

Interventions

Once you have made an interpretation of the problem-solving dynamics you have observed, what are you going to do about it? Will you hire the performance coach or the diversity trainer? Or both? Will you share your interpretation at that meeting, try it out with a smaller group, or wait until the next meeting? Your next move, your intervention, should reflect your hypothesis about the problem, be considered an experiment (by yourself and maybe others), and be in the service of a shared purpose. Well-designed interventions provide context; they connect your interpretation to the purpose or task on the table so people can see that your perspective is relevant to their collective efforts. If they cannot see the relevance, they might write you off as if you were riding a personal hobbyhorse ("That's Jack's issue"). Good interventions also take into account the resources available in your organization. For example, you probably would not propose an intervention consisting of a massive top-to-bottom diversity or performance coach program if you had just cut bonuses by 50 percent. Moreover, in crafting an intervention, you should consider where you "sit" in the organization and what that implies for your chances of success. What you should do might be different if you were the CEO, the only other woman in the group, or the newest member of the team. Finally, in designing an intervention, consider the skills and resources in your own tool kit. What are you really good at doing? And what kind of interventions are at the edge of your competence? Some people, for example, are much better at managing a group of ten people in a meeting than they are at managing a more intimate one-on-one conversation. The more you have in your tool kit, the greater the range of interventions you will be willing and able to launch, and the more likely they will generate the desired results.

At the same time, practice designing interventions that are outside your comfort zone. Everyone has their own repertoire of options that they draw on when they take action to address a challenge. People become used to (and good at) intervening in a specific and narrow set of ways. They become familiar. Regrettably, they become familiar to the organization, too. This predictability can limit your effectiveness. Other people will know what is coming from you, and they will know how to deflect it. For example, if you are really good at engaging in emotional persuasion, they will know to stay calm and take you out of your best format.

Strengthening your ability to design interventions that lie outside your comfort zone takes practice. But it is a vital component of effective leadership. It will help you tailor your interventions to each unique situation and make you less predictable. And that makes it harder for others to neutralize you.

Experiment and Take Smart Risks Smartly

When you are dealing with adaptive challenges, there is no obvious answer to the question "What is going on here?" Trying to define the problem at hand is a contentious act in itself. Managing this ambiguity requires courage, tenacity, and an experimental mind-set: you try things out, see what happens, and make changes accordingly.

When you adopt an experimental mind-set, you actively commit to an intervention you have designed while also not letting yourself become wedded to it. That way, if it misses the mark, you do not feel compelled to defend it. This mind-set also opens you to other, unanticipated possibilities. (You are undoubtedly familiar with the stories about the ways Benjamin Franklin and Thomas Edison produced their great inventions by accident, while pursuing some other purposes entirely.) Thinking experimentally also opens you to learning: you stay open to the possibility that you might be wrong. Finally, an experimental mind-set facilitates the iterative nature of the adaptive leadership process: you make an intervention based on your interpretation of the situation, and you see what happens. You use the results of your experiment to take the next step or to make a midcourse correction.

Holding incompatible ideas in your head at the same time is a little like deciding to get married. At the moment you decide that this is the person you want to spend the rest of your life with, you have to fully embrace your choice; you have to believe wholeheartedly that it is the right decision. But your practical self also knows that you probably would have fallen in love with someone else under different circumstances. So how can your intended be the only "right" one for you? If you treated the decision to marry this particular person at this particular moment as a 51–49 question rather than a 90–10 question, you would never take the leap. The same paradox applies to adaptive leadership interventions. You have to run the experiment with full and hopeful conviction.

F. Scott Fitzgerald once said that "the test of a first-rate intelligence is the ability to hold two opposed ideas in mind at the same time and still retain the ability to function."[5] In the realm of adaptive leadership, you have to believe that your intervention is absolutely the right thing to do at the moment you commit to it. But at the same time, you need to remain open to the possibility that you are dead wrong.

Still, adaptive leadership is about will *plus* skill. Effective interventions can torque the odds of both survival and success more in your favor. An intervention that has only, say, a 50–50 chance of success might have a 60–40 chance if you design it skillfully. The tools and resources in this book will help you do that.

Engage Above and Below the Neck

If leadership involves will and skill, then leadership requires the engagement of what goes on both above and below the neck. Courage requires all of you: heart, mind, spirit, and guts. And skill requires learning new competencies, with your brain training your body to become proficient at new techniques of diagnosis and action.

You might think about this idea as the convergence of multiple intelligences (intellectual, emotional, spiritual, and physical) or the collaboration among physical centers (mind, heart, and body). But the central notion is the same. Your whole self constitutes a resource for exercising leadership.

One distinctive aspect of leading adaptive change is that you must connect with the values, beliefs, and anxieties of the people you are trying to move. Being present in that way is tough to do unless your heart is part of the mix as well. Acts of leadership not only require access to all parts of yourself so that you can draw upon all of your own resources for will, skill, and wisdom; but to be successful, you also need to fully engage people with all these parts of yourself as well.

Leadership is necessary when logic is not the answer. Leading adaptive change is not about making a better argument or about loading people up with more facts. Take cigarette smoking. Suppose you have a friend, Ian, who smokes. If Ian is like most smokers, he knows full well that the habit is bad for his health. More white papers on the dangers of tobacco and more pictures of diseased lungs are not going to change his behavior. Whatever is keeping him stuck in the habit is going on below the neck. To "move" him off of tobacco, you would have to understand and address the needs that are making him smoke, such as, it gives him pleasure, reduces his anxiety, or reminds him of his beloved dad.

The same is true for exercising leadership. You are trying to move people who have not been convinced by logic and facts. They prefer the status quo to the risks of doing things differently. They are stuck in their hearts and stomachs, not in their heads. To move them, you need to reach them there. If you are not engaged with your own heart, you will find it virtually impossible to connect with theirs.

Connect to Purpose

It makes little sense to practice leadership and put your own professional success and material gain at risk unless it is on behalf of some larger purpose that you find compelling. What might such a purpose look like? How can you tell whether a particular purpose is worth the risks involved in leading adaptive change in your organization? If you try to achieve this purpose, will you produce results valued in your organization? These are tough questions that you can answer only by articulating your own personal values.

Clarifying the values that orient your life and work and identifying larger purposes to which you might commit are courageous acts. You have to choose among competing, legitimate purposes, sacrificing many in the service of one or a few. In doing so, you make a statement about what you are willing to die for, and, therefore, what you are willing to live for.

We work with a lot of people in public K–12 education. Teachers, superintendents, parents, principals, central office administrators, and elected school committee members have a range of personal, professional, and sometimes ideological commitments that frequently stand in the way of collective action to address their adaptive challenges. In the heat of difficult conversations and tough choices, they often become distracted from their shared purpose: education of young people. Simply asking, "How does this new policy connect to our purpose? How does it help us educate kids?" can help people focus on finding ways to compromise some of their vested interests.

For example, teachers may have to give up a measure of autonomy by sitting in each other's classrooms to help each other improve. They might have to find ways to better engage parents and families in young students' education, even though they have never taken a course in parent engagement and they get almost no encouragement or help from the education system to do so.

The notion of purpose plays just as powerful a role in corporate life. One of our clients, a fast-growing marketing firm, had come to a crossroads. It had risen quickly to become the number two firm in its industry. But growing quickly was no longer an adequate beacon to guide the company into the future. Questions had begun cropping up: Who benefited from the growth? Was further growth possible or even desirable? From where was that growth likely to come? Tensions had arisen between the creative people and the sales staff over who deserved credit for the company's rapid expansion and therefore whose values would drive the future. The firm, while enormously successful, had lost its way. Members of the top team initiated a conversation about purpose. The discussion was uncomfortable for all of them, but it eventually helped them clarify what the next stage in the company's life might look like and what its new orienting principles might be.

Defining a shared purpose is often a challenging and painful exercise because some narrower interests will have to be sacrificed in the interests of the whole. But it is also a valuable corrective. When you face a tough decision, or when prospects for success look bleak, reminding one another what you are trying to do provides guidance, sustenance, and inspiration.

CHAPTER 3

Before You Begin

PRACTICING ADAPTIVE LEADERSHIP is difficult on the one hand and profoundly meaningful on the other; it is not something you should enter into casually. Here are four tips to consider before you step out there.

Don't Do It Alone

Sounds easy and obvious, but we have seen over and over again how people who are trying to do the right thing end up out on a limb all alone. It is not only lonely out there; it is dangerous. Those who see your good works as a threat will find you a much easier target if you are out there by yourself.

If the peril is so obvious, why do so many people end up going it alone? Three reasons: first, their opponents will do whatever it takes to make them vulnerable. For example, they might say something like, "You know I disagree with you, but I admire your courage in fighting for what you believe in." Who would not like the sound of that? So you are happy to oblige, by isolating yourself even more.

A much more subtle danger comes from friends. It usually works something like this. Your allies sense that you are fully committed and that you enjoy the plaudits that come from being out there on the front lines. They say to themselves, "Well, as long as he's willing to go out there and test the ice, good for him. If the ice is strong enough, we'll follow." They clap harder as you inch your way across the frozen lake, so you think they are right behind you. But when you look back, you see them still onshore, waiting to see what happens so they can make sure it really *is* safe for them to follow you. To keep you motivated, they might say something like, "You know, until you came to this company, no one understood our issues, no one spoke for us. We owe you so much. You are indispensable." That sounds good, too. Makes you feel warm all over. Want to hear it again? Just inch farther out onto the ice. But there is a way to avoid making this mistake: when someone tells you how wonderful you are, listen for a little voice inside yourself saying, "I know I'm terrific, but I'm not *that* terrific." That little voice is sending you a signal that something else is going on.

The third reason that you may end up too far out there by yourself is a function of your passion and commitment. Your belief in what you are doing is indispensable to your willingness to take the risks of leading adaptive change. But that same belief can also make you vulnerable. It is so easy to get so caught up in the cause that you do not notice danger signals. So your intervention fails.

We recently had a conversation with one of the people central to advancing the United States' ultimately unsuccessful bid to host the 2012 Olympics in New York City. He recounted how he was so fired up by the cause, believed in it so deeply, was so committed to the connection between the Olympics and the post-9/11 resurgence of the city he loved, that he could not read the smoke signals and never saw that the decision makers did not see things as "clearly" as he did. Thus he was unable to step back and make the midcourse corrections that might have made the story turn out differently.

Whether you are taking on a small initiative (such as planning to raise a difficult issue at a team meeting) or a large one (like our friend and the New York Olympics bid), do not go it alone. Find partners who will share the dangers and the exposure. Together, you'll stand a far better chance of avoiding attacks from opponents and keeping your initiative alive.

Live Life as a Leadership Laboratory

Opportunities to exercise adaptive leadership come before you every day. They come at home with your family; at your workplace; and in your civic, religious, and community life. Look for them, and try to take advantage of them.

For most people, including us, it is all too easy to let those opportunities slip through the fingers. There are lots of rationales, lots of stories, lots of excuses. "I'm too busy." "I've got to put three kids through college." "In this job market, I've got to hold on to what I have." "We four siblings only get together a couple of times a year. I can't ruin things by bringing up the issue of moving Mom and Dad into an assisted-care facility." "I'm on this nonprofit board to give something back to the community. I don't want to create trouble by pointing out that we're not practicing our stated values." "This is my church. I am a member of the vestry to further my spiritual life, not to force parishioners to face the uncomfortable reality that we're spending money faster than we're taking it in and at some point, probably long after I am gone, reality will catch up with them. I'll just increase my annual donation, do my part, and let it go at that."

The purpose of this book is to help you see and take advantage of adaptive leadership opportunities more often than you have before, and on behalf of what you care most deeply about. It's not meant to move you from exercising leadership 25 percent of the time to doing it 75 percent of the time. Going from 25 percent to just 30 percent would make a major difference in your professional and personal life, as well as to your purposes in your family, your job, and your community.

To move the adaptive leadership needle, you have to be willing and able to see opportunities where you might have missed them before. Start by recognizing that those opportunities are present everywhere and every day in your life.

After his first near fatal bout with cancer, Marty's friend and longtime Boston talk show host, the late David Brudnoy, wrote a book called *Life Is Not a Rehearsal.*[1] It was his own way of saying that his experience with the disease taught him to live life in the present. But whether you think it is all a rehearsal for something else, or whether you think it is all in the moment, either way, opportunities for exercising leadership are also learning opportunities. Leadership is an experimental art. We are all at the frontier. And one way of reconciling the rehearsal versus living in the present conundrum is to think of your life as a leadership laboratory. In that laboratory, you are continuously facing opportunities for learning how to be more effective in living a meaningful existence, and for making more progress on life's deepest purposes and leading meaningful change. Seeing life as a leadership lab enables you to try things out, make mistakes, strengthen your skills, and take pleasure in the journey as well as the fruits of your labor.

> *The difference between a beginner and the master—is that the master practices a whole lot more.*
>
> —Yehudi Menuhin

Resist the Leap to Action

Adaptive leadership may come intuitively and spontaneously to some, but for most people, it requires a lot more reflection. Many iconic practitioners of leadership in recent history, such as Nelson Mandela, Mohandas K. Gandhi, Martin Luther King Jr., and Mother Teresa, were notably reflective, as well as people of action.

Yet in organizational life, particularly in times of stress or crisis, pressure mounts to take quick action. That pressure plays into many people's strengths. You may have been there before. You know how to rise to the occasion. Even if you do not have the foggiest idea of what to do, you have a strong incentive to give in to others' demands that you: "Do something!"

Of course, emergency management is a needed skill. Saving people's lives when they are trapped in a burning building is as important as any other human endeavor. But adaptive leadership is difficult and dangerous in different ways than rescuing people from a fire. Adaptive challenges are hard to define and typically require people to reinterpret and question their own priorities, as well as their habits of thinking and behavior. When leading adaptive change, you will be courting resistance by stirring the pot, upsetting the status quo, and creating disequilibrium.

Sorting through an adaptive challenge takes time and reflection. Resist the pressure to do something, and spend more time diagnosing the problem, even if taking that much time feels excruciatingly uncomfortable. Give yourself license to assess your own skills and to determine whether you are the right person to intervene or someone else would have a better chance of success. Take time to inventory the risks, to yourself and your organization, and to ask yourself whether the potential rewards are worth the risks.

Discover the Joy of Making Hard Choices

Leadership is a difficult practice personally because it almost always requires you to make a challenging adaptation yourself. What makes adaptation complicated is that it involves deciding what is so essential that it must be preserved going forward and what of all that you value can be left behind. Those are hard choices because they involve both protecting what is most important to you and bidding adieu to something you previously held dear: a relationship, a value, an idea, an image of yourself. Marty often uses the metaphor of getting divorced with children, something he and Ron have both experienced. If you have gone through that, you might relate directly, as well as metaphorically. You tell yourself that you believe in self-fulfillment, but also you believe just as strongly that you would never do anything your kids would experience as deeply harmful to them. Those are both important values, equally compelling in the abstract. But then you decide to get divorced, and all of a sudden instead of two number one values, you have a number one and a number two. You are, in your own eyes and in the eyes of your family and your community, a different person, and not necessarily more admired. It is a painful process, but a revealing and liberating one as well.

Acknowledging that you have opted not to exercise leadership because there's something more important to you is a step toward self-knowledge, Socrates' definition of virtue (as reported by his student, Plato). When you take responsibility for the choices you make, you understand a little more about who you are. Choices between multiple deeply held values are not matters of right and wrong, but moments of clarification, painful as those choices may be to make.

You know best who you really are by watching what you do rather than listening to what you say. The only way you can really know what you believe in comes from the times when one belief comes into conflict with something else you say you believe in. It does not mean much to say you believe in something if it is so far down on your list of cherished values that you never have to act on it. There are many more people who "believe in ending world hunger" or "believe in saving the environment" than those who actually do anything on behalf of their belief beyond voting for politicians who share their view or making a few behavioral changes (such as sending a check to a charity or turning off a few lights in the house).

Here's an everyday example of the way loyalties shape everyday beliefs. We have a friend who for twenty years thought of himself as someone who liked Chinese food, even though he never partook. Then one day he was with a group of friends who suggested they go out for Chinese dinner. He was taken aback when he heard himself say, "Let's go somewhere else. I really don't like Chinese food." So, why had he been holding on to the idea that he did? After thinking about it for a while, he began to see that his commitment to Chinese food was actually a commitment to his family. When he was growing up, he and his parents and his siblings went out for Chinese dinner most Sunday nights. It was a family ritual. If he acknowledged disdaining Chinese food now, he would have experienced it (and very likely his parents would have similarly experienced it) as a criticism of his family's practices. Holding on to beliefs or practices often is a commitment to the source of those beliefs or practices rather than to the belief or practices themselves.

If you want to exercise adaptive leadership more than you have in the past, you will have to make some different choices from those you have made before. You will have to risk whatever commitment or concern held you back on behalf of something else that you have been saying is more important to you. Some wise person once told us that the sign of being an adult is saying a hard no once a day. Saying a hard no is a clarifying act, a step toward self-knowledge, a commitment to stand up for something even when it is hard to do so. Finding the joy in making such a personal, purposeful declaration is the flip side of grieving for what you will have to give up to lead adaptive change.

PART TWO

DIAGNOSE THE SYSTEM

IN MEDICINE, DIAGNOSIS COMES BEFORE treatment. As in the television show *House*, teams of doctors, nurses, technicians, scientists, and other health-care professionals devote extraordinary talent, skill, and energy to identifying the problem. Occasionally, the illness is identified backward by trying a particular treatment and seeing whether it works, but more often, tests, time, thought, and discussion are devoted to assessing the problem first. Treatment comes second.

In organizational and political life, people often jump to treatment without stepping back to clarify the nature of the problem itself, making enormous investments in solutions, rolling out large-scale new strategies and programs, without knowing as much as they should about the situation. As the United States learned in the war in Iraq, countries even go to war sometimes without adequately assessing the situation: Were there really weapons of mass destruction in Iraq? Did the United States have the manpower to fight in Iraq, secure the peace in Iraq, and at the same time finish the job of securing and stabilizing Afghanistan? Did the government have the public commitment and the funds to stay the course, if protracted, and what were the odds that it would be protracted? What impact might a protracted war have on many other national and global economic, social, and political priorities?

When the chief of staff of the U.S. Army, General Eric Shinseki, told Congress before the war that hundreds of thousands of troops would be needed to win the war and secure the peace, the secretary of defense, Donald Rumsfeld, categorically disagreed. After Baghdad fell, Shinseki reiterated the need for more troops and was fired for saying so.

In medicine, when two highly skilled experts strongly disagree on the diagnosis and therefore the treatment, they remain in the diagnostic mode, probing to find out whose interpretation of the facts is closer to the truth, gathering more data, and, at most, taking action in small steps in an experimental way to generate more data. Only in nearly hopeless and desperate situations, would they take the risk of a major treatment intervention under great uncertainty about the nature of the problem itself. Many treatments are too dangerous and costly to try them without having some level of confidence that your diagnosis is accurate.

Too often, people trying to address tough issues are too smart for their own good, throwing guesses at tough problems, seeing the shapes they recognize because they fit what they know already, without even knowing that they are doing so. Impatient with the diagnostic process, and sensitive to the urgency with which the people around them look to them to be quick and decisive, they move with resolve. Indeed, people get rewarded for decisiveness and resolve and take pride in it, too. Sometimes decision and resolve are great virtues, but sometimes they push organizations into the wild blue yonder.

CHAPTER 4

Diagnose the System

THE FIRST STEP in tackling any adaptive challenge is to get on the balcony so you can see how your organizational system is responding to it. Informed by this perspective, you will gain a clearer view of your company's structures, culture, and defaults (its habitual ways of responding to problems). You will grasp the nature of the adaptive challenges at hand. You will map the networks of political relationships that will be relevant to how effectively you mobilize people to deal with that challenge. And you will assess your enterprise's overall capacity for adaptation, by considering distinguishing characteristics of an adaptive organization.

The Elegance and Tenacity of the Status Quo

We start with the assumption that the status quo functions elegantly to solve a stream of problems and opportunities for which it has already evolved. Yesterday's adaptive pressures, problems, and opportunities generated creative and successful responses in the organization that evolved through trial and error into new and refined structures, cultural norms, and default processes and mind-sets. In other words, yesterday's adaptations are today's routines. Yesterday's adaptive challenges are today's technical problems.

Of course, organizations, like all human systems, are highly complex. And the structures, culture, and defaults that define and maintain them prove tenacious. But they are tenacious for a reason. It took a long time for them to develop into self-reinforcing systems. They would have perished already if they were not fit to thrive in at least yesterday's world. That they may be at risk today, lingering more than thriving, does not diminish the extraordinary functionality of the adaptations they achieved to the challenges they faced in previous decades.

Systems become tenacious quickly. From the first day in the life of an organization, the elements begin taking shape: the structures, culture, and default responses. People make decisions about how to interact with each other, which ideas will be shared and which will not, what jokes are appropriate and funny, who gets the floor during debates and meetings, and what kinds of performance will be rewarded. Founders, CEOs, and senior vice presidents may strive to transform the organization's structures, culture, and defaults, but they often fail. An organizational system takes on a life of its own, selecting, rewarding, and absorbing members into it who then perpetuate the system.

Have you ever started a new job, gone to your first staff meeting, and asked yourself, "What have I signed up for? How will I ever fit in here?" And then, after several weeks pass and you've attended more staff meetings, you begin acting more like the other people around you? If so, you've experienced the power of an organizational system to sustain itself.

As early as the second gathering of any group of individuals, the structures, cultural elements, and defaults that make up the organization's system begin to take root. Behaviors begin to transform into patterns, and the patterns over time become entrenched. Everyone present contributes to the creation and maintenance of the system with every action they take.

Six months into a new job, you are probably no longer even aware of your organization's unique systemic characteristics. You have begun dressing like everyone around you, exchanging the right kind of jokes, using the appropriate tone of voice when speaking to your boss, and doing what it takes to get what you want from those around you, be they superiors, subordinates, or peers. You have learned how to succeed in the organization.

Every organization defines "success" in terms of different desired outcomes, whether it is improving profitability, saving the world from the scourge of AIDS, enhancing market share, improving public education, or creating breakthrough offerings. And the behaviors that help generate those desired outcomes get rewarded and celebrated, while those that do not get devalued.

Appropriate behaviors are reinforced in explicit ways, such as in the criteria for annual reviews, promotions, awards, bonuses, and retention. But they also get reinforced implicitly, such as whom the boss acknowledges and ignores in staff meetings, which stories get told and retold about the organization's best and worst moments, and what people tell one another about how to get ahead in the organization.

When Marty first started teaching at the Kennedy School, he had a conversation about his opportunities at the school with one of his mentors on the faculty. During the discussion, the mentor suddenly broke off in midsentence and said, "You know, Marty, I'm willing to have this conversation with you anytime, but only in private; you should never discuss this with more than one other person in the room." The message was clear: in this organizational system, it was considered inappropriate to be explicitly ambitious. If you discussed your normal human career ambitions openly, you could be seen as grasping for power and status. And your peers and superiors would likely interpret your behavior to mean that you cared more about your own future than about your scholarship responsibilities.

Over time, the structures, culture, and defaults that make up an organizational system become deeply ingrained, self-reinforcing, and very difficult to reshape. That makes sense when things are going well. But when something important changes—as with the economic and financial crises that began in 2008, or in more normal times when a new competitor enters the industry, the organization's founder leaves, customers' preferences shift, or new laws are passed—the system's tenacity can prevent it from adapting, from learning to thrive in the new context.

Many organizations get trapped by their current ways of doing things, simply because these ways worked in the past. And as tried-and-true patterns of thinking and acting produced success for the organization, they also produced success for the individuals who embraced those patterns. The people who rose to the top of the organization because of their ability to work with the system as is will have little interest in challenging its structures, culture, or defaults. Moving away from what has worked in the past is especially difficult for people in midcareer who have enjoyed considerable professional success. We knew a stockbroker on the East Coast, for example, whose huge firm dismissed the technology boom as a fad throughout the 1990s. The broker was still encouraging clients to buy AT&T as an anchor stock well into the company's downward spiral. We did some leadership development work at AT&T during those years and saw firsthand how difficult it was for many managers to see the warning signs that so many of those outside the organization recognized. In this case (as in many others across an array of industries), people were so immersed in their organization's system that they couldn't see the adaptive challenge staring them in the face. And as long as they were blind to that challenge, they could not make the changes needed to remain competitive in a shifting landscape.

As John Gardner, former U.S. cabinet secretary and founder of Common Cause and Independent Sector, put it: "All too often, on the long road up, young leaders become 'servants of what is' rather than 'shapers of what might be.' In the long process of learning how the system works, they are rewarded within the intricate structure of existing rules. By the time they reach the top, they are very likely to be trained prisoners of the structure. This is not all bad; every vital system reaffirms itself. But no system can remain vital for long unless some of its leaders remain sufficiently independent to help it change and grow."[1]

Adaptive challenges have unique characteristics. For example, take the challenge of trying to keep your best people from leaving for another organization.

1. *Input and output are not linear.* Your strategy produces unintended consequences. (You have increased salespeople's bonuses, but even more of them have defected because they look more successful to competitors.)

2. *Formal authority is insufficient.* The formal authority of your position is not enough to effect change. (You tell sales managers to spend more time mentoring high-potential associates, but they do not comply.)

3. *Different factions each want different outcomes.* A change you propose is praised by one group of employees but protested by another. (When you suggest that managers begin to hand off their most profitable clients to top associates so they can

develop new business, the managers grumble about losing long-standing relationships and easy reorders and giving their subordinates greater opportunities to replace them.)

4. *Previously highly successful protocols seem antiquated.* The tried-and-true techniques that worked for you in the past seem antiquated, not adequate for the new challenge. (Paying Gen Xers more money does not seem to buy their loyalty.)

Clearly, adaptive challenges comprise a tangle of interdependent threads. One of those threads is that your organization (as a system) reflects characteristics of the larger system (the industry or sector) in which it is embedded.

Take the main sectors operating in many economies: not-for-profit, private, and public. Each has distinctive characteristics that make them less able to adapt to new realities. For example:

- In the *not-for-profit sector*, organizations are typically mission driven. They tend to value consensus decision making, with everyone having a voice in tough decision making. That also gives everyone a veto.

- In the *private sector*, organizations are typically driven primarily by profit and operate in a highly competitive environment. They tend to protect historically but diminishingly profitable business lines even as the competitive marketplace changes around them.

- In the *public sector*, organizations tend to be risk averse, security oriented, and insulated from the pressure to adapt from marketplace competition.

Understanding that you are operating in multiple systems at the same time is an essential component of identifying and addressing adaptive challenges.

ON THE BALCONY

- Think about the sector in which your organization sits: not-for-profit, private, or public. How does that sector's distinctive culture affect the way your organization operates? What is the impact of this reality on your organization's ability to deal with adaptive challenges?

- List several of your organization's or family's distinguishing norms. What is their impact on your group's ability to deal with adaptive challenges?

ON THE PRACTICE FIELD

- Gather your direct reports. Ask them to describe what they see as the most difficult part of their transition into their current job and what strategies they used to ease the transition. Discuss whether these strategies have enabled them to cope better with the distinctive adaptive challenges of transitioning into a new role.

- Think about a recent crisis or challenge your team experienced. With your team, trace the events leading up to the challenge, as far back as you can. Identify the different outcomes people desired and the roles people played outside of their formal job to generate those outcomes. Ask what valuable new behaviors, attitudes, and ways of doing things emerged during this process of generating the desired outcomes. How might these new strengths be used to deal with adaptive challenges that arise in the future?

Every organization is not only one overall system but also a set of subsystems. We encourage you to look at three components to start with as a way into a multidimensional look at what is happening around you. The components are *structures* (for example, incentive programs), *culture* (including norms and meeting protocols), and *defaults* (routine processes of problem solving and ways of thinking and acting). These subsystems powerfully shape how people respond to and try to deal with adaptive pressures.

Discover Structural Implications

An organization's formal structures create the playing field and rules for all activities that take place in the overarching system. For example, structures may reward certain behaviors or attitudes (such as not making mistakes or bringing in new business or customer satisfaction) and implicitly discourage other behaviors and attitudes (risk taking or increasing business from existing clients or focusing on improving employee morale). Organization charts, reporting and communication protocols, laws and bylaws, employment contracts, hiring practices, and compensation plans are examples of such structures. Each structure can enhance, or constrain, an organization's ability to adapt to changes in the business landscape. "Merrill Lynch's Story" shows an example.

Merrill Lynch's Story

In the late 1990s, financial services giant Merrill Lynch began developing a division focused on providing 401(k) services, a field where robust competitors had a considerable head start. The pay structures for the 401(k) sales force were based on the company's existing corporate model. Specifically, the company determined bonus pay for the sales force (which typically made up a significant portion of salespeople's annual income) by how people within the institution regarded each of them and how well he did against sales targets. The formula made sense for the firm's established divisions. But it fell flat in the fledgling 401(k) division, where big growth would not occur until managers and sales reps had learned the business. Hampered by the traditional pay structure, the new 401(k) division could not attract the best and the brightest from within the bank. Worse, some of the most promising folks left for more lucrative opportunities at other companies.

To succeed in the 401(k) business, employees had to build external networks and sell unfamiliar new products. But that all-important bonus was still based on exceeding sales targets, so salespeople (understandably) focused their efforts on selling established products to existing clients. The compensation structure was nurturing behavior that generated success in other parts of the organization, but that same behavior undermined the new division's efforts.

The company eventually changed the bonus criteria for 401(k) division sales. Of course, this move sparked some tension in other divisions that continued to operate under the old system. But the 401(k) business soon began generating a substantial new revenue stream, and the firm became a significant player in the 401(k) field.

Take some time to get on the balcony and consider your own organization's structures and their impact.

ON THE BALCONY

- What behaviors do your organization's compensation and recognition systems encourage? Discourage? How well do the encouraged behaviors support the organization's strategic goals?

- What does your company's organization chart say about which functions and roles are valued most? Valued least? Looking at who has direct access to whom, what might this imply about who is designed to work together and who in isolation?

- How are departments or teams organized in your enterprise? Who reports to whom? What does this suggest about who has input into decision making?

- Recall the last senior manager or executive hired by your organization. How did the process work? Who did this person formally meet inside the organization? What does all this imply about how the new person is supposed to interact with the organization?

- What do the size, criteria for membership, election system, and payment of the board of directors tell you about how decisions are made and what and how value is recognized by the organization?

ON THE PRACTICE FIELD

- With your team, write the organization's mission on a whiteboard or flip chart. Draw two columns underneath. In the left column, list all of the organization's structures that support the mission. In the right column, list the structures that impede the mission. Here's a quick example:

Our mission: Improve quality of life for people in need

Structures supporting the mission	Structures impeding the mission
• Hiring practices emphasize recruiting people with a not-for-profit background and long track records of public service.	• Awards and other forms of recognition go primarily to those who get the biggest financial gifts from donors. Employees who find nonfinancial ways of serving our clients (such as establishing community mentoring programs) receive little recognition.

Surface Cultural Norms and Forces

An organization's culture is made up of its folklore (the stories that people frequently tell that indicate what is most important), its rituals (such as how new employees are welcomed into the company), its group norms (including styles of deference and dress codes), and its meeting protocols (like modes of problem solving and decision making). All of these cultural ingredients influence the organization's adaptability.

Unlike structures, the culture of an organization is not usually written down or formally documented, so it may be hard to describe in precise terms. But like structures, culture still powerfully determines what is considered acceptable and unacceptable behavior.

Think about your family as an organization you know well. What are the cultural rules about displaying emotion? Are emotional responses an appropriate element of robust interaction or frowned upon as a sign of weakness? Which emotions are OK to express? Under what circumstances? For example, in many families it is inappropriate to exhibit anger. Sometimes it is sadness or negativity that is forbidden, and, conversely, we even know families where the culture says that life is very difficult and displaying happiness means that you are not taking life seriously enough or not struggling hard enough or are naive. How does your family do on that score? (Most families we know are doing well if they are good at displaying any anger, negativity, or happiness, never mind all three.) Marty remembers being told when he was very young that if he did not have something good to say about someone, then say nothing. When Michael Dukakis ran for president in 1988 and was criticized for his analytical response to being asked what he would do if his wife were a rape victim, he responded by saying that he was taught at a very early age not to display his emotions. How long does it take after the norm of not displaying anger is established before members of the family are so out of practice that they have lost the capacity to do so?

Adaptive leadership requires understanding the group's culture and assessing which aspects of it facilitate change and which stand in the way. Too often, people taking on tough issues in organizational life do not devote enough time to this diagnosis, perhaps because an organizational culture feels less personal than community, ethnic, or family cultures do. But in organizations, each person both shapes and is shaped by the enterprise's culture, just as in their family.

How do you get on the balcony to diagnose your organization's culture? Begin by looking for four cultural flags: folklore, rituals, norms, and meeting protocols.

Folklore

In organizations, just as in any community, people make sense of the events and circumstances around them by developing enduring folklore, such as stories, jokes, and legends. Folklore has staying power because it embodies images and ideas that symbolize what matters most to people in the enterprise. These stories are told over and over again, at the coffee machine, in the cafeteria, during orientation programs, and at good-bye parties for departing staff. They endure because they contain truths about how the organization functions and what its members consider important.

But because folklore is so resonant and powerful, it can also obscure other important information. To get the full story about how your organization operates, you need to unpack each story and read between the lines, looking for clues about what is allowed as well as what is off-limits. Your findings will tell you something about how risk accepting, determined, value anchored and flexible the organization is, and therefore how well positioned it is to adapt to change.

Here are some characteristic themes that often show up in organizations' folklore:

- What happened when someone disagreed openly with the boss

- Why someone (especially a senior manager or executive) was fired or resigned from the company

- How the person with the longest tenure in the organization managed to achieve such longevity

- Why the founders created the organization, and why they left (or stayed)

- What happened at last year's holiday party that people are still talking about

- What happened at the last off-site for senior managers

- Who wields the real power on the board

- Who the CEO confides in and listens to
- How the organization scored a big success or recovered from a big failure

ON THE BALCONY

- Think about two or three people who were fired, who left your organization voluntarily, or who were given big promotions. What was the official company story about what happened to each of them? Was the story told in the hallways any different? If so, how? What do the various stories suggest about how the organization defines appropriate and inappropriate behavior? What do they suggest about the adaptability of your organization?

ON THE PRACTICE FIELD

- Ask each member of your team to write a brief, anonymous story about an incident or event in the organization that they think reveals the enterprise's values. Collect the stories and share them at the next retreat. (In our consulting practice, after each piece of client work, we do an after-action review where we describe and analyze our contribution to the outcome by focusing on both successful interventions and failed ones. Frequently in these meetings when we begin to analyze what went wrong, the lead consultants cannot see their own contribution to it. When these meetings are effective, they represent the value we place on being on the leading edge of our own practice in working to affirm our strengths, discover our blind spots, and develop new diagnostic and action options.)

- Ask members of your team to sit with you one-on-one and share a two-minute story about the organization's biggest success in the last six months. Videotape each account. Then gather your staff together to collectively watch all the stories in one sitting. Discuss what the stories, as a group, suggest about the organization's culture. For example, perhaps a theme of determination, or of inflexibility, crops up in most or all of the stories. Talk about what the stories suggest about your firm's adaptability.

Rituals

Every organization has rituals, practices that people repeat time and again under similar circumstances. Rituals can range from birthday parties, regular meetings, and holiday parties to support of charitable efforts and celebrations of special occasions and professional successes (such as winning a new client, finishing a big project, or retiring after many years of service). By determining which rituals your organization has established and which it does not have, you can tell a lot about the enterprise's adaptability. That, in turn, can help you figure out how to frame an adaptive challenge so that people are motivated to take it on. For example, if your company routinely celebrates big, collective successes, then build in events to acknowledge milestones of progress long before it is possible to reach completion. If your company likes celebrating individual success, then build in acknowledgment programs that honor new and smart risk-taking behaviors.

ON THE BALCONY

- List your organization's rituals. What do the rituals celebrate or acknowledge? Professional accomplishments? Making time for family life? Interaction across the organization? What do the rituals suggest about your firm's adaptability?

ON THE PRACTICE FIELD

- Identify a behavior that would make the enterprise more adaptable, and design a ritual that you think would encourage that behavior. For example, to foster an environment where people felt safer taking risks and making mistakes, Marta, a manager in a large sales organization, created a "best failure" ritual. At every Monday-morning staff meeting, the employee who learned the most from a mistake during the previous week shared what they learned, and then received a funny prize and a round of applause for contributing to the team's education.

Group Norms

Group norms govern how people relate to one another in an organization and can further illuminate the adaptability of an organization. Early in his career, Alexander interviewed for a job at Microsoft. He wore jeans because his friends at the company had told him that everyone wore jeans at work. He did not get the job, and later learned that no one was expected to wear jeans until *after* they had been hired. In addition to matters of attire, group norms can govern behaviors such as:

- Who gets to call whom by their first name

- What's appropriate gift giving in the organization

- Whether, how, and where people socialize

- Whose doors remain open, or closed

- What jokes are OK to tell, and which are bad form

- Who sits with whom in the cafeteria

Together, these norms can give you data and clues about how adaptive the organization is. In a basic frame, you can look at whether the norms create opportunities for learning or reinforce the status quo. If the same people always sit with the same people at lunch, this reinforces the old norms of the organization. If people are always sitting in new combinations, there may be a higher chance of cross-fertilization and new ideas happening.

ON THE BALCONY

- What behaviors are considered inappropriate in your organization? Yelling? Heated debate? Casual attire? Long lunches? Long weekends? Leaving at five o'clock instead of later? What do these rules suggest about your group's culture and its adaptability?

- Recall your first day on the job at your organization. What group norms initially struck you as surprising? Have you internalized those norms? If so, how quickly did you do so? What does this imply about the ways that your organization reinforces the status quo?

ON THE PRACTICE FIELD

- Think of a norm that would help your organization be more adaptable. Get two or three of your colleagues on board and start doing it whenever appropriate. For example, perhaps you would try out a norm that says, "People should spend five minutes at the end of meetings to reflect on the team performance and individual effectiveness." Begin to practice this norm in small ways at work and watch what happens.

Meeting Protocols

You can learn a lot about your organization's adaptability by looking at its meeting protocols. Protocols include what kinds of meetings are held regularly, who gets invited to them, and how the agenda is established. They speak to how power is distributed in the organization and what information is exchanged.

But some additional questions can reveal even deeper aspects of an organization's culture and thus its adaptability:

- Are meetings designed primarily for decision making or information sharing? Is there room for creative thought and learning from mistakes, or are they mostly for getting direction from the authority?

- If decisions are made at the meetings, what is the decision rule? How are decisions made? Do members discuss and then advise the chair, leaving the decision to her, or is a majority, supermajority, or consensus required for decisions? How does the decision-making rule reflect the context and purpose of the decision? Are all decisions made by one rule, or are different rules used for different problems and situations?

- Are attendees authorized to speak on subjects beyond their own areas of expertise? If so, are the new ideas integrated into thinking or just noise? Do people value nonjudgmental brainstorming, out-of-the-box ideas, and far out possibilities?

- To what extent are attendees expected or required to share the meeting's content with their subordinates? When the information is shared, what work is done to integrate the information into the current reality?

- What role does the most senior person in the room play during the meeting? (Facilitator? Decision maker? Inquisitor? Provocateur?) Does the person create space for conflict or marginalize it?

ON THE BALCONY

- Watch closely what happens at the next staff, team, or executive-team meeting that you attend. Then answer the questions listed above. What do your answers tell you about your company's culture and adaptability?

ON THE PRACTICE FIELD

- If you regularly convene meetings as part of your job, start every meeting with a new practice that you have not used before that encourages people to learn from and adapt to change. Here are some suggestions: Have everyone meditate for one minute. Solicit the most important lesson of the week. Ask people to spend more time discussing an idea that demands more attention. Cite a mistake that was made from which others can learn.

  Whatever new practice you decide to try, explain to everyone that it is an experiment. At the end of each session and at the end of the month, ask people what they thought of the practice, what they see as its advantages and disadvantages. Observe whether and how the meetings change as a result of the new practice. Are there more ideas being exchanged? Is there more participation from usually quiet attendees? More debate?

Recognize Default Interpretations and Behavior

In addition to structures and culture, an organization's problem-solving defaults can provide insights into the way your organization operates as a system—and its adaptability. Defaults are the ways of looking at situations that lead people to behave in ways that are comfortable and that have generated desirable results in the past. Organizations fall back on defaults because they are familiar *and* they have proved useful for explaining reality and solving problems in the past. When people in an organization find that a certain response to a particular type of situation worked well previously, they will likely repeat that response whenever they encounter an apparently similar situation. After all, why tamper with success? But the more a default continues to work, the more it gets repeated. And the harder it is for the organization to change when new realities require a different response. "Defaults in the Middle East" is one example.

A default interpretation, leading to a default response, puts people on familiar ground and plays to their organization's strengths. But in several respects, it can also be a constraint. It can blind people to a wider array of solutions and ideas that might generate even more value.

Also, a default that works in one setting, at one moment in time, may not necessarily work in another place or time. Because people tend to interpret new situations in ways that confirm the default, they fail to recognize the distinctive qualities of a new situation and thus cannot develop fresh solutions. Finally, an organization's default responses become predictable, enabling competitors or other adversaries to use that predictability for their own purposes. For example, extremists in the Middle East can easily hijack any progress toward peace because they know that violence will predictably generate a violent response in a cycle of reinforcement that puts the moderates on the defensive. After each turn of violence, moderates within each community are attacked for even considering compromises with the enemy toward peace. Or, to take another example, in political campaigns one technique for changing the content of the debate is to challenge the opponent with a provocative advertisement, knowing that doing so will produce a reaction, which can then be fodder for another advertisement and so on, having the effect in a very short time of displacing the central conversation.

Not surprisingly, defaults can greatly constrain an enterprise's adaptability. Have key elements in the business landscape changed?

Defaults in the Middle East

During and immediately following the war between Israel and Hezbollah in southern Lebanon in the summer of 2006, the American Jewish community responded to the crisis by creating the Israel Emergency Campaign (IEC). In a matter of weeks, the IEC raised $300 million to help rebuild the northern part of Israel, which had been devastated by Hezbollah missiles, and to aid families who had been displaced. It was a remarkable response. It was also a default response, a predictable reaction based on a tried-and-true response to events. The war fit the paradigm: Israel's survival was at stake, and the American Jewish community must support its defense and reconstruction.

The funds raised during the IEC undoubtedly contributed significantly to Israel's recovery. But this default response prevented members of the American Jewish community from considering a broader range of responses that might have generated an even better outcome. Was it possible to frame the American Jewish community's role differently—for example, as a partner in security rather than as a rescuer? For example, one senior authority in a major Jewish organization suggested in an e-mail to his network of colleagues that funds could be raised to support the rehabilitation of not only northern Israel but also southern Lebanon, which had also been devastated. His proposal received no support and even generated some considerable pushback. He backed off, and his idea went nowhere. In the end, much of the Lebanese reconstruction went by default to Hezbollah, which used the opportunity to solidify its patron-client relationship with Lebanese in need of help.

Are new behaviors required to deal with those changes? An adaptive organization looks beyond its defaults when confronted with a new challenge. "Fresh Eyes at Global Insurance" provides an example.

Overriding your organization's defaults often means taking on behaviors that feel uncomfortable and risky. But it is worth sticking with those behaviors if the situation warrants them. Indeed, it is a default's very familiarity that causes organizations to cling to it long after it has stopped being so widely useful.

Fresh Eyes at Global Insurance

A multinational company we'll call Global Insurance (GI) demonstrated its capacity for looking beyond its own defaults after merging with a similarly sized firm. GI's board and the CEO realized that the hardest aspect of the merger was going to be talent management. So, for the first time in GI's long and distinguished history, a successful senior executive from the sales side was moved laterally to serve as the corporate vice president for human resources (HR). The intent was for HR to be managed by someone who had a deep understanding of the business and long-standing credibility with the company's revenue-producing side. The appointment raised the HR function's visibility and status. People within the function and leaders from other functions began taking HR more seriously. As a result, their behavior changed. For example, the HR function shifted its role from just providing new skills and transactional personnel administrative services to helping cultivate and support important new business initiatives. Other executives in the business actually started asking HR for help. Thanks to these new behaviors, the top team aligned around strategic business initiatives and resource allocations, and two competing internal departments began working together on an integrative marketing strategy.

ON THE BALCONY

- Identify a default interpretation that your organization regularly makes. What view of the world is it based on? What predictable behavior does it generate? What created the default? In what situations has the default worked well? In what situations has it proved less effective? What's different about those two types of situations?

ON THE PRACTICE FIELD

- The next time you attend a meeting, track your own energy level as if you were operating a heart monitor. Note what causes your energy level to increase or decrease: is it around content, or conflict, or moving to action? Where you react is a great indicator of your default interests and where you may need to stretch beyond them.

- Study the body language of your employees during a presentation. Notice when people perk up and pay attention, when there is an immediate physical response to something said, and when the energy seems to seep out of the audience. What do your observations suggest about your company's defaults?

CHAPTER 5

Diagnose the Adaptive Challenge

A DAPTIVE CHALLENGES ARE difficult because their solutions require people to change their ways. Unlike known or routine problem solving for which past ways of thinking, relating, and operating are sufficient for achieving good outcomes, adaptive work demands three very tough, human tasks: figuring out what to conserve from past practices, figuring out what to discard from past practices, and inventing new ways that build from the best of the past.

Many people apply solutions that have worked in other situations in the past but fail to take sufficiently into account the value-laden complexity of the new problem situation. The complexity is not just analytical complexity in the way that difficult economics or engineering problems have uncertainty and complexity associated with them. They have human complexity because the problems themselves cannot be abstracted from the people who are part of the problem scenario itself. So the analysis must take into account the human dimensions of the changes required, the human costs, paces of adjustment, tolerances for conflict, uncertainty, risks and losses of various sorts, and the resilience of the culture, and network of authority and lateral relationships that will need to backstop the tensions and pains of change.

The failure to take into account the diagnosis of the human aspects of adaptive challenges, and the tendency to treat the diagnostic task like any other analytical, expert task that can be separated from the cultural and political human dimensions of the situation, is a primary cause of low implementation rates, whether of doctors' exercise and diet regimens for patients; brilliant public policy analysis performed in universities, think tanks, and government agencies; or well-considered strategic plans developed by the major business consulting firms.

Separating a situation's technical elements from its adaptive elements, listening for clues in what people are saying about the problem, and looking for adaptive challenge archetypes can help.

Determine the Technical and Adaptive Elements

Leadership begins, then, with the diagnostic work of separating a problem's technical elements from its adaptive elements. The task is to appreciate, value, and take in what the experts say, but then go beyond their filters to take into account the cultural and political human requirements of tangible progress. Anybody operating with a theory of leadership that assumes that experts know what is best, and that then the leadership problem is basically a sales problem in persuasion, is in our experience doomed at best to selling partial solutions at high cost.

Adaptive challenges are typically grounded in the complexity of values, beliefs, and loyalties rather than technical complexity and stir up intense emotions rather than dispassionate analysis. For these reasons, organizations often avoid addressing the value-laden aspects and try to get through the issue with a technical fix. For example, we have worked with health-care organizations that have tried to contain costs by introducing new technology, rather than looking at the highly valued processes and procedures that contribute to the problem. Typically, the new technology has created its own set of adaptive issues (e.g., medical personnel who do not want to give up face-to-face patient contact in favor of e-mail) and has not produced the desired cost savings. One way you know that there is an adaptive challenge facing your organization or community is that the problem persists even after a series of attempted technical fixes.

But even when people feel a genuine interest in naming the adaptive challenge, doing so is difficult. People are enmeshed in their defaults, and it's difficult to gain the balcony perspective needed to more completely define the problem. Attempts to describe the situation can lead to one or more of the following stories:

- *Where's Waldo?* Presenters tell a long, complicated story about the problem situation and its history, but the story makes no mention of their own roles, interests, stakes, or contributions to the problem.

- *Community of jerks.* The story goes something like this: "If all the jerks I work with would just shape up or get out of the way or agree with me or do their jobs or do what I say . . . we wouldn't have this problem."

- *End world hunger.* The story is that the problem is so big, so important, and so noble that no one can be faulted for taking it on and failing.

- *Breakfast of champions.* The story is that the organization has a huge, incredibly difficult challenge that it has already solved.

How do you know whether you and your team are confronting an adaptive challenge? Look for two characteristic signals: a cycle of failure and a persistent dependence on authority.

A Cycle of Failure

The most common leadership failure stems from trying to apply technical solutions to adaptive challenges. Authorities make this mistake because they misinterpret or simplify the problem, fail to see how the organizational landscape has changed, or prefer a "solution" that will avoid disruption or distress in the organization. Sometimes throwing a technical fix at the problem will solve a piece of it and provide a diversion from the tougher issue, though only temporarily.

Understandably, people gravitate toward technical solutions, especially those that have worked in the past, because they reduce uncertainty and are easier to apply. The tendency will often persist even when the evidence of failure is clear: "Let's try it again, this time with more enthusiasm and attention." (Remember the old saw, often attributed to Albert Einstein, that defines insanity as trying the same thing over and over again and expecting a different result?)

These failure cycles can unfold over short or long time frames, depending on the nature of the problem and the applied technical solution. It is also quite difficult to see these cycles in real time, without the benefit of hindsight. You have to get on the balcony and look for indicators early on and midstream, which is particularly hard to do when you think you've found a painless way to move forward. "A Failure Cycle at Work" gives an example.

A Failure Cycle at Work

A retail company that sold mostly to U.S. federal agencies expanded its territory beyond Washington, D.C., to New York. The field staff had a difficult time selling the product under the company guidelines that had been developed for D.C. As was the custom, they wrote a memo outlining the situation, a friendly e-mail addressed to corporate headquarters and discussing how the New York metro market was different. They got no response. There was no change in the company's policies or practices. And no improvement in New York.

The staff wrote a longer, more detailed e-mail that took a tougher-sounding stance. Still nothing changed. Then they wrote a really harsh e-mail. That produced a response: a key person on the field staff was fired.

The increasingly aggressive e-mails did not help corporate headquarters adapt to a new reality. It was easier for corporate to fire the "troublemaker" from the field staff than to treat the New York initiative as an adaptive challenge that needed to be addressed.

ON THE BALCONY

- Think of a problem you have tried (and failed) to fix multiple times. What solution have you attempted to use? What story have you been telling to explain why the problem remains unfixed?

- Identify a major challenge facing your organization. Which elements of the challenge are technical, and which are adaptive? Which are so intertwined as to be indistinguishable at first glance? Consider the relative degree of difficulty you are facing in trying to manage the technical versus the adaptive elements of the challenge you have identified.

ON THE PRACTICE FIELD

- Meet one-on-one with each member of your team. Ask each person to name the most pressing adaptive challenge confronting the team. Ask each to then tell a story about why the problem has not yet been addressed. Videotape each story, and then watch the team's "film shorts" together as a group. Discuss what you are seeing, and explore the advantages and limitations of the current ways of thinking expressed in the stories.

Dependence on Authority

From the moment humans are born, they turn to those in authority to provide answers, comfort, sustenance, and safety. Their first concern as newborns is to find the milk supply and then to figure out how to keep it flowing. Babies do whatever is necessary to make that happen: laugh, cry, smile, or whine. As with other mammals, this dependence on authority is hardwired into human DNA. Teenagers develop more complex and nuanced relationships with parents, teachers, coaches, and other authority figures. But even rebellious teenagers and otherwise self-sufficient adults often look again to authorities to provide direction, protection, and order when problems arise.

Holding authority figures responsible for causing and/or fixing organizational problems makes sense when it's a technical problem that fits their authoritative expertise. But what happens when an adaptive challenge lurks beneath the surface? Authority figures typically try to meet these challenges just as if they were technical problems because that is what people expect of them, and that's also what they've come to expect of themselves. Usually, they think that's what it means to be the "go to" person. But authorities cannot solve an adaptive challenge by issuing a directive or bringing together a group of experts, because the solutions to adaptive problems lie in the new attitudes, competencies, and coordination of the people with the problem itself. Because the problem lies in people, the solution lies in them, too. So the work of addressing an adaptive challenge must be done by the people connected to the problem. And those in authority must mobilize people to do this hard work rather than try to solve the problem for them.

We have earlier identified characteristics of adaptive challenges. Each of the characteristics is a flag or a signal for diagnosis; table 5-1 connects the characteristics with a social flag that can give you a starting point for your diagnostic work.

A Basic Diagnostic Framework

Diagnosing an adaptive challenge is a challenge in itself. At best it requires some of the skills we are discussing in this part plus a healthy dose of willingness to step into the unknown. That is why reality testing is so important. But there are a series of questions that we have found useful for you to use in framing this piece of work:

- What is the mission or purpose of the organization or group facing the challenge?

TABLE 5-1

Identifying a primarily adaptive challenge

Concept	Identifying flag
Persistent gap between aspirations and reality.	The language of complaint is used increasingly to describe the current situation.
Responses within current repertoire inadequate.	Previously successful outside experts and internal authorities unable to solve the problem.
Difficult learning required.	Frustration and stress manifest. Failures more frequent than usual. Traditional problem-solving methods used repeatedly, but without success.
New stakeholders across boundaries need to be engaged.	Rounding up the usual suspects to address the issue has not produced progress.
Longer time frame necessary.	Problem festers or reappears after short-term fix is applied.
Disequilibrium experienced as sense of crisis starting to be felt.	Increasing conflict and frustration generate tension and chaos. Willingness to try something new begins to build as urgency becomes widespread.

- Does the current challenge emerge from changing values or priorities within the organization or changing conditions externally?

- What are the adaptive aspects and the technical aspects of this challenge?

- Where am I in the organization, and what is my perspective on the challenge?

- Who are the relevant parties to the challenge, and what are their perspectives?

- Where does the conflict emerge—at the level of orienting values and mission, or at the level of objectives, strategy, and tasks?

- Are there internal contradictions, breaks in the linkage that ideally should coherently connect the orienting values and mission of the organization through its strategy, goals, objectives, and action plans down to the concrete level of its operations close to the ground?

- To test ways to frame the adaptive work, start at high levels of abstraction, at the level of orienting purpose and values, where it is likely that most of the relevant parties agree. Then ask, "What would it take to do that?" to get down to the next lower level of abstraction. Keep asking that question, getting more and more specific, until the conflicts begin to emerge. Then frame the work at the lowest level of abstraction where people agree just above the level where the conflict begins to emerge.

- What work avoidance mechanisms might have been operating to control the conflict and maintain the equilibrium?

- What authority and resources do I have to manage the organization and the environment? How well positioned am I to intervene? What assumptions am I making here that might be constraining me?

- What strategies have I tried? What happened? What strategies have I thought of but been unwilling to try? Why? What strategies might work that I am unwilling to even consider? Again, what assumptions am I making that might be constraining my imagination of possible interventions?

ON THE BALCONY

- Choose an adaptive challenge your organization currently faces, and identify the people who have been involved to date in trying to solve it. Who are they? What degree of authority do they possess? How effective have they been so far? Brainstorm ideas about others who should get involved in the problem because they are part of the problem, but have not been drawn into the process yet.

ON THE PRACTICE FIELD

- Over the next week, look for signs of dependence on authority figures to address adaptive challenges in your organization. Look for where people are asking their senior authorities what to do rather than make more of their own decisions and run more of their own experiments. At the end of the week, meet with your team, name the signs you have noted, and ask team members to add to your list before you collectively try to dig into any aspects of the adaptive challenge itself.

Listen to the Song Beneath the Words

To identify the adaptive challenges confronting an organization, look beyond what people are saying about them. We call this listening to the song beneath the words. There is so much more data than just the actual words being said. Look for the body language, eye contact, emotion, energy. For example, pay as much attention to what is *not* being said as you do to what *is* being said. If people around you are focusing their stories on team dynamics but not on how to produce the outcome, that may indicate there is a problem with being accountable for the outcome. Also watch for behaviors that seem at odds with people's statements and with company policies. For instance, look for unusual factions or alliances as well as informal authority relationships that differ from the organizational chart. These may indicate where informal authority within the system is placed. Finally, notice whether there are any disproportionate reactions to proposals regarding possible solutions to the problem. A response that seems out of scale with the suggested idea or initiative is a strong sign that something else is going on, something more than a simple solution to this one issue.

ON THE BALCONY

- Think about the formal and informal interactions you have had recently with your boss to address an adaptive challenge or other problem. Try to identify the song beneath your boss's words. What story might your boss be telling others to convey who she is or what she is already doing to solve the challenge? What would be her version of the encounter with you? Ask yourself what steps you could take or data you could collect or observe that might confirm or challenge your hypothesis regarding what your boss's song is about. Try to discover the people tugging at her sleeves and talking in her ear. What stakes and loyalties do they represent to her?

ON THE PRACTICE FIELD

- During your next retreat or staff meeting, ask members of your team to write a sentence or two expressing the song of each other participant. That is, how does each person wish to be seen by the others? For example, we have a colleague who always usefully sings a purpose song: "Why are we doing this? What is our mission?" Reading others' descriptions will give everyone the opportunity to understand that they may be communicating unintended messages or may be overplaying a message.

Four Adaptive Challenge Archetypes

Adaptive challenges come in many shapes and forms. Often, they represent complex shifts in the organizational landscape (such as changes in technology, customer preferences, or market dynamics) that require a complex response. We have seen four basic patterns that are particularly common. Usually these overlap in any setting, and by familiarizing yourself with these archetypes, you can more easily identify and begin to diagnose the adaptive challenges facing your own organization. The four archetypes outlined will help you distinguish a complex, primarily technical problem from a complex, primarily adaptive challenge, allowing you to marshal the right resources and strategy.

Archetype 1: Gap Between Espoused Values and Behavior

How you behave can at times differ from what you say you value and believe about yourself. For example, our friend Harold thinks of himself as someone who wants to end world hunger. Yet when he looks back over the past year to see how he has invested his time and energy, he realizes that, in actuality, he has done little to mitigate the problem. A CEO we know named Alice always tells her family, and us, that she is committed to balancing her nonwork obligations with her professional duties. But when she steps back and compares how much time she is spending at the office or on business trips versus at home with her family, she realizes the scales are tipped heavily toward work. Roberto, a member of the management team at a professional services firm, assured us and his employees that a key part of his job is to help them develop their professional skills. But when he analyzed how much effort he really put into activities such as giving them stretch assignments and coaching them, he saw that he had actually done little in the way of developing his people. In all three examples, there's a gap between the person's espoused values and his or her behavior.

After Alexander and his wife, Yasuko, had their first child, our colleague Jeff Lawrence advised him, "Worry not that your child listens to you; worry most that they watch you." Jeff was riffing on the old saw "Actions speak louder than words." And research shows that the human brain responds more to visual cues (including what a person is doing) than to auditory cues (such as what they're saying they intend to do).

Just as individuals can have a gap between what they say they value and how they actually behave, so can organizations. Why? Closing that gap might well be painful, traumatic, impossible, or disruptive. And making a long list of "core values" (such as "treating one another with utmost respect," "appreciating differences," "putting the customer first," and "making the world a better place") makes people in the organization feel good about themselves and their enterprise, even if they are actually doing little beyond the bare minimum to live those values.

In many organizations, particularly often in large professional services firms, there is a gap between the organization's espoused values and its actual behavior when senior authorities advocate collaborative behavior but reward individual performance. Operating across boundaries to break down the silos will not be achieved just by telling people at staff meetings they should do it. Closing that gap is a difficult adaptive challenge because people in the organization have been successful through their patterns of behavior and will want to continue to do what earned them success, especially when they still are recognized and rewarded for doing so.

Individuals and organizations alike come face-to-face with their real priorities when the gap between their espoused values and their behavior can no longer be ignored. You know whether you and your company really care about something when that value collides with preferred behavior. "Closing the Gap in Civil Rights" shows an example from American history.

Closing the Gap in Civil Rights

Martin Luther King Jr.'s civil rights initiative pushed Americans to face up to a yawning gap between their espoused values and their actual behavior. When King stood on the steps of the Lincoln Memorial in August 1963 and delivered his renowned speech, he was giving voice not just to his own dream but to America's: "I . . . have a dream. It is a dream deeply rooted in the American dream." That dream had first been articulated by the nation's founders (even though some owned slaves) and was expressed powerfully again in Abraham Lincoln's Gettysburg Address. The country was dedicated to the proposition that all people are created equal. And by giving this dream such powerful language, King made it come alive. His work on behalf of civil rights for African Americans forced people to acknowledge the contradiction between the espoused, shared dream of equal opportunity and the reality of segregation and racism in daily life. The disturbing images of racist conflicts depicted on television brought that contradiction home, literally. People could no longer ignore the fact that the country was not living up to its most cherished values.

ON THE BALCONY

- Think of a gap between an espoused value and an actual behavior that currently exists in your organization. In what way does the gap's existence fulfill a need or desire for the individuals whose behaviors do not reflect the espoused value (such as your boss, yourself, your peers, and your employees)? What do these individuals stand to lose if they were to change their behaviors to better reflect the espoused value?

- Put yourself in your boss's shoes. Better, get into your boss's head. Describe the story the boss recounts at night about what happened that day, about what is most important, and why things are the way they are. Now look at a piece of what you experience as "dysfunction" in your team. In what way does it serve you or your boss to let it continue the way it is? How does it make your or the boss's life easier to have it just the way it is? Which of the boss's needs, interests, loyalties, or values are served by the current situation?

ON THE PRACTICE FIELD

- Over the next two weeks, track your team's activities in thirty-minute increments. For each increment, identify the type of challenge you are working on (primarily technical or primarily adaptive). Then track the values motivating the team to work on this activity. Review the record to see how you are spending your time across different challenges.

- Think of an important change that people in the organization have been talking about for a long time. Now one-on-one, engage them in a conversation about why the organization, and maybe they in particular, haven't done more to make it happen.

Archetype 2: Competing Commitments

Like individuals, organizations have numerous commitments. And sometimes these commitments come into conflict. For example, a multinational consumer products corporation with operations in numerous countries tries to create one unified brand while also seeking to preserve the unique brand associations it has in each country where it operates. A law firm wants to grow its practice while also allowing older partners and those with family responsibilities to work shorter hours. A human rights organization needs to raise more funds, which requires additional staffing, but it also wants to cut costs.

To resolve such competing commitments, organizational leaders must often make painful choices that favor some constituencies while hurting others. And this constitutes another adaptive challenge archetype. Because these decisions are so difficult, many leaders simply avoid making them, or they try to arrive at a compromise that ultimately serves no constituency's needs well. As a result, the organization's commitments continue to be in conflict.

The hard fact is this: when an organization's commitments are in competition with one another, people in authority can resolve the situation perhaps only by making decisions that generate losses for some groups and gains for others. There is rarely a way to get around it (except through avoidance). Win-win solutions are ideal, but not common with strategic choices. When we hear someone talk about "win-wins," we wonder whether anything really lasting is going to change. When competing commitments need to be resolved, the questions are, how will the decision be made: through a mandate from on high, by majority rule, through consensus where everyone involved must agree? What groups are going to lose something as a result of this decision, and what precisely are they going to lose?

ON THE BALCONY

- Think of several commitments that are currently competing in your own organization. How are people in your organization currently dealing with this situation? What are the consequences, positive and negative, of this way of coping?

ON THE PRACTICE FIELD

- The next time you're in a staff meeting and you realize that there are several commitments competing with one another in your

team, acknowledge the situation verbally. Name the commitments
that seem to be in competition, and ask meeting participants to
add their own impressions. Keep the conversation focused on the
commitments themselves and not on the people, not on who is
supposed to be fulfilling them and how they are falling short.

Archetype 3: Speaking the Unspeakable

Whenever members of an organization come together and have a conversation, there are actually two types of conversation going on. One is
manifested in what people are saying publicly. The other is unfolding in
each person's head. Only a small portion of the most important content
of those conversations (radical ideas, naming of difficult issues, painful
interpretations of conflicting perspectives) ever gets surfaced publicly.
Most of the time, the public discourse consists primarily of polite ban-
ter or debate that falls short of naming, let alone resolving, conflict.

There are always a thousand reasons not to speak the unspeakable.
For one thing, the organizational system does not want you to say these
things out loud; doing so will generate tension and conflict that will
have to be addressed. Indeed, anyone who has the courage to raise
unspeakable issues may become immediately unpopular and could lose
standing in the organization (or even her job).

The presence of a senior authority in the room makes it even riskier
(and thus less likely) that someone will give voice to the unspeakable.

But getting people to share what seems unspeakable is essential for
an organization that hopes to move forward in the face of changing priorities or external conditions. Only by examining the full range of perspectives can a group of people increase their chances of developing
adaptive solutions.

ON THE BALCONY

- Think back to the last tough conversation you had in which you or
  someone else gave voice to the unspeakable. What enabled this to
  occur? (For example, did someone else ask each person to give voice
  to a heartfelt but unpopular perspective? Was there a disturbing

incident that everyone noticed was undermining the rest of the meeting? Did someone just get fed up?) What happened as a result of the conversation?

Then think of a recent conversation in which the unspeakable remained unspoken. What results came from that conversation? How do the results of the two conversations compare in terms of their usefulness to your organization?

ON THE PRACTICE FIELD

- During your next conversation with your boss, purposefully share more of what you are thinking than you would normally share. For instance, if you do not typically express concerns about ideas your boss is proposing, try expressing one. Frame it in neutral rather than judgmental language, such as "I'm worried that these design changes you are describing will put the project behind schedule and over budget. Can you tell me more about how this would work?" not "We cannot make these changes; they're too expensive and time-consuming." See what happens.

- The next time you are attending a meeting, draw two vertical columns on a piece of notepaper. In the right-hand column, write down statements or questions voiced by you in response to someone's comment. Write these contributions word for word. In the left-hand column, write what you were really thinking when you made your statements or asked your questions. Look at the two lists, and ask yourself what differences between the two columns suggest about what might be considered unspeakable in your organization.[1]

  For example, suppose you work for a mobile telecommunications firm whose established markets have become saturated. The company is considering ways to generate new revenue streams. You manage the company's North American regional operations. You're in a meeting attended by other regional managers as well as the vice president of strategy development. Table 5-2 is a quick example of how your left-hand/right-hand column writings might look.

TABLE 5-2

What I thought and what was said

What I thought	What was said
	Joe, VP: "So, we really need to think about how we can generate new kinds of revenue. Expanding into emerging markets is one idea I'd like us to explore."
"Oh no. If we expand into emerging markets like China, Africa, and India, where will that leave me and my team? We'll get a lot fewer resources if the company steps up operations in those other regions."	**Me:** "There's a lot of potential in emerging markets."
What's unspeakable: the loss of status and power that could happen to my group (and other groups managing established markets) if our company dramatically changes its growth strategy.	

Archetype 4: Work Avoidance

As we discussed in part I, in every organization people develop elaborate ways to prevent the discomfort that comes when the prospects of change generate intolerable levels of intensity. For example, managers form a new subcommittee that has no real power or influence to effect the proposed change. Executives hire a diversity officer so no line manager has to take responsibility for increasing diversity in his or her own department. People blame external forces (fickle consumers, an unscrupulous new competitor) for the company's loss of market share. They change the subject or make a joke when someone insists on discussing the problem. Or they treat an adaptive challenge as a technical problem—for example, by moving a retail item to a more prominent position in a store when sales are down due to better competitors' products in the marketplace. These behaviors are all ways of avoiding the harder work of mobilizing adaptive change.

We find two common pathways in the patterns by which people resist the potential pain of adaptive change: diversion of attention and displacement of responsibility. Such defensive behaviors are sometimes deliberate and strategically protective against the threats of change, but sometimes they are unplanned, poorly monitored or unconscious reactions. Reality testing, the effort to grasp the challenge fully, is often an early victim of the social and personal unrest associated with adaptation. People may initially assess and address problems realistically. But if this does not pay early dividends, moving into a protective posture may take precedence over enduring the prolonged uncertainty associated with weighing divergent views, running costly experiments, and facing the need to refashion loyalties and develop new competencies.

With sustained distress, people may focus on just getting by. They often produce misdiagnoses: a society may scapegoat a faction because of a dominant perception that it is indeed responsible for the problem. More severe patterns of avoidance are generated by prolonged periods of disequilibrium. In a classic study of thirty-five dictatorships, all of them emerged in societies facing crisis.[2] The Great Depression of the 1930s generated such deep yearnings for quick and simple solutions in many countries around the world that groups in them lost the capacity to critically and open-mindedly reality test different strategies for restoring their own local and national economies. A reversion to narrower identity groups took hold. Charismatic demagoguery, repression, scapegoating, and externalizing the enemy were all in play, leading to the catastrophes of World War II.

Here's a list of work avoidance tactics:

Diverting Attention

- Focus only on the technical parts of the challenge and apply a technical fix.

- Define the problem to fit your current expertise.

- Turn down the heat in a meeting by telling a joke or taking a break.

- Deny that the problem exists.

- Create a proxy fight, such as a personality conflict, instead of grappling with the real problem.

- Take options off the table to honor legacy behaviors.

Displacing Responsibility

- Marginalize the person trying to raise the issue—that is, shoot the messenger.

- Scapegoat someone.

- Externalize the enemy.

- Attack authority.

- Delegate the adaptive work to those who can't do anything about it, such as consultants, committees, and task forces.

ON THE BALCONY

- What are the work avoidance tactics most often used in your team, department, or organization?

- What routines has your organization developed to leap to action by throwing a technical fix at a problem without addressing the under-lying adaptive issues?

ON THE PRACTICE FIELD

- Discuss work avoidance tactics with members of your team. Together, identify a complex problem your team is currently facing, and list all the tactics the team is using to reduce the stress associated with dealing with the issue. During an upcoming meeting, encourage team members to point out instances when anyone in the group is using one of the techniques. For example, a team member might raise her hand and say something like, "When John put up the graphic showing our decline in client-satisfaction ratings, Sheila made a comment about how we can't keep up with our clients' ever-changing tastes. In my view, we can't afford to blame external forces for the problem we're discussing."

- Sometimes, work avoidance mechanisms are easier to identify than the issues being avoided. The timing and nature of the work avoid-ance mechanism often provide a clue to the conflicting perspectives on the adaptive issues that remain hidden. What issue was surfacing or being discussed at the time when the group generated a work avoidance mechanism? What was the work avoidance mechanism? Did anyone intervene to redirect the group's attention to the issue, or try to surface conflicting perspectives?

- When your organization or team goes through a period of stress and discomfort, where do the symptoms appear? Who is embodying the stress for the team? Interview that person to learn what that person is dealing with on behalf of the team; discover the sources of stress: competing values, suppressed perspectives, protecting against losses?

CHAPTER 6

Diagnose the Political Landscape

UNDERSTANDING THE POLITICAL relationships in your organization is key to seeing how your organization works as a system. And this activity, what we call thinking politically, can help you design more effective strategies for leading adaptive change. The key assumption behind thinking politically is that people in an organization are seeking to meet the expectations of their various constituencies. When you understand the nature of those expectations, you can mobilize people more effectively.

People in organizations are under the same kinds of pressures as politicians. Talk with legislators anywhere in the world, and you will find them very respectful of the competing interests among their constituencies. They also know that whenever they negotiate allocation of resources with peers and constituencies, someone will win and someone else will lose. A legislator may say to her colleague, "I'd love to support your idea for the new industry regulations. I actually agree that it would benefit our region and our state in many ways. But I have a real problem back home in my district, because there are a thousand people whose livelihoods depend on a company that operates in that industry. Your proposal would weaken the industry's competitive positioning and may put that company out of business. What can I do?" This politician will likely be seen by peers as honorable, not selfish. And her colleagues will probably help her go back to her constituents and equip them to face the difficult challenges on the horizon, perhaps by amending the legislation to pace the change and give time for that district to do its adaptive work, either by the company itself becoming more competitive or by the community attracting other jobs.

Legislatures are virtually the only place in professional work where people routinely put their real stakes right on the table, in full view. In legislatures, the personal stakes tied to the need to represent one's community are the units of currency around which all engagement is conducted. In most organizations, doing that is taboo. You rarely see a person in business say something like, "Listen, I cannot possibly sell that new process to my team. I'm really going to have a problem with my salespeople because they're so committed to doing it their way. They'll run me out of here if I order them to adopt the new process you're describing."

Still, small *p* politics exists in every group of human beings, from families to huge multinational corporations. Some people control resources and define goals, and individuals must negotiate to determine who gets what and who's going to do what to achieve the desired goals. Thus, managing the politics in your organization, no matter how distasteful that may seem, is essential to leading adaptive change.

Marty's mentor, the late Elliot Richardson, who was elected lieutenant governor and attorney general of Massachusetts and served in more federal cabinet-level positions than anyone else in U.S. history, called politics "the most difficult of the arts and the noblest of the professions."[1]

To think politically, you have to look at your organization as a web of stakeholders. For each stakeholder, you need to identify her:

- *Stake in the adaptive challenge at hand.* How will she be affected by resolution of the challenge?

- *Desired outcomes.* What would she like to see come out of a resolution of the issue?

- *Level of engagement.* How much does the person care about the issue and the organization?

- *Degree of power and influence.* What resources does the person control, and who wants those resources?

Equally important, you must identify each stakeholder's:

- *Values.* What are the commitments and beliefs guiding the behaviors and decision-making processes?

- *Loyalties.* What obligations does the person have to people outside his or her immediate group (such as long-standing customer or supplier relationships)?

- *Losses at risk.* What does the person fear losing (status, resources, a positive self-image) if things should change?

- *Hidden alliances.* What shared interests does the person have with people from other major stakeholder groups (for example, with peers in another department) that could lead the person to form an alliance that could build influence?

How do you answer these questions? The best way is to gather information directly from the stakeholders themselves. But if you are in a senior authority role, the people you interview may not be completely honest with you. Thus you may need to make judgment calls and interpret some of what you hear. For example, a direct report who says he is not afraid of losing his job but who works late every night may be more afraid than he is letting on (or even acknowledges to himself). You may also need to make the data-gathering process safe for stakeholders—for instance, by talking around the watercooler, going out to lunch, or watching a sports game together. Finally, you can use third-party data (such as through a common colleague) to further interpret what you are hearing from the relevant stakeholders, although any one third party has their own filters and interests through which they are absorbing and relaying the data.

Take a closer look at the last four stakeholder questions listed above. At the end of the chapter is a worksheet (see table 6-1) that should help you map your stakeholders according to what you know about them.

Uncover Values Driving Behavior

When you want to drive adaptive change in your organization, and others are getting in your way, it is natural to view in less-than-charitable ways those who are impeding progress, as you understand it. You tell yourself, "That marketing vice president who is sabotaging my initiative just wants to make sure he gets his year-end bonus." You start viewing these stakeholders as two-dimensional characters rather than real human beings with legitimate aspirations and needs. In reality, each of these "characters" has a much more complex set of concerns and priorities than the one you might be imagining.

You need to understand that complexity. It is not about being more sympathetic. It is much more tactical than that. By identifying your stakeholders' strongest values, the things they care most about, you may be able to find another way for the resisters among them to serve those values than by opposing your proposed change.

People think of themselves as holding many values simultaneously. But they will focus on only a few of those values when the going gets rough. Those are their core values. Something that is seventh on your list of the things in which you believe might as well not be on the list at all. There are so many more important values to be served, and you have limited time and energy. Think of a manager you know who is "committed to diversity" but who never seems to make much progress on it because the unit's profitability or their own career advancement is actually more important to them and is tied to other metrics.

To mobilize stakeholders to engage with your change initiative, you have to identify their strongest values and think about how supporting your program would enable your stakeholders to serve those values.

In recent work we did with a group of public school superintendents, we were exploring the issue of extending the school day by half an hour. Almost immediately, the group began disparaging the motivations of the teachers union and custodians as self-serving. They said the union and custodians would not want to extend the school day because they did not want to work any harder in a longer day. It was difficult for the superintendents to consider the possibility that the teachers and custodians may have had honorable reasons for opposing the longer school day, such as preventing burnout among teachers, preserving class preparation time, giving students time to engage in outside activities, promoting their own healthy family life, or that the custodial staff believed they needed that time to clean the school and make sure it was safe for students.

Acknowledge Loyalties

No stakeholders operate solo. They have external loyalties, to people outside their group and to the people behind the ideas that matter to them. When representatives from a teachers union enter a bargaining session, they intend to fight not only for their own interests but also for the interests of those they represent: the team members who selected them to go to the meeting, the union members and their families, their peers in other unions who have expectations of them, and the organization itself. All of these other parties are counting on the representatives to protect their jobs and provide them with some security so they can make the mortgage payments and have time for their own children as well. The representatives may also feel loyal to an idea about the role of unions. Perhaps they read a biography of the revered labor leader David Dubinsky twenty-five years ago in graduate school, or they worked with farm worker rights activist César Chavez the year after graduation. How could they ever let those icons down?

For any stakeholder, having to disappoint his own constituencies is immensely difficult. Again, the ongoing conflict between the Israelis and the Palestinians in the Middle East is illustrative. The conflict involves different religious groups, factions within each of them, and stakeholder groups in each country in the region and further abroad. The senior authorities in each of these groups are under immense pressure to give up nothing that is important to their own people, whether it is land, the dream of a hopeful future, or respect from other groups.

In the 1980s, Alexander was in the Crown Heights section of Brooklyn, New York, after rioting had broken out between members of the area's neighboring black and Jewish communities. He was working with a group that brought blacks and Jews together for a series of meetings to discuss how they could get along more peacefully. Extraordinary conversations emerged. But these exchanges never translated into real change outside the meeting-room walls. Alexander's group had not adequately diagnosed the two sides' external loyalties. It had not understood what was at stake for each side in shifting some of the long-held loyalties that anchored deeply held beliefs about one another.

One way to understand the challenges raised by external loyalties is to use the metaphor of a vegetable stew. To make a good vegetable stew, you have to cook the ingredients just enough that they give up some of their original color and taste; otherwise, you'd have a pot of crunchy vegetables, not a stew. But if you cook the vegetables *too* much, each of them will lose so much of its distinctive qualities that you will end up with a pot of undifferentiated mush.

Imagine these vegetables as stakeholders, and suppose you get the stew just right. When those carrots and onions go back to carrot-land and onion-land, having sacrificed some of their distinctiveness in the interests of contributing to the stew, their old friends and family at home will notice they have changed. "You . . . smell like an onion," the carrots will say. "You're not one of us anymore. You've sold out. We sent you there to represent us and champion our views to the others, not come back contaminated with *their* juices on *you*. What did they do to you there?"

That presents a real problem for those well-intentioned returning carrots. Reentry would be a lot easier if the carrot came back completely unchanged, if it could mask what had changed, or if it could quickly revert to its old familiar carrot self. For each stakeholder in your change initiative, the knowledge that he is going to have to return to "carrot-land" (or "onion-land" or "lentil-land") can put up a huge barrier to collaboration.

In leading adaptive change, broaden your focus beyond just the people in the room, the players most directly involved. Take into account the people outside the room about whom the players care. And consider how you might help each stakeholder in the room to engage their constituencies outside the room in the questions and solutions you are exploring at the table.

In a sense, we are asking you to imagine that every working group is like an elected group of legislators or a city council, with each representing a set of constituents with a mix of expectations asking to be satisfied. Figure 6-1 illustrates a working group brought together to work on an adaptive challenge, each seeing it differently because each represents the perspectives of his or her faction, guild, division, or subset in the community.

Alexander and his colleagues were asking people in Crown Heights to bring together a stew of racial and religious factions and create a

FIGURE 6-1

The politics of change

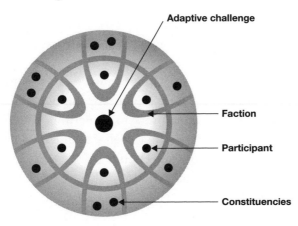

community with some shared purpose and identity. But his group did not take the crucial step of preparing the participants for what would happen to them as they began to share and learn from each other's perspectives. As a result, blacks returning to their community were seen as having been tainted by the Jews. It was the same story for the Jews. Those who participated in the sessions were seen as being disloyal to their own when they returned to their neighborhoods. Each stakeholder had to reestablish how they were still Jewish or black and show how they had not given anything up to the other party. The promising ideas that emerged during the conversations never bubbled over into the streets.

The vegetable stew metaphor for the politics of change applies in any type of organization. A few years ago, we worked with a global energy company that had recently acquired a similarly sized firm in a related business. The top team, comprising the senior staff from both companies, met regularly and talked through all the accommodations that had to be made to unify their operations and cultures. But after a year of working together, they realized that the accommodations they had planned so carefully in the big conference room had not come to pass in their respective organizations. This was in part because they themselves were not willing to make any changes that would cause their old colleagues in the legacy companies to see them as disloyal.

They had not prepared themselves or one another for the leadership tasks of mobilizing adaptive work among each of their own peoples.

Name the Losses at Risk

As we have discussed, exercising adaptive leadership requires distributing significant losses. The people you are asking to make changes experience your initiative as a threat to something they value. What they value might be some deeply held belief about right and wrong or about the way the world works or should work. Or it may be nothing deeper than a desire to maintain what is stable, predictable, and familiar in their lives. Resistance to change stems from a fear of losing something important.

So it follows that one element of thinking politically involves ferreting out the losses you are asking people to take. What aspect of their self-image or identity are you threatening? What advantages or benefits do they fear losing if they go along with you? You need to identify those potential losses and then help people survive them.

Identifying the losses is not easy. Often people hide them because they sound embarrassingly self-serving and self-protective. Start by assuming that potential losses exist for each stakeholder group in your organization. Then look for what each group considers most important and most at stake (noble values and less noble ones), even if they do not seem imperiled to you. Review the following list of potential losses to begin getting some ideas:

- Identity

- Competence

- Comfort

- Security

- Reputation

- Time

- Money

- Power

- Control

- Status

- Resources

- Independence

- Righteousness

- Job

- Life

For example, a group of managers in a not-for-profit may fear the loss of future earning potential if they had to acquire new skills to meet an adaptive challenge. But because making more money is not an espoused value in most not-for-profit entities, managers may not openly express this fear. And that means you will have to dig it out or interpret the behavior that masks that concern.

Realize Hidden Alliances

When you are trying to lead adaptive change, you can expect to encounter hidden alliances between people from different stakeholder groups, alliances that can make or break your change initiative. Identifying these connections can help you figure out ways to leverage supportive alliances and soften opposing ones.

An incident from Marty's experience in the Massachusetts state legislature many years ago offers an example. Lawmakers had proposed new legislation easing adoption laws by permitting cross-religious adoptions. Some religious groups and social conservatives represented in the legislature strenuously opposed the change, and the bill had failed several years running. Then advocates of the new law began looking into which members of the house had been adopted, which of them had adopted children or adopted siblings, and which had other personal connections with adoption (for example, they had spouses or close friends who were adopted). The advocates began using those personal connections to adoptions with the resisters to tap into and elevate a different value—friendship or family rather than their religious loyalty or social conservatism—which enabled many of the formerly resistant representatives to view the new laws as resonating with a different one of their deeply held beliefs and loyalties. Eventually, the proposed bill became law. "Generating Alliances in a Law Firm" gives an example of how we helped one client identify and generate alliances within a group of resistant stakeholders.

How can you identify and generate hidden alliances to lead adaptive change? Look at your enterprise's organization chart. The boxes in it represent the stakeholder groups (such as divisions and functions) that are most obvious and formal. Identify subgroups within each group that may have something in common that crosses the formal reporting lines, functions, and hierarchical levels in the chart. For example, people of the same race or gender who work in different functions or at different levels in the organization may align behind their shared interests, concerns, and values. Their common causes may enable you to mobilize them to engage with your change initiative.

Generating Alliances in a Law Firm

Jerry, a partner in a large law firm, wanted the company to take on more pro bono work, as a way for the practice to give back to the community. But the firm had traditionally focused sharply on maximizing billable hours. Still, many productivity mavens in the practice were also competition mavens who took great interest in published rankings of law firms. Companies' quantity of pro bono work was one of the items ranked.

Jerry could have crafted his pitch by simply emphasizing the altruistic value of pro bono work. But he took a savvier approach. He won over some of the competition mavens by pointing out the firm's relatively poor widely published ratings on pro bono work. And he began looking for causes and charities close to some of the productivity mavens' hearts. By encouraging them to contribute time to those causes, he was able to promote an increase in pro bono work among that faction as well.

The list is endless, but here are several subgroups that can get you thinking about possible hidden alliances you could leverage to drive adaptive change in your organization:

- Line managers and staff

- New people in the organization and old-timers

- Those nearing retirement and those with a longer view

- Empty nesters and parents with kids at home

- People across racial, political, ethnic, or other divides of "difference"

- Employees and consultants

- People hired by the current CEO versus those hired by someone else

- Those who deal directly with customers and those who do not

ON THE BALCONY

- For your own team, think about what keeps you from being more daring in your organization. If you were to record the voice in your head telling you to not take more risks, whose voice is it and what is it saying? What is holding you back from taking risks, pushing your agenda, raising the heat?

ON THE PRACTICE FIELD

- Identify an adaptive challenge you want to see addressed in your organization and a change initiative you think would help to address that challenge. Fill out the worksheet in table 6-1 to document your thinking about the stakeholders for this initiative.

- List stakeholder subgroups that may share things in common around which they could form an alliance to support your initiative. List where they sit in the organization (for instance, which function and which level in the organizational hierarchy) and what they have in common (race, age, family obligations, tenure, and so forth).

- Develop a new strategy for helping each stakeholder group endure the losses that may come if your change initiative were to be implemented.

TABLE 6-1

Adaptive challenge and proposed change initiative

Adaptive challenge:

Your proposed change initiative:

Stakeholder (individual or group)	Relationship to the issue?	Preferred outcome?	Noblest values?	Loyalties?	Potential losses?

CHAPTER 7

Qualities of an Adaptive Organization

D IAGNOSING THE ORGANIZATIONAL system, the adaptive challenge at hand, and the political landscape in an enterprise takes time, careful thought, and courage. You have to improvise creatively and responsively as you engage stakeholders inside and across the boundaries of your organization. Some organizations have the keen external sensors, internal norms and a critical mass of people to do this. What distinguishes these enterprises? What makes some organizations more adaptive than others? We've identified five key characteristics:

1. Elephants in the room are named.

2. Responsibility for the organization's future is shared.

3. Independent judgment is expected.

4. Leadership capacity is developed.

5. Reflection and continuous learning are institutionalized.

After looking at each of these in turn, we will offer a worksheet (see table 7-1) that helps you assess how well your organization stacks up against these characteristics and begin thinking about how the enterprise could increase its adaptive capacity.

Name the Elephants in the Room

In any meeting in any organization, there are really four meetings taking place at once. First, there is the public, explicit conversation, the ostensible reason for coming together. Second, there is the informal chat, hallway conversation, or premeeting meeting that took place before the meeting but that did not include everyone who was at the meeting itself. Third, there is the set of internal conversations unfolding within participants' heads related to the meeting agenda. These internal conversations often consist of balcony reflections, observations and interpretations about what is being said about the difficult issues that have not been openly acknowledged, those elephants in the room that no one is mentioning. Fourth, there are the meetings after the meeting, those conversations that occur at the coffee machine or by e-mail soon after everyone streams out of the conference room. Those exchanges are about what really happened during the meeting, the unspoken agendas and the tense moments that came and went without being publicly discussed.

In a highly adaptive organization, no issue is too sensitive to be raised at the official meeting, and no questions are off-limits. Someone who senses early changes in the external environment that would disturb current operations if those changes were taken seriously has the freedom to say so. It is not only all right to challenge the senior authority who represents and often protects those operations; it is expected. Indeed, when someone asks a hard question or raises a difficult issue, people in authority provide some protective cover for that courageous individual and help keep the issue alive, even if the issue makes them or others in the room squirm with discomfort. Crises are identified early on, long before they reach unmanageable proportions. Participants establish rituals and procedures designed to ensure that the elephants get acknowledged and discussed. Hidden perspectives get put on the table fairly quickly.

Andy Grove attributed Intel's agility, in part, to an attitude of almost paranoid vigilance scanning for emerging threats and opportunities externally and internally, in the marketplace and within the company. In that same spirit, the chair of any meeting might routinely ask something like, "What are we missing? Is there an angle we haven't yet discussed?" or "Is there anything simmering below the surface that we need to talk about before we break up?"

Share Responsibility for the Organization's Future

In most organizations, people have titles and they work in clearly defined teams and departments. We all need these labels and functional boundaries to have clarity about our roles in the organization and the structure of our reporting and lateral professional relationships. But titles and functional boundaries can also create a local orientation that sparks a desire to protect one's turf, erodes loyalty to the organization as a whole, and (most important) inhibits the enterprise's ability to operate across boundaries as needed to adapt to change.

In an organization with a high capacity to adapt, people share responsibility for the larger organization's future in addition to their identification with specific roles and functions.

This sense of shared responsibility for the whole manifests itself several ways in organizational life. At meetings people comment on and raise issues that are not within their own portfolios. If a complex problem arises in one department, the heads of other departments view it as their problem, too. Compensation and reward systems are weighted toward the performance of the whole company rather than that of individual units. Cross-functional problem solving is routine; departments often lend their people to other departments, and people deep down in the organization worry about issues and concerns that go beyond their own immediate assignments. At the front line, for example, Toyota is famous for having established a norm by which assembly line workers are encouraged to stop the production process if they see a problem, even beyond their specific role.

Value Independent Judgment

An organization will be better equipped to identify and grapple with adaptive challenges if its people do not expect the CEO and other senior authorities to always have the answers. In such organizations, high-level executives and managers speak up on issues that are not within their own bailiwicks and more freely change their positions after robust conversation among colleagues. "Sticking to your guns" is not the highest value. When President John F. Kennedy gathered a team of people in October 1963 to help him develop the best way to respond to the Cuban Missile Crisis, he invited some members because of their specific expertise and others because he valued their judgment, regardless of their formally defined roles. During the deliberations, participants in the group changed positions frequently as arguments were made, refined, fleshed out, and amended. In an organization where people are valued for their judgment, the question asked is not "What would the people above me in the hierarchy do?" but "What do I think is the best thing to do here in the service of the mission of the organization?" And in those organizations, there is a palpable norm of pushing decision making and idea generation down deep into the organization.

Build Leadership Capacity

Organizations enhance their ability to handle adaptive challenges by ensuring a healthy pipeline of talent. This is not about sending people to seminars. A commitment to individualized professional development comes from understanding that the courage to make needed change resides in people who have a long-term perspective and a stake in the organization's future. Adaptive CEOs understand that they, not their vice president of human resources, are the company's chief personnel officer. Jack Welch was famous at GE in large part because of the seriousness with which he took on that job. Adaptive executives and operations folks understand that their most vital responsibility is getting the right people in the right roles doing the right jobs.

Beyond selection, leadership development is a line manager's daily responsibility. Training and development processes like those we design in our consulting services are no substitute for regular on-the-job debriefing. Leadership is practiced in the details and must be learned close to where the tire hits the road. In an organization that sees the talent pipeline as central to its adaptive potential, people deep in the organization need clear on-the-job guidance to learn where they can make their greatest contribution going forward and what must happen to maximize their potential.

Succession plans are another clear indicator of how well an organization stacks up on this dimension. We often ask executives whether they have identified the two or three people with the capacity to do their jobs better than they can and, if so, what they are doing to nurture and mentor these individuals. GE, for example, has a rich history of succession planning. In fact, the planning process used by CEO Reginald Jones to promote Jack Welch in 1981 is classic among Harvard Business School case studies. But many organizations have better-developed *non*succession plans than succession plans. Managers at one corporation with whom we worked dealt with their high-turnover problem by reframing it as a success. They recruited terrific young people, assuming they would stay around only for a few years before moving on. That way, they could take credit for giving talented young people needed experience, invest little or nothing in their development, and (by the way) ensure that those bright young folks would never go after their own jobs. Not surprisingly, with few people on hand to take a long-term view of the business and to feel a personal investment in the organization, the enterprise was unable to see the external changes that were making the company less relevant to customers and other constituencies.

Institutionalize Reflection and Continuous Learning

Adaptation requires learning new ways to interpret what goes on around you and new ways to carry out work. It's not surprising, then, that in organizations with significant adaptive capacity, there is an openness and commitment to learning. Developing these cultural norms, however, is easier said than done. As people move up the hierarchy in an organization, it becomes increasingly difficult to acknowledge that they don't have all the answers. After all, they have been rewarded for being able to solve problems and take decisive action. As a result, senior executives at many organizations are often much more willing to sponsor learning opportunities for their direct reports than for themselves. But being open to learning is a critical capacity for anyone seeking to enable their organizations to adapt. People at all levels in the enterprise must be able to acknowledge what they do not know and need to discover. In today's world, even the most experienced experts are in over their heads. Adaptive challenges cannot be solved by taking a course, hiring a consulting firm, or copying other companies' best practices. Instead, people throughout the organization must open themselves to experimentation, giving up some old truths that have become irrelevant with changes in the business, social, or political landscape.

What does a continuous-learning mind-set look like in action within an organization? Here are some signs:

- People who make mistakes or experiment with new ways of doing things are not marginalized. Instead, they are treated as founts of wisdom because they have had experiences that the organization needs to capture. For example, at one global bank, the CEO regularly identifies those responsible for big mistakes, helps them tease out what they have learned, and then sends them around the world sharing their new knowledge with colleagues.

- When strategic decisions need to be made, the perspectives of frontline people are considered. Executives and managers know that some of the most useful knowledge resides in those out in the field or on the assembly line, those who deal with the organization's day-to-day realities because they have their hands on the customers, products, and key constituencies. These organizations build their employees' input into the strategic planning process.[1]

- Retreats and off-sites are regularly scheduled and include people from all levels of the organization. These gatherings are two-way conversations instead of one-way lectures or mandates delivered from on high. A diverse group sets the agendas, and they leave space for issues that weren't anticipated in advance.

- When something bad happens (a client is lost, a bid is rejected), the news is acknowledged and the event is debriefed for its lessons, not treated as a cause for punishment.

- Through sabbaticals and leaves of absence, senior people are encouraged to get away from the office to refresh themselves and gain new perspectives.

- Communication and interaction are nurtured across all formal and informal boundaries. The organization brings together units or factions that do not regularly do business with one another, separated by function, level of authority, geography, age, or nationality. Executives and managers try to put people face-to-face with "the other," both within and outside the organization, to generate additional learning opportunities. By shadowing one another to learn about other jobs and perspectives, people get another angle on the whole.

- Executives encourage pure reflection as well as more disciplined processing of complex dynamic situations. For example, some gatherings are scheduled with no agendas, just to give people a chance to test different interpretations of current, past, and future realities.

- The organization supports coaching for those in top positions, knowing that simply having a sounding board outside the organization can prevent the insularity that undermines adaptability.

- People view the latest strategic plan as today's best guess rather than a sacred text. And they expect to constantly refine it as new information comes in.

ON THE BALCONY

- What are the structures put in place to capture learning? Are the important lessons from experience left to the individuals to capture, or are there mechanisms for collective learning? Are there after-action reports or team debriefings? When next year's budget and plans get made, what motivates the changes from the previous year? When people fail in the organization, what happens? Are they marginalized or are lessons learned?

ON THE PRACTICE FIELD

- How does your organization stack up against the five distinguishing characteristics of adaptability? Have yourself and each member of your team fill out the survey in table 7-1, where you each rate the organization on the five adaptability criteria, using a scale of 1 (low rating) to 10 (high rating). Collectively discuss and interpret the data. Ask yourselves, should we try to increase any of those numbers? And if so, what would it take from each of us to do that?

TABLE 7-1

Survey: How adaptive is your organization?

Adaptability criteria	Description	Rating (1 means "very low"; 10 means "very high")
Elephants in the room	How long does it take for conversations to get from inside people's heads to the coffee machine and then to meeting rooms? How quickly are crises identified and bad news discussed? Are there structures, incentives, and support for speaking the unspeakable?	1 2 3 4 5 6 7 8 9 10
Shared responsibility	To what extent do people in your organization, especially those in senior management, act from the perspective of and for the betterment of the whole organization, as opposed to worrying about and protecting their individual groups or silos?	1 2 3 4 5 6 7 8 9 10
Independent judgment	To what extent are people in your organization valued for their own judgment rather than their capacity to divine the boss's preferences? And when someone takes a reasonable risk in service of the mission and it doesn't work out, to what extent is that seen as a learning opportunity rather than a personal failure?	1 2 3 4 5 6 7 8 9 10
Develop leadership capacity	To what extent do people know where they stand in the organization and their potential for growth and advancement? Do they have an agreed-upon plan for how they are going to reach their potential? And to what extent are senior managers expected to identify and mentor their successors?	1 2 3 4 5 6 7 8 9 10
Institutionalized reflection and continuous learning	Does the organization carve out time for individual and collective reflection and learning from experience? To what extent does the organization allocate time, space, and other resources to get diverse perspectives on how work could be done better?	1 2 3 4 5 6 7 8 9 10

PART THREE

MOBILIZE THE SYSTEM

IN PRACTICING ADAPTIVE LEADERSHIP, you make interventions that, though sometimes unwelcome, are designed to help people in your system (your organization, team, community, society, or family) address worthy challenges. For example:

- Frustrated in its attempts to persuade the school administration to broaden its focus to incorporate new technology, which the administrators neither understood nor valued, the school's advisory committee resigned en masse.

- Unable to convince the HR department to move from a transactional orientation to a strategic partnership with the rest of the company, the CEO challenged the culture by moving a highly successful sales vice president into the vice president for HR role.

- Violating the family's deeply held cultural norms, a son risked disrupting the family Christmas dinner by raising the question of Grandma's "forgetfulness" and whether she was beginning to undermine the equanimity of the entire family.

Interventions to diagnose and mobilize adaptive work will take the form of questions, process ideas, frameworks, single change initiatives, as well as a strategic sequence of efforts that engage different individuals and subgroups in different ways at different points in time. In this part, we focus on action: the practices of leadership on adaptive issues from preparation to implementation. Whatever form your interventions take, if successful, they are likely to have certain qualities:

- Pointing to a long-term solution (rather than a quick fix) to the adaptive challenge

- Framing the challenge and offering interpretations of the issues and the current realities that will make some people uncomfortable

- Using the discomfort to drive progress rather than repressing or temporizing to restore the more comfortable status quo

- Leveraging unusual networks of relationships throughout your organization

- Strengthening your organization's adaptive capacity to deal with an ongoing stream of adaptive challenges in the future

The first step toward effective action is nonaction: the ability to avoid the all-too-common impulse to leap into action when an adaptive challenge rears its head.

Are you a problem-solving junkie? When a problem shows up, do you dive right in and start working it through, determined to clean up the mess? Have you been rewarded professionally and personally for your willingness and ability to take problems off of other people's shoulders and fix them?

Often the most powerful thing you can do to help your organization is to buy time rather than apply quick technical fixes that may have worked in the past. Remember the adage "If all you have is a hammer, everything looks like a nail"? When you are dealing with an adaptive challenge, your hammer will not help. Difficult as it may be, you will have to holster the tool, slow down, and get your group to think before acting.

This is not easy in today's fast-food, hurry-up-and-get-on-with-it world. But it is essential. If you occupy a position of authority in your organization, you may find it easier to apply the brakes once you've identified your own vulnerability to taking decisive action under pressure. If you do not have much authority, you will have to employ more dramatic techniques to buy time to get a better diagnosis and then engage experimentally toward a solution. You will likely meet resistance and be accused of "standing in the way of progress" or "being too negative."

You need some nonconfrontational ways to slow down your organization's momentum. Here are some ideas to get you started:

- Ask more questions rather than issuing more directives.

- Softly exercise a veto by withholding your support for a decision if your support is essential for its successful implementation.

- Build extra time into meeting agendas so that the adaptive challenges do not get either bypassed in favor of more immediate concerns or treated with short-term technical fixes.

- Expand the circle of individuals who need to be consulted in exploring possible solutions to the problem.

- Arguments about fact questions are often a way to avoid addressing the hidden conflicts. Distinguish the facts on the table and then engage real conflicts in perspectives and values.

Once you have staved off a leap into action, you can begin designing and implementing interventions to address the challenge.

CHAPTER 8

Make Interpretations

EFFECTIVE VISIONS HAVE accuracy and not just imagination and appeal. Providing thoughtful, accurate interpretations that get at the essence of the complex reality you observe in your organization is enormously helpful to people. An incisive statement of the key issues that underlie a messy, complexified discussion orients people and helps focus attention productively. Although people may balk at your interpretation, having one on the table to discuss, revise, and amend is profoundly useful. But the interpretation also has to capture key realities. Dreams and fantasies are essential sources of new ideas and hope, but adaptive solutions have to capture and build from today's realities toward new possibilities.

Often the default interpretations people use to explain problematic realities conveniently serve to shield them from the need for them to change. In any organization of human beings, people will tend to glom onto interpretations of reality that do not call for them to take personal responsibility for the problem.

For example, middle managers from different industries, countries, and cultures will differ on many things, but they will often agree that "it's senior management's lack of commitment to innovation that is causing us to lose market share." Though that accusation may be partially accurate, the prevailing interpretation fails to explain the lack of leadership from middle management—that is, its failures of courage, imagination, or strategic and tactical effort.

Or people will embrace interpretations suggesting that low-cost solutions are available. People are routinely elected to public office by telling constituents that they will not have to suffer losses in order to meet the challenges at hand. Senators Obama and McCain were no different in that regard during the 2008 campaign.

After the 9/11 attacks, Americans understandably wanted to believe that the international terrorist threat could be removed without having to make major sacrifices in the form of higher energy prices, strict conservation measures, or loss of life, and significant changes in the roles that Americans play in the world. Politicians, Democrats and Republicans alike, colluded to perpetuate that fantasy. Who is going to vote for a politician who demands tough sacrifices that include, at the very least, the need to raise taxes to pay for major new expenses? The preferred message was, "Resume your lives. The government will go after the perpetrators and take care of the problem. A few will courageously make the ultimate sacrifice, but we will do everything we can to keep those casualties to a minimum." The messages were reassuring and therefore appealing; but they were unrealistic.

Figure 8-1 shows the shifts in interpretation that people in an organization must experience before they can effectively grapple with an adaptive challenge. Your job in exercising adaptive leadership is first to wean people away from interpretations on the left-hand side of the chart (where people define problems as technical, benign, and individually caused). Then you need to nudge them toward interpretations on the

FIGURE 8-1

Making the interpretation mind-shift

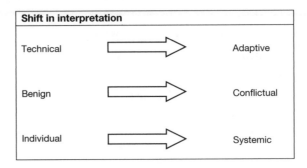

right-hand side (where they define problems as adaptive, conflictual, and systemic).

This means that one of the first overall tasks of leadership is to educate the people around you—junior, senior, lateral, and across boundaries—that adaptive challenges are fundamentally different from technical problems. You need to create the latitude to treat each kind of situation differently—technical problems with expertise, and adaptive challenges with leadership. When people begin to accept that many problems can be treated with authoritative expertise, but that many cannot, you will have more leeway to mobilize more widespread engagement, experimentation, discovery, and costly adjustment. You can be directive and efficiently authoritative when needed for technical problems without being accused of being too controlling or autocratic; and you can be questioning and improvisational with a focus on processes of inclusion and experimentation when needed for adaptive work without being accused of weakness or lack of direction.

As people begin to identify the *adaptive* elements of the challenge, they will legitimize the need to learn new ways, begin to identify the losses that they will have to take in order to make progress (such as giving up a legacy product or relinquishing highly valued autonomy in exchange for an infusion of capital), and shift their mind-set from conflict avoidance to conflict resolution.

If you can make interpretations that surface the *conflictual* aspects of the problem, you can lead people to begin identifying which losses are negotiable and which are not, engage in the courageous conversations needed to work through those conflicts, and create an environment in which the conflicts can be surfaced and managed so that new adaptations emerge.

If people see the issues as *systemic rather than personal*, they will begin to look for the leverage points in the system (such as a tradition of protecting underperformers or centralized control) as targets of attention to effect change. By making systemic interpretations, you can help them think politically and map the issue's stakeholders, spot opportunities to build unusual alliances, and determine what is at risk for each stakeholder group.

This shift to the right-hand side of the interpretation chart can begin to happen during any conversation, formal or informal, where default interpretations are being tossed around. But getting people into the habit of interpreting events systemically and politically rather than at the individual and interpersonal level will need reinforcement over time. Here are some questions you might ask to push the conversation to the right-hand side of the chart:

- Is there any part of this situation that is new to us and that therefore might need a different strategy than what we usually do?

- Who are the key stakeholders in this situation, and how might they be positively affected or negatively affected? How would they describe the situation and the stakes for them?

- How generalized in our organization is the urgency to do anything about it, or do we have to figure out a way to ripen the issue?

- What are the adaptive elements of this situation, and what are the technical aspects?

- Are we the only ones in this organization or industry facing this situation? What responses are others making?

The following guidelines can help you lead the interpreting process in your group.

Notice When People Are Moving Toward the Left Side of the Chart

People gravitate toward interpretations that are technical rather than adaptive, benign instead of conflictual, and individual rather than systemic. You can begin by noticing when members of your organization are doing this, and simply by pointing it out. Signs of unproductive interpretation crop up in the way people talk about the situation. Table 8-1 shows examples and suggests questions you can ask to nudge people away from the left-hand side of the chart.

In addition to interpreting reality in ways that suggest easy, painless solutions, people look mostly to their immediate environment for information to determine what's going right and wrong in their organization (for instance, staff competence and company rules). What is in your immediate environment will tend to occupy most of your time and energy. Of course, it is natural that you would want to use what you see

TABLE 8-1

Signs of unproductive interpretation

This kind of comment . . .	Suggests that people see the problem as . . .	You can encourage a shift by asking questions such as . . .
"If we only had better direction from the CEO . . ."	A deficiency in the authorities, not the organization's vision, mission or strategy	"What pressures is the CEO up against? What are his constituencies, and what do they expect him/her to deliver?"
"We'll have this worked out in no time . . ."	Short-term, not long-term	"Do you think we have the will to try to deal with the causes of the problem rather than the symptoms?"
"This will be an easy fix."	Technical, not adaptive diagnosis	"Maybe this is a problem that a consultant cannot fix?"
"We can't seem to carry out our good ideas."	Incompetent execution, not a problematic business model	"Maybe our product, even though we love it, is not what the market wants?"
"This will be a win-win."	No one needs to suffer any pain to solve this problem	"What losses do the people who oppose this step think they are going to take?"

around you to make sense of the world, to use the data that is right before your eyes. But this tendency can cause you to stay on the left-hand side of the chart—in particular, to interpret problems as technical and individual rather than adaptive and systemic. We worked with a firm where the key employees colluded with the founder in keeping him in a paternal role, long after the firm needed someone at the top to be less protective. They focused their frustration on his "intrusiveness" without being able to see how they both helped to keep him in that role and were helped by doing so.

To counteract this habit, bring information from outside your group members' experience into the conversation. It might have been useful, for example, for the members of that company to have heard, read, and discussed stories of other founders who wanted and were seduced into continuing to infantilize the staff. Or explore the perspectives and interests of people outside their normal range of vision. Perhaps it would have been useful for them to have videotaped one of their top team meetings to be able to see the dynamic from the balcony.

"Seeing an Adaptive Problem as a Technical One" shows how one large law firm struggled to shift its interpretation mind-set from the left side to the right side.

Seeing an Adaptive Problem as a Technical One

A large law firm declining in prestige found that its earnings per partner had slumped. The partners felt that if they could begin to hire more candidates from big-name law schools, these trends could be reversed. Instead of examining the full set of forces behind these adaptive challenges, the partners interpreted the problem as a technical one that could be solved with a technical fix: hiring from the top law schools.

The opportunity to put this fix into action soon arrived. Evelyn, a summer associate who had graduated in the bottom half of her class from one of the top law schools in the country, had expressed interest in being hired permanently. She mentioned this interest to Charles, one of the senior partners. She also told Charles that she had slept with another senior member of the firm, and Charles had the sense that she was willing to sleep with him as well if it would help get her an offer. Charles did not know whether to provide this information to other members of the hiring committee. He was worried that if the committee knew of Evelyn's liaison with the senior firm member, members would feel forced to hire her so she would not accuse the partner of sexual harassment. He decided to keep the information from the hiring committee and use his credibility to talk them out of hiring her "on the merits." He was successful in doing that, but he realized later that the underlying adaptive issues (upholding standards of professional conduct by dealing with the partner involved in the liaison, risking turmoil and a lawsuit, and the deeper causes of the firm's downward spiral) were not going to go away.

Reframe the Group's Default Interpretations

Every organization has default interpretations, entrenched ways of perceiving and responding to reality. And every group within an organization has its own defaults. These may stem from distinct departmental perspectives. (For example, with one of our software clients, the R&D department always addressed declining market share by advocating for the development of a slew of new features for the company's products.) Senior authorities often powerfully reinforce default interpretations by offering them early on in the diagnostic process or by devaluing alternatives.

Default interpretations work much of the time because they do capture elements of reality, at least superficially. Interpreting systemic events in terms of individual motives and interpersonal competition often carries a surface piece of the truth. And sometimes it is a useful piece because knowing someone's personal motives alone will enable you to speak to their elemental interests. However, personal motives are profoundly influenced by the context in which that person operates: their constituencies and loyalties, that is, the water they are carrying for others from the various expectations they are trying to meet, including the people whose authorization they need for both legitimacy and to maintain their jobs.

Looking beneath the surface of our default interpretations at the individual level, you are led back to a systemic perspective for interpreting individual behavior. What you really want to interpret are the needs of those constituencies that pull the strings.

To move people away from their default, personalized, interpretations, the following process can help:

1. *Figure out the group's default interpretations.* If it is not obvious, get on the balcony and track the group's responses to several different problems, looking for patterns. For example, do group members generally seek someone outside (a new competitor, a supplier) to blame for their problems? Do they usually expect senior authorities to address the issue? Do they tend to blame particular managers for their lack of imagination or courage? Do they look for external expertise, yet another consultant, to provide a magic bullet?

2. *Name the default.* If your group has a high level of tolerance for difficult conversations, name the default interpretation you are seeing, and invite people to explore how it inhibits their creativity and adaptability. Otherwise, use a less direct approach: ask questions that stimulate a conversation that might surface other interpretations. Here are some suggestions:

   - What are the assumptions that have led us to see the problem in this way? How accurate are those assumptions? Are there things we can do to test them?

   - Are there any other ways to see this problem that we haven't yet discussed?

- Who else in our organization cares about this problem, and how might they describe the situation?

Generate Multiple Interpretations

If people have arrived at only one interpretation of the situation, the options for action are often severely limited; any one interpretation will tend to drive toward a single solution or a small set of solutions. To expand the array of options, encourage people to come up with more than one possible interpretation. Use what-if questions; for example, "What if we found that customers *do not* value the kinds of features we're adding to our products? What might that suggest about the causes behind our loss of market share?"

It is always possible to come up with multiple interpretations of any situation. Sometimes a simple structural change can generate and legitimize the airing of different views. We have learned this the hard way in our after-action reviews as a consulting practice. When we debrief an engagement, the consultant who has served as the lead on that engagement will usually provide a story, an interpretation, of what happened during the project. We have always strived to be a collegial group, and early in the history of our practice, those of us who were not involved in a particular engagement were reluctant to challenge the lead consultant's interpretation.

But we saw that this approach limited our learning. So we began working in pairs in even our smallest client engagements. That way, the lead consultant had help in understanding our work with the client as the engagement unfolded and also could contribute a second perspective after the assignment was completed. We began to work toward a norm where there were always at least two and sometimes three or four interpretations available in our engagement debriefings from which to improve our services.

It takes some practice to hold open more than one idea about reality, particularly when those multiple ideas conflict with one another. Once your people have generated several interpretations of their collective challenge, your goal is to help them keep those interpretations alive instead of gravitating prematurely toward one of them. Watch carefully what happens when more than one interpretation is on the table.

Which gets affirmed; which gets rejected? Factions within groups will be attracted to the interpretations that favor their own interests. Here are some reasons:

- The favored interpretation connects to one subgroup's deeply held values and interests. For example, in a law firm where growth has slowed, one senior lateral hire ascribed the firm's lack of greater revenue to the unwillingness of the longer-tenured partners to work as hard as the new laterals do. In contrast, the dominant faction of careerists in the firm focused on the challenge of integrating the new laterals.

- The losses appear significant. Members of the subgroup avoid an interpretation that suggests adaptive work with tough trade-offs is necessary. In the law firm example, the firm's careerists want to avoid having to diminish the firm's tradition of honoring longevity in financial and other nonmaterial ways.

- The issue is not yet ripe. Subgroup members avoid dealing with an issue they are not ready to address. By focusing on the difficulty of integrating new laterals, the firm avoids the much tougher issue of what to do with revered senior partners who are no longer performing at a high level.

- The prevailing interpretation reduces conflict. The law firm addressed the lateral integration problem by adding a lateral to the management committee rather than surfacing the deep value conflict between the new senior hires and the careerists.

When you try to keep several different interpretations alive, you will probably experience pushback. Each member or faction in the system will emphasize their favored interpretation over the others. So try to spread around the responsibility for working through alternative interpretations. For example, break the group into subgroups. Assign each subgroup one possible interpretation, and have them flesh it out and generate ideas for taking action. Analyze the various interpretations. Which ones make people feel uncomfortable? Which ones veer toward the right-hand side of the chart? Once multiple options are on the table, ask people, "How would we know whether one of these interpretations is more accurate than the others?" Produce some low-risk experiments that might test the interpretations that seem to generate more energy, maybe even more negative energy. Think of the process as iterative and improvisational. You will probably find that some interpretations have more juice, more reaction, and more staying power in the conversation than others.

Audition Your Ideas

You have your own default interpretations and thus are going to be drawn to certain interpretations over others. To combat this tendency, think of yourself as in the role of auditioning your interpretation rather than advocating it energetically. Get in character by fully investing in your view when you offer it. Then pull yourself out of that role and watch and listen for other members' feedback on your interpretation. Observe the reactions or nonreactions. We were at a corporate retreat recently where the firm was trying to understand whether anything was to be learned from the fact that a disproportionate percentage of women in the last year had left the firm. One member of the firm suggested that the basic principles on which the firm rested were heavily biased toward a direct and aggressive way of looking at the world associated more with men than with women. It was a disturbing idea, but the person who offered it exercised restraint in letting the group react in its characteristically direct and aggressive way, neither defending nor explaining his view further, until several minutes later when he was able to ask his colleagues to make sense out of the way they handled the idea. He would never have been able to generate all that data to support his interpretation had he followed it with a continuing and spirited explanation and defense!

Generate a Diversity of Interpretations

Adaptive work involves orchestrating multiple and passionately held points of view. In an ideal world, people would not be threatened by the existence of contrasting viewpoints. Instead, they would view them simply as different pieces of the larger picture that everyone needs to see. The more different pieces of the puzzle are laid out on the table, the more you know what you are really dealing with, and the better equipped you are to generate interventions that will help you sequence and solve the most pressing shared difficulties.

We have already likened adaptive work to evolutionary biology. In the realm of evolution, sexual reproduction generates the most options for adapting to the new challenges and opportunities facing a species. Cloning may maximize efficiency, enabling the mass production of identical individuals. But it does not produce the diversity and innovation that enable creatures to thrive in new ways and in challenging environments. Likewise, the capacity to orchestrate multiple interpretations of an organizational challenge is more likely to produce innovative insights than relying solely on one person's viewpoint.

Sure, bringing in a diverse range of interpretations can be a nuisance. Creativity is less efficient than alignment, producing more friction and taking up time, but it is only less efficient when you are dealing with a technical problem for which authoritative knowledge and alignment with it will most efficiently produce solutions, as in an emergency room. But when you are dealing with an adaptive challenge that requires creativity, you have to tolerate the pains of processes that increase the odds that new ideas will lead to new adaptive capacity.

To build a diversity of interpretations into your working group, organization, or community, keep the pot simmering just enough to get ideas rubbing up against each other. You will know you have gotten it right when people start considering and understanding each other's viewpoints and start discussing potential solutions that make sense across the table.

CHAPTER 9

Design Effective
Interventions

EFFECTIVE INTERVENTIONS MOBILIZE people to tackle an adaptive challenge. They may be designed to make progress at any point in the process: for example, to surface a difficult issue, quash a diversion, or move people forward through a difficult period. Effective interventions are based on interpretations of the situation that are anchored on the right-hand side of the interpretation chart (see figure 8-1), in the adaptive, conflictual, and systemic characteristics of the organization's challenge.

Even if you tactically need to move to the left column temporarily to speak to someone's personal stakes and personal interpretations of others, staying anchored in the systemic view gives you a place to bring people as you help them depersonalize the situation.

At whatever stage of the process you are intervening, here is a checklist, a series of practices that can make your interventions more effective. They are presented as they might be employed more or less sequentially, but you can think of them as individual practices as well.

Assume the need for midcourse correction in whatever you do. Each intervention generates information and responses that may then require corrective action. Maintain the flexibility to move, reflect, and move again.

Step 1: Get on the Balcony

This takes the famous "count to ten" one leap further. Do not just count to ten. Observe what is going on around you. Stay diagnostic even as you take action. Develop more than one interpretation. Watch for patterns. Reality test your interpretation when it is self-serving or close to your default. Debrief with partners as often as you can to assess the information generated by your actions, and the interventions of others, in order to think through your next move.

Step 2: Determine the Ripeness of the Issue in the System

Look again at the disequilibrium diagram in part I (see figure 2-4). Where would you put your group or organization on the diagram? How resilient and ready are people to tackle the issue? An issue is ripe when the urgency to deal with it has become generalized across the system. If only a subgroup or faction cares passionately, but most other groups in the system have other priorities on their mind, then the issue is not yet ripe. Determining ripeness is critical because a strategy of intervention to ripen an issue that is only localized is different from a strategy to deal with a ripe issue that is already generalized.

For example, the issue of environmental protection has had a deeply passionate constituency for decades. But until recently, not many people cared across the larger national or international landscape. For years, many environmental organizations focused on attention-getting strategies to distribute the urgency. Some of those strategies, such as Greenpeace's picking public fights and the Sierra Club's lawsuits, were intentionally provocative. But after decades of gradual impact, with the help of the noticeable effects of global warming and the efforts of Al Gore and many others, the issue has ripened considerably around the world. Many environmental organizations understand that their strategy will now need to change from adversarial to various forms of collaboration (even with former adversaries) as well as more graceful prodding, to achieve not only widespread changes in public policy and business practices but also change in the way billions of people around the world choose to behave.

The ripeness of an issue, then, is a critical factor in planning a strategy of intervention. Is the urgency localized in one subgroup and not yet widespread across the larger system? Or, on the other hand, are people avoiding the hard work of dealing with the adaptive challenge at hand because the pain of doing so has reached too-high levels of disequilibrium? Is the prevailing momentum to treat the situation as a technical problem or as an adaptive challenge?

Your answer to these questions will affect how you frame your intervention strategy and the timing of your actions. For example, suppose the top team in a company keeps focusing on squeezing more business out of its one big customer rather than dealing with the problem of overreliance and its need to diversify its customer base and offerings; they have all grown up with that customer and they are not sure they would be competent at marketing to others or developing new products and services. They are in the middle of an economic crisis, so their anxiety level is already pretty high. You see the current crisis as an opportunity finally to ripen the question of overreliance and the need for a new business development strategy, but in every meeting, the discussions remain stubbornly focused on that one customer, along with some short-term cost cutting. In this case, you may want to frame your interventions carefully, finding allies, affirming the need for cost-cutting measures to buy time, and creating informal processes for asking questions that gradually draw attention to the adaptive possibilities, rather than go it alone in meetings and directly challenge their work avoidance.

When Marty worked for the governor of Massachusetts, the top team held a meeting with the governor every morning to resolve issues and plan approaches. The members of the team sat in assigned places around a large oval table, and the governor went around the table in the same order every day. Each person was asked whether there was an issue to discuss, and each issue was addressed when raised. Marty was the last one in the queue. Every morning, when it finally was his turn, he had to take the temperature of the group to assess where they were on the disequilibrium chart at that point in order to decide which, if any, of the issues he wanted to raise the group still had the tolerance to handle. Sometimes he assessed the situation well, pushing them to the limit but not beyond it; but often, especially when he cared a lot about something, he raised the issue, when it might better have been left for another day.

Step 3: Ask, Who Am I in This Picture?

How are you experienced by the various groups and subgroups? What role do you play in them? What perspectives on the adaptive issues do you embody for them? Because they are comfortable with the way you usually act, they are probably quite proficient at managing you in that role to ensure that you do not disturb their equilibrium.

Consistency is a high value in management but a significant constraint in leading adaptive change.

You will have to be less predictable than usual to get their constructive attention and make progress on an adaptive issue. For example, suppose you are the one who always presents ideas. When you propose your intervention, group members may respond with silence, because they have become accustomed to relying on you to do all the thinking and talking. If this is the case, stop talking. Wait for someone else to come forward to contribute opinions or to offer additional ideas. If you are usually soft-spoken and deferential, be more passionate or perhaps authoritative, and vice versa. If you are singing a song you have sung often before without great success, get someone unexpected to sing it for you.

Step 4: Think Hard About Your Framing

Thoughtful framing means communicating your intervention in a way that enables group members to understand what you have in mind, why the intervention is important, and how they can help carry it out. A well-framed intervention strikes a chord in people, speaking to their hopes and fears. That is, it starts where they are, not where you are. And it inspires them to move forward. As we've noted, Martin Luther King Jr. anchored his dream in the American dream. By doing so, he reminded Americans of the starting point for their nation, challenging people to give life to their dream, not only his own.

Think about the balance between reaching people above and below the neck. Some groups and some people need data first, before the emotion. For others, it is the reverse. Connect your language to the group's espoused values and purpose. Consider the balance between strong attention-getting language and language that is so loaded as to trigger flight-or-fight responses rather than engagement.

Step 5: Hold Steady

When you have made an intervention, think of it as having a life of its own. Do not chase after it. The idea will make its way through the system, and people will need time to digest it, think about it, discuss it, and modify it. If you think of it as "yours," you are likely to get overly invested in your own image of it.

Once you have made an intervention, your idea is theirs.

You cannot control what people do with your intervention. So as this process unfolds, resist the impulse to keep jumping in with follow-ups like "No, what I really meant is . . ." or "Didn't you hear me?" or "Let me say that again" or "You misinterpreted what I said." Let people in the system work with your idea without your getting too attached to it. Listen closely to how various subgroups are responding to your idea, so you can calibrate your next move. Watch for the ways and the elements of it that are taking hold. Watch for avoidance mechanisms, like an allergic-like immediate rejection, or silence.

Your silence is itself a form of intervention. It creates a vacuum for others to fill. The key is to stay present and keep listening. But the silence of holding steady is different from the silence of holding back. Your silent presence communicates and helps to hold the attention of people to the perspective you have offered. And by staying present, patiently, sometimes for weeks, you can then listen carefully, collect information, and figure out what to do next.

Holding steady is a poised and listening silence. People will appreciate, even if they never say so, the patience and respect it shows. In contrast, holding back is a form of withdrawal, perhaps out of frustration or resignation that your point of view has not been adopted in the form or at the speed you want.

Holding back communicates, too. People will pick up your impatience and frustration, and may interpret it as annoyance on your part with their responses and with them. Your annoyance becomes unwittingly your next intervention and is likely to draw attention to you personally rather than the content of your offering. Instead of saying to themselves or to each other at the coffee break, "Did we misunderstand what he said?" they will more likely say, "What's wrong with him?"

Step 6: Analyze the Factions That Begin to Emerge

As people in your own close-in group begin to discuss your intervention, pay attention to who seems engaged, who starts using your language or pieces of your idea as if it were their own. Listen for who resists the idea. Use these observations to help you see the contours of the factions the various people represent on the issue. Faction mapping of your close-in group will give you valuable information about the ways the larger system of people will deal with the issue, which is critically important because refining and implementing your change initiative will usually require the involvement of people from different functions and departments in the larger system.

Step 7: Keep the Work at the Center of People's Attention

Avoiding adaptive work is a common human response to the prospect of loss. Even if nearly all of the cultural, institutional, political, and personal DNA is honored and conserved on the road to new adaptive capacity, the prospect of having to experience some incompetence, some disloyalty, and some direct losses will cause people to flinch.

Avoidance is not shameful; it is just human.

Expect that your team will find ways to avoid focusing on the adaptive challenge in doing their diagnosis as well as in taking action. Resistance to your intervention will have less to do with the merits of your idea and mostly to do with the fears of loss your idea generates. Often this is on behalf of their own constituencies, people (or ideas) who are not present but to whom they are accountable: "Sounds good, but what does this mean for the people back in my department? How would I take this idea back to them without their being furious at me?"

It falls to you, your allies, and others who lead in the system to keep the work at the center. Frequently, people will want to distract themselves by putting the personal issues and power manipulations at the center of attention. The problem becomes, "The CEO is just stuck in his old ways. He lacks courage," or "People around here are just in it for themselves," or "This team isn't working well," rather than "We're losing market share; we'd better figure out why," or "The technology is evolving quickly, and we're already falling behind the curve," or "We say we support innovation, but we don't put any resources behind it."

Begin by trying to understand the impact of new directions on the factions, the constituents behind the people in your working group, and how the pleasure or displeasure of those constituents is then going to play out in the behavior of that person. When you find that your terrific idea becomes a headache for someone in your group, the explanation is usually that it represents a headache to some key people in their authorizing environment, key people to whom they look to maintain their credibility, reputation, and formal and informal authority. So, although that person's personal motives are relevant, they do not provide a sufficient explanation of the background for their resistance to showing more courage in tackling the problem that you see.

Then think about how you can help with their problem, even if it is a problem the resister does not want to acknowledge. Depending on the personalities and culture of communication in your setting, you may want in some way to suggest, "Perhaps I can go to your team and present our new strategy so you will not have to do it alone." Or, "I know your folks have been asking for an upgrade in their technology for over a year. I want to make sure you get credit for making that happen at this moment."

A second strategy is to help them, the resisters who are worried about their own people, interpret their constituents' resistance in terms of threat and loss rather than intransigence, cowardice, or lack of creativity. Dealing with the fears of loss requires a strategy that takes those losses into account and treats them with respect.

Finally, get allies. You need to share the burden of keeping the work at the center of people's attention. You never want to be isolated on the point. Allies are critical in keeping you straight and in distributing the heat for knocking people in the system out of their comfort zone. The need for allies introduces our next chapter.

ON THE BALCONY

- Each of the seven steps can be understood as a skill set. Rate yourself on a scale from 1 to 10 for each of the seven steps. What are your strengths? Where do you need to build your skills?

ON THE PRACTICE FIELD

- The next time you are in a meeting, notice what is going on in your head while others are speaking. Are you judging their ideas or comments? Rehearsing what you are going to say when it is your turn? In what ways are you staying on the dance floor and leaping into action? Practice avoiding this mental leaping by listening to others and trying to figure out on whose behalf are they speaking, whose perspectives are they representing, and how you can give your perspectives context within the current concerns and subject on the table.

CHAPTER 10

Act Politically

WE HAVE USED the phrase *thinking politically* to describe the leadership task of understanding the relationships and concerns among people in an organization. People who think politically discern the formal and informal exercise of power and influence among individuals in their organization. They take time to understand the interests, loyalties, and fears of everyone who has a stake or might be affected by the change. And they understand that relationships count. Ignore the human complexities when you try to lead adaptive change, and you greatly reduce your chances of succeeding—to say nothing of surviving.

By *acting politically*, we mean using your awareness of the limits of your own authority, and of stakeholders' interests, as well as power and influence networks in your organization, to forge alliances with people who will support your efforts, to integrate and defuse opposition, and to give valuable dissenting voices a hearing as you adjust your perspective, interventions and mobilize adaptive work. We offer the following six guidelines for acting politically and some exercises to help you put these ideas into practice.

Expand Your Informal Authority

Consciously expand your informal authority. The more informal authority you have, the less you will need to transgress expectations, with all the risks that entails (point A in figure 10-1), to lead adaptive

FIGURE 10-1

Expanding your informal authority

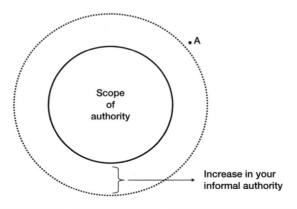

Scope of authority

• A

Increase in your informal authority

Twisting in the Wind

In 1971, Miles Mahoney became the head of a Massachusetts state agency with responsibility for housing and economic development. Mahoney took on the enormous challenge of trying to stop a large redevelopment project in Boston called Park Plaza that had enormous political and financial momentum. He believed that the project was inconsistent with the spirit (and perhaps the law) of urban redevelopment policy. But he was new to the job and new to Massachusetts. He had a decent résumé, but he had not demonstrated his managerial, political, or technical competence in this arena. His bosses, peers, and employees watched him and waited rather than actively backing him up.

Mahoney could have taken steps to augment his informal authority. He might have taken on a few smaller challenges to show his abilities, run his department smoothly for a while, and built up his professional network. These efforts would have added credibility, expertise, relationships and political capital. And with that, he might have eventually excelled at the job for which he had a significant measure of formal authority, although he likely would still have had to tolerate losing on the issue of Park Plaza. His lack of significant informal authority left him isolated, and the opposition that had solidified against him ultimately cost him his job.

change. "Twisting in the Wind" shows an example from the realm of public policy illustrating what can happen when you *do not* enhance your informal authority while seeking to lead major change.

When you see a difficult adaptive challenge on the horizon, develop a plan for building up your informal authority regarding that challenge. Here are some ideas:

- *Strengthen your relationships.* In particular, forge strong connections with people who have big stakes in the challenge, whatever their perspective on it. Listen to them to comprehend their interests and loyalties.

- *Score some early wins.* Solve some of the technical aspects bundled with the adaptive challenge. For example, if Mahoney's enduring purpose was to create a more robust role for the state in the urban renewal process, he could have begun to do so by being involved in some smaller projects, rather than taking on one of unprecedented size and scope in the state's largest city, one that already had enormous political momentum behind it when it came across his desk. You build credibility with your subordinates, peers, and bosses by scoring early wins. They in turn will give you more slack as you move them to follow you into the unknown territory of adaptive change.

- *Address interests unconnected to the adaptive challenge.* Mahoney had many opportunities to support other initiatives of some of the players who he needed to have on his side, or at least not arrayed against him, if he wanted to take on the challenge of stopping Park Plaza.

- *Sell small pieces of your idea.* Take small steps, run pilot projects, and try experiments related to your intervention idea, rather than pitching a large rollout of a program that comes with major costs and losses. If these small pieces prove out, you may be able to get more authorization to implement the entire idea.

ON THE BALCONY

- With whom do you have the most informal authority or influence: Peers? Subordinates? Superiors? External parties such as customers or suppliers? From whom might you need more informal authority? Why? How might you build relationships with these individuals to expand your informal authority?

- There are many ways to expand your informal authority. You do not have to reinvent yourself in the process. What is your style for building informal authority with others? How does it change in different social contexts: work, family, community? For example, do you form close bonds by sitting around and telling interesting stories? Making jokes? Delivering above expectations? Doing favors? Listening attentively? Drawing out other people's stories? What's your style? And what additional styles could you master?

ON THE PRACTICE FIELD

- Identify a person with whom you want to have more informal authority. Then practice overdelivering on your commitments to that person for three weeks.

- Become a master of ceremonies. Design new activities to bring people together. Whether it is getting drinks after a tough meeting, organizing lunches, or celebrating someone's success, help connect people to you and to each other to build your relationship capital for times when the going gets tough.

- Try getting to every meeting early and leaving every meeting late. Spend the time before the meeting connecting with other participants and afterward reflecting on the meeting with some of them. The moments after a meeting present priceless opportunities for you to strengthen bonds, get a sense of what people think of ideas discussed during the meeting, and identify emerging alliances and factions.

Find Allies

Trying to lead an adaptive set of interventions without allies is like braving Buffalo, New York, in the dead of winter without a warm coat. That is especially true when you attempt to lead change in a group or organization of more than twenty people. In such settings, the complexity of the political landscape is way beyond anyone's ability to navigate alone.

Before you go public with your initiative (whether through making a big announcement or simply raising the subject at a meeting), you need to line up enough support to keep your intervention (and you) alive once the action starts. Where to start building alliances? Review the worksheet you filled out in part II, chapter 6, "Diagnosing the Political Landscape" (see table 6-1). Identify which stakeholders are most likely to be interested in supporting your cause. Potential allies have interests and perspectives of the adaptive challenge closely aligned with yours and will gain the most if your intervention succeeds. Also look for stakeholders with interests that are different from but not in conflict with your own and would be served by partnering with you. For example, there may be people who see long-term gains from partnering with you or with some of your other partners, even if they have no particular interest in the issue at hand. In addition, stakeholders who owe you something or who share a history with you (for instance, they went to the same school or shared some difficult professional or personal experience) also could be allies, as are those who see you as representing something positive for the organization, such as core values, the future, or diversity. Moreover, pay particular attention to identifying unlikely allies. For instance, someone who has opposed your initiatives in the past or comes from a part of the organization that often competes with yours would be especially compelling. Connections with unlikely allies could make a strong impression on those who oppose your change initiative or have not yet decided how they feel about it. Especially be aware of subfactions across different parts of your organization (such as through shared experience) that might provide an opportunity for you to gain some allies in a department or function that is not especially supportive of your intervention.

Allies operate across boundaries and therefore have another set of loyalties beyond their loyalty to you or your perspectives. They may well be close personal and family friends, but operating across an organizational boundary means they will sometimes have competing loyalties. Understanding their loyalties allows you to protect these very good and sometimes long-standing relationships. (See "What Happened to Harry?")

What Happened to Harry?

In a high-level engineering department in the auto industry, Jack had a good relationship with Harry, a colleague and peer with whom Jack had worked well on cross-functional projects in the past. They were given the challenge to design the base of a new car that could be easily adapted to European as well as American standards and markets, and they needed to collaborate with engineers in both Germany and Detroit to do so. However, the two countries had never done this before. Harry and Jack worked for different design teams in Detroit, and it seemed to Jack that Harry was quite sympathetic to his point of view on the design challenge and the need to engage the German team. The two of them spent a lot of time talking about the issues, synergies, and efficiencies to be gained. And Jack also felt that on an intellectual and even emotional level, he and Harry were kindred spirits.

While preparing for an important series of design meetings, Jack checked in with Harry, who nodded and smiled as Jack described his innovative ideas. Jack thought Harry's responses were insightful and encouraging. It all looked hopeful, and Jack felt certain that Harry would back his interventions wholeheartedly when it came time to roll into action.

A week later, during the first major redesign meeting with Jack, Harry, and numerous other Detroit people involved in the initiative, Harry acted like an entirely different person from the one Jack thought he knew. Jack's idea was high on the agenda, and everyone had received a written briefing

Stay Connected to the Opposition

One of the more obvious lessons Americans have learned from the United States' involvement in Iraq is that Saddam Hussein had a major community of allies on his side. The Sunnis who inhabited Baghdad and the central region of the country, and who constituted the politically dominant minority of Iraq's population, backed him passionately and wanted to maintain their dominance over the Shiites and Kurds. Had the United States' administrators understood what was at stake for these various ethnic communities in Iraq, they may have developed beforehand. But Harry sat there completely silent when Jack asked everyone to respond and to explain how they might go about presenting the idea to their teams back in their own departments. Jack felt blindsided. His instinctive interpretation was that Harry had turned out to be untrustworthy or maybe even a liar. At best, it looked as if he were a coward. Jack felt disappointed and deceived, and stopped talking with Harry.

But Harry was none of those things. Harry might have done better to let Jack know that he was going to have a problem backing him up, but in fairness, most people aren't very good at conversations when they're disappointing people they like and who count on them. In fact, Jack had completely failed to appreciate that Harry had serious reasons to be of mixed minds. On one hand, Harry agreed that change was needed and even shared Jack's enthusiasm for coming up with an integrative and more modular car design. On the other hand, Harry had a major problem with his own team in going in Jack's direction. Long-standing loyalties to his people were at risk if he were to ask his team to change how they worked so radically. Nothing in Jack's proposal took these changes into account, so Harry balked. Jack only saw what he wanted to see when Harry nodded and smiled. But Jack never really asked whether his approach was going to cause problems.

Instead of taking it personally and withdrawing, Jack should have made inquiry his next move. He should have sat down with Harry and asked, "I'm sure you've got good reasons for holding back. What have I missed?"

---

a far more effective strategy for constructing a set of relationships across each ethnic and religious boundary. Instead, they tended to assume that all ethnic groups in Iraq had a shared interest in being "liberated" from Hussein's tyranny by U.S. forces. That was largely true for the Kurds. And it was somewhat true for the Shiites, though less so because they were afraid of American hegemony and therefore felt more ambivalent about their "liberators." But the Sunni Arabs did not en masse feel liberated when U.S. forces entered Iraq. They felt captured. The Iraqi military, mostly Sunni, was largely disbanded rather than reintegrated. Having lost its connection to the core opposition in the streets and among the military, the United States was forced to start from scratch in building an Iraqi security force. This gave ample time for an emboldened insurrection to build. And years, lives, and trillions of dollars were lost. Only with the success of U.S. military efforts to make connections with the opposition—Sunni insurgents who began to tire of insurrection and consider changing course to ally with the Iraqi government—did the tide begin to turn in 2007–2008, bringing some measure of stability to Iraq. Without this "Awakening," no surge of American troops in 2007 would have made a difference.[1]

Connecting to the opposition was not an easy task. The military officers who first began to sense the change of heart among insurgent commanders and wanted to seize the opportunity to gain new indigenous allies ran into opposition up their own chain of command among officers who refused to risk trusting and supporting insurgents against whom they had lost troops even in previous days. Loyalty to the soldiers they had lost took precedent. Indeed, it took months of effort with junior officers leading upward, along with changes in senior command, to get key commanding officers on board with building these new alliances.[2]

Look again at the worksheet in table 6-1. Who is most likely to oppose what you're trying to do? Potential opponents are stakeholders who have markedly different perspectives from yours and who stand to risk losing the most if you and your initiative are go forward.

Once you've identified the opposition, stay close to them, spend time with them, ask for their input on your initiative, listen closely to their reality (especially where it differs from yours), and take their temperature to assess how much heat you are putting on them and how desperate they are becoming. Regularly get together for coffee, include them in meetings, and let them know you value their perspective and insights on your intervention. Of course, it is not a lot of fun to spend time with "the enemy." Recently, we had a hard time persuading the CEO of a governmental agency who was pushing for adaptive change to spend time with officials from the union that represented many blue-collar employees and fought him at every opportunity. Understandably, he did not look forward to the abuse he received at meetings with these officials. But it was critical for him to do so if he hoped to win some of them over, find a more integrative solution, or at least prevent them from stopping his work.

Resisters to your initiative are people who feel most threatened by it. They may believe that they will not be able to make the changes you recommend, that they might lose their job, or that they'll be worse off in some way if the initiative is carried out. You may agree or disagree with their perception, but it is their perception that counts for your purposes. Resist any temptation to try "straightening them out." Our experience suggests this would be a fool's errand and could actually set you back by stiffening their resistance. (Nobody likes being told that they "shouldn't feel that way.") Instead, accept that what you're trying to do is not in their interest. Compassion and empathy have their own reward in heaven, but they are also critical tools for comprehending the potential losses at stake for your opposition.

Authentic empathy has consequences. If you really understand the losses that your initiative would inflict on your opponents, you have to take responsibility for inflicting them. From your perspective, you did not create the adaptive challenge at hand, and your purpose is simply to mobilize people to grapple with the problem; you are not deliberately trying to make their lives miserable. It might be a lot harder to keep pushing your initiative forward single-mindedly when you have compassion for the people who will have to bear the losses.

Second, your stakeholders will be looking to you to project certainty and thereby diminish their worry that the costs they will pay might not be worthwhile. Empathizing with your opponents might lead you to ask yourself, "Am I really doing the right thing?" If you start doubting your cause, you may end up revising your plan or even abandoning it, or undermining the confidence of some allies.

So why force yourself to spend time with your resisters? First, you will never seem as evil in person as you can be in people's imagination. Simply spending time in their presence can help take the edge off their hostility and thus soften their determination to block your efforts. For just this reason, when Marty was advising clients on media relations, he always encouraged people to accept invitations to go on hostile talk-radio shows or speak before opposition audiences. "Gerald Ford's Story" shows another example.

There is another reason to make yourself spend time with resisters: by meeting with them, you can acknowledge the sacrifices you are asking them to make and how difficult and painful those sacrifices may be. For some people, that is all they need to hear in order to begin feeling

Gerald Ford's Story

During his tenure as U.S. president, Gerald Ford went before the Veterans of Foreign Wars of the United States (VFW) to announce that he was granting a limited amnesty for some Vietnam War protesters. He was bent on healing the emotional wounds that the United States had sustained from both the Watergate scandal and Vietnam. He knew he had a much better chance of achieving this goal if he delivered the message of amnesty to a group that was likely to oppose it strongly. He believed that some subfactions within the VFW, those who most highly valued courage as well as those who had estranged family members who had protested the war, would be much less likely to oppose the amnesty plan if Ford displayed the courage and compassion to tell them about it first before presenting it to the rest of the nation.

---

less hostile toward you and your idea. Some may actually become supporters, while others may at least tone down their opposition.

Finally, spending time with the opposition enables you to assess firsthand how much pressure they feel from your initiative. You can then calibrate your tactics accordingly. For example, suppose you meet with union officials to discuss a cost-saving initiative that would require greater employee contributions to their generous health benefit plan. Watching body language and nonverbal cues in informal conversations might well give you information that you could not get in a more formal setting to indicate the importance to the membership of maintaining the current benefit as compared to other potential cost-cutting measures.

Manage Authority Figures

Your boss and other senior authority figures are essential to any intervention you try to lead. To sustain their support, you need to do more than just figure out how they feel personally about the adaptive issue you are seeking to address. First, you need to prepare them for the disequilibrium you are going to generate in the organization. Second, once the disequilibrium sets in, you must "read" them for signals suggesting how much heat the organization can stand.

In those consulting engagements in which we are asked to work primarily with people one or two levels below the CEO and executive team, we have learned to interact first with those top-level authority figures. At the very least, we describe to them the pushback they can expect to experience once the intervention rolls into action. And we try to give them a taste of what that pushback may look like at its worst (complaints of confusion, conflict, or urging that we be fired after the first day of a three-day program), so they can understand on a more visceral level what their colleagues will be going through. We use their responses to this information to better customize and calibrate our work. "Managing the Board at SAS Airlines" provides another example of how this process can work.

Managing senior authority figures has numerous benefits when you are trying to lead adaptive change. People who sit at the top of an organization see a bigger picture than those at lower levels. A CEO of a publicly held company stays in touch with needs and trends in the external environment, while most of the rest of the people in the organization are sheltered from the direct pressure of Wall Street or the media. Thus chief executives can see the external consequences that might result from your activities.

But top executives also have a broader internal view. A CEO gets feedback and pressure from a huge range of constituencies inside the organization. So he is a good barometer of how the whole organization is responding to your initiative.

And that can help you assess how your intervention is faring in the organization at large. The clues are all there if you look for them: observe how the senior authority relates to you in private and public settings, what he says about the initiative, and how this individual uses his political capital. These observations can tell you a lot about the pressures the CEO is experiencing as a result of your work. Armed with that knowledge, you can better calibrate the heat produced by your efforts than if you were just relying on the information you get firsthand.

Managing the Board at SAS Airlines

In his now classic book *Moments of Truth*, Jan Carlzon, former CEO of SAS, Scandinavian Airlines, describes how he managed his superiors, the members of SAS's board, while leading a change initiative related to improving customer service.[3] Carlzon had decided that to remain competitive, SAS had to give frontline employees more freedom to serve travelers better and therefore improve customer loyalty. To exercise this power, ticket handlers, flight attendants, and baggage handlers needed more latitude to make decisions that would sometimes cost the company money in the short run (such as providing refunds or putting people on other airlines' flights). Carlzon knew that making this initiative deliver as promised would require widespread cultural change (and spark a lot of disequilibrium) in the organization.

To prepare his board for tolerating this disequilibrium and supporting the risks and investments he would need to lead the intervention, he held a series of meetings with the board in which he pushed them hard to imagine just how much pressure they would be getting to undermine his plan. Had he not taken this step, people in the company who opposed this redistribution of power—and there were many, particularly at the high levels of management—may have gone to the board and bad-mouthed this "heretic" who had somehow "manipulated" himself into the office of CEO. And board members may have begun questioning their support of Carlzon's intervention.

But Carlzon had more in mind than just preempting this sort of sabotage. He involved the board also to benefit from their knowledge. Carlzon was stepping into unknown territory. Airline companies did not generally operate the way he had envisioned for SAS. He benefited from the accumulated wisdom of board members, many of whom were elders in business and politics and had helpful ideas for how to manage the intervention.

Take Responsibility for Casualties

Adaptive change results in casualties: people in the organization who lose something they value, whether it is a familiar way of doing things, status, jobs, or in the military, their lives. If you are trying to exercise adaptive leadership, you will need to shoulder responsibility for these inevitable casualties. That means paying attention to them: spend time with them, acknowledge your role in their difficulties, and find ways to help them endure the experience or get on with their lives in another way. When you take responsibility for casualties in these ways, some of them may even rise to the occasion and support the intervention despite the fact that it puts them in jeopardy.

As important strategically, you are also communicating to the allies of those who have become casualties: if these allies see you treating their friends humanely, they may have more positive feelings about you and your initiative. If they see you treat their friends callously, they will have one more good reason not to come on board.

Finally, you send the message that you are accountable for the outcomes of your decisions and actions. And that may encourage similar accountability throughout the organization.

Protect and Engage the Voices of Dissent

The voices of dissent are naysayers, the skeptics, who not only question this initiative but question whatever is on the agenda for today. They are princes of darkness, often resting on the negative. But they are valuable for implementing adaptive change because they are canaries in the coal mine, early-warning systems, and because in addition to being unproductive and annoying much of the time, they have the uncanny capacity for asking the really tough key question that you have been unwilling to face up to yourself or that others have been unwilling to raise. In many organizations, dissenters get marginalized, silenced, or even fired, which deprives the organization of their valuable, if unpopular, service.

How can you protect the voices of dissent? If you have formal authority in your organization, keep in mind that when someone expresses a contrary idea or asks a disturbing question during a meeting or conversation, everyone will observe your response to decide how they should react. Thus it is vital to demonstrate openness to seemingly subversive or revolutionary ideas.

Consider a meeting in which someone voices concern that a new strategy may not be consistent with the company's values. By allowing this concern to be raised and explored, you may unearth a wide range of perspectives that would otherwise be unspoken, and you will learn more deeply about individual and collective values of the team.

If you are not in an authority role, you can still protect dissenters by taking them seriously and listening to them, trying to find the useful insights in what they're saying without necessarily endorsing their perspective. Just urging others to let the dissenter finish the diatribe or asking the group whether there is anything to be learned from the outburst will not only protect that voice but nurture other challenging voices as well.

Here are several additional tips for ensuring that minority perspectives receive a hearing in your organization:

- Make careful interventions following a disturbing one, to keep it alive.

- Create formal space on meeting agendas for brainstorming, exploring innovative ideas, and acknowledging the "elephants in the room," the sensitive, unacknowledged issues in the group.

- Pair high-potential new hires with veterans who can help them navigate the organization's political minefields.

- Give annual awards for the most helpful dissenting views.

- Create outside forums, brown-bag lunches, retreat spaces, and other occasions that take people out of their usual roles and make it safer to put radical ideas on the table.

- Hang around after a meeting has ended, so you can support informal debriefings when some otherwise unspeakable ideas are given voice.

- Build an anonymous input box, and then read the comments from it at every staff meeting.

ON THE PRACTICE FIELD

- Think of an adaptive change intervention you are considering in your organization. Fill out the worksheet in table 10-1 to develop strategies for acting politically with each of the five groups we have discussed in this section: allies, opponents, senior authority figures, casualties, and dissenters.

TABLE 10-1

Worksheet: strategies for acting politically

Your adaptive change initiative:

1. Allies

Who might be your allies?	Why might they be allies?	What's their main objective? (Support you? The initiative itself? The organization?)	How can this ally best help you successfully implement your intervention?

2. Opponents

Who might be your opponents?	Why might they be opponents?	What do they stand to lose if your initiative succeeds?	How might you neutralize their opposition or get them on your side?

3. Senior authorities

Who are the senior authorities most important to your intervention's success?	Why are they important?	What signals are they giving about how the organization perceives your intervention?	What might you say or do to secure their support as your initiative is being implemented?

TABLE 10-1 CONTINUED

4. Casualties

Who will be casualties of your intervention?	What will they lose?	What new skills would help them survive the change and thrive in the new organization?	How might you help them acquire those skills?	Which casualties will need to leave the organization?	How could you help them succeed elsewhere?

5. Dissenters

Who are the dissenters in your organization—those who typically voice radical ideas or mention the unmentionable?	What ideas are they bringing forth that might be valuable for your intervention?	How might you enable their ideas to have a hearing?	How can you protect them from being marginalized or silenced?

CHAPTER 11

Orchestrate Conflict

O RCHESTRATING CONFLICT is a discipline. It requires seeing the process as a necessary step in the journey toward a better future, tolerating the moments your people are not working well together, and believing that working through some rough patches will help to solidify their collective effort and commitment.

For example, we have been working with a large school system where the high school teachers say they want the majority of the school's graduates to go on to college. Currently, only small percentages manage to do so, but the teachers union has fought almost every initiative proposed that some people thought might help close the gap, such as longer school days and fewer social promotions (letting students move up into the next grade in spite of poor performance). From the teachers' perspective, they are already overworked and underpaid, and spend too much of their time dealing with disciplinary issues rather than teaching.

To narrow the gap between the aspiration and current reality, the superintendent had to find ways to bring those conflicts to the surface and have the teachers themselves work them through, without her becoming the issue by attempting to resolve those issues for them. Surfacing those value conflicts and holding steady while the teachers did their work took faith, courage, and discipline. After a great deal of angry interchange, even to the point of yelling and screaming, with a restrained superintendent not showing her hand but keeping teachers in the conversation with each other, the teachers began to face the gap between their aspirations for their students and the current reality of their union's position by developing some of their own ideas for change.

Everyone has a particular capacity for tolerating conflict. Some people are comfortable working through conflict, while most avoid it entirely or try to get through it as quickly as possible. But surfacing the relevant conflicts is essential when an organization is falling short of its aspirations. To do this well requires an approach to conflict that teases out the *unacknowledged* differences in perspectives on the work issues that may be preventing the organization from reaching its espoused aspiration. It requires acknowledging the many competing visions, values, and views that may be alive in the organization even if they are not articulated.

As you might imagine, orchestrating conflict is not easy. For the orchestrator, it often requires tolerating a lot of hostility. And for many people, sitting in the stew and heat of conflict can be extremely challenging. That is why most organizations respond to conflict, or potential conflict, in other ways that are simpler, but ineffective. For example, they:

- *Do nothing.* This is the easiest response. Organizational systems reward people who do not upset the equilibrium, who do not make things messy by bringing conflict out into the open. But when people allow the conflict to stay unresolved, the organization often remains unchanged.

- *React by flight or fight.* In the high school example, the superintendent had to work hard to keep some teacher factions in the game, the ones that would have preferred to keep things calm and unresolved. Similarly, she had to work with other factions that wanted to avoid any real resolution by blaming without responsibility and arguing without listening.

- *Look to authority.* People in the organization prefer to rely on those with formal authority to resolve the conflict. Authorities are often expected to do what they can to preserve the calm, which does not foster change. If the superintendent in our high school case had decided the issue herself, resolved it as a strong authority person is expected to do, she would have become the issue, deflecting attention to her own behavior and choices rather than the real work of teachers in getting more kids to stay in school, do well, and go to college.

We borrow the term *orchestration* from music because of the way composers approach the uses of dissonance and consonance in the creation of harmony. Composers treat dissonance as an essential component of harmony. Very few pieces of music or kinds of music use only sounds that are consonant with one another, like Gregorian chant. Using only consonant sounds gives music a timeless, motionless feel to it. Dissonance creates tension in the music, causing the listener to naturally want some kind of resolution. Composers know this, so they put two or more dissonant notes together that do not sound quite right, and then they create different kinds of resolutions to the tension by putting together consonant tones that do sound right. To a composer, the art of harmony is the creative uses of dissonance and consonance, woven together to create tension, a sense of forward motion, resolution, and then tension again until, usually, there is a final resolution.

Forward motion in organizations and communities is also a product of differences that generate creative tension and that, properly orchestrated, will resolve into a more integrated whole. The voices and perspectives that do not sound quite right together, and may never sound quite right together in isolation, are woven into a larger composition, and as part of the whole picture, they become essential. The working through of their differences provides the hope that some new synthesis will emerge, a new experiment and new capacity. People learn by encountering different points of view, not by staring at themselves in the mirror or engaging just those with consonant views.

If you want to generate progress on adaptive issues, you have to seek out, surface, nurture, and then carefully manage the conflict toward resolution, rather than see it as something to be eliminated or neutralized. Think of organizational harmony as the artful use of conflict to produce new resolve. Conflict is an essential resource in getting to the real, as opposed to superficial, harmony.

"Seven Steps to Orchestrating Conflict" describes how to start the process of surfacing and working through conflict in order to move forward on adaptive issues. You can think of the steps as the process agenda for a single event, such as a multiday off-site retreat, or as a process strategy for making progress over a period of time involving multiple, shorter interventions.

Seven Steps to Orchestrating Conflict

1. **Prepare.** Before bringing your organization's factions together and surfacing the conflict, do your homework. Where does each faction stand on the key elements of the conflict? What do they care about the most? What losses do they fear? Talking to them in advance helps you acquire the informal authority you will need to retain their trust when the rough moments come.

2. **Establish ground rules.** Propose rules making it safe to discuss the conflict, such as committing to confidentiality, staying in the room with PDAs and computers off, depersonalizing the conflicts, and brainstorming. Set the agenda. Frame the issues with the overall mission and the current adaptive challenge. Tell them that it is up to everyone to keep the work issues at the center of attention at all times. To warm up, you might use exercises and cases from other settings to work the issues by analogy rather than directly.

3. **Get each view on the table.** Invite each faction to articulate the values, the loyalties, and the competencies that inform each of their perspectives on the adaptive challenge and its various related work issues. What commitments do they have to others who are not in the room, and what perspectives do those people have on the challenge? What do they see as their potential and nonnegotiable losses?

4. **Orchestrate the conflict.** Starkly but evenhandedly, articulate the competing claims and positions you are hearing. As people begin to appreciate how deeply held the competing values are and how committed each faction is to avoiding taking any losses, the tension will rise. Look for signs that people are seeking to avoid the conflict, such as trying to minimize the differences or change the subject. As orchestrator, keep reminding people of the purpose, why it is that they are going through this hard patch.

5. **Encourage accepting and managing losses.** Give each person or faction an opportunity to reflect more fully on the nature of the losses they would be asking each of their factions to accept. Tell them that

some losses will be necessary, but give everyone time to sit with these losses (maybe hours, but also maybe days, weeks, or months). Ask them to consider how they are going to deal with constituents, and how they might go about refashioning constituents' expectations and loyalties. Ask them to continue to reflect among themselves while maintaining confidentiality.

6. **Generate and commit to experiments.** Discuss individual experiments for dealing with constituents and collective experiments for tackling the adaptive challenge. Generate a consensus to go with several experiments for tackling the adaptive challenge, in sequence and/or at the same time, as it makes sense, with a shared commitment to get back together to evaluate the results of both kinds of experiments when enough data has been generated for lessons and insights.

7. **Institute peer leadership consulting.** Individual and collective commitments to go forward will be hard to make because they require decisions about who will take what losses, how each of them will bring the agreed-upon next steps back to their own constituents, and what adaptations each of their constituent groups will need to make to implement the collective experiments. To maximize the chances of success, move the members of the group into peer consulting, where they begin systematically to consult to one another on the leadership headache they have just given each other. How can they help each other analyze the sources of resistance each should expect from their own people? How can they redesign some of the experiments and their implementation to take these resistances into account—for example, by pacing, sequencing, or framing cross-boundary projects? People in positions of authority generally hold their leadership issues close to the vest, keeping them private. So asking them to consult to one another establishes a new norm and may be difficult at first. You want your team to have a shared responsibility for the whole in which one person's issue is an issue for everyone.

Orchestrating conflict requires courage, to different degrees for different people. Here are some suggestions based on characteristics we have seen when people have tried to lead adaptive change in this way:

- *Push the boundaries of your own tolerance for conflict.* Orchestrating conflict requires tolerating a high degree of conflict yourself, perhaps more than you are comfortable with.

- *Play with the bad guys.* You will have to interact with hostile or antagonistic factions, and engage them on their own terms, not yours, even when their terms make no sense to you. And that means you will probably take some heat from the people you consider your core constituents, your primary loyalties, perhaps the division from where you came. ("Why are you even sitting down at a table with those guys?")

- *Accept support from people whose reasoning you would reject.* Bringing antagonistic groups together often means allowing them to voice arguments you may personally find distasteful or even abhorrent. The motives and rationale for factions agreeing to engage or agreeing then to a particular course of action may differ widely. What you are looking for is progress on the issue, and people will get there in their own ways. With one of our clients, a professional services firm, the gap between the espoused values and the current reality was maintained powerfully by the compensation system. Aligning the compensation system with their values was a heated process. There were not only winners and losers in material terms, but some folks were willing to go along with the new system for reasons that we found uncomfortable, such as devaluing certain product lines they did not respect.

- *Adapt your communication style.* Orchestrating conflict successfully can mean having to change your communication style to help adversarial factions work through the issues. For example, you may have to display more confidence or hopefulness than you really feel to keep others from getting up and stalking out of the room. Or you may have to get forceful or even angry even if you do not like to appear that way. If adapting your communication style or demeanor makes you feel manipulative or inauthentic, keep reminding yourself of the purpose: helping the parties

be more authentic so they can identify, examine, and move
through their conflicts toward some integrative solution.

The following practices can help you surmount these difficulties and
boost your chances.

Create a Holding Environment

A holding environment consists of all those ties that bind people
together and enable them to maintain their collective focus on what
they are trying to do. All the human sources of cohesion that offset the
forces of division and dissolution provide a sort of containing vessel in
which work can be done. In fact, every group—from a family to an
international organization—provides a holding environment, either
weakly or strongly, for its members to collaborate productively. We
have used the analogy of a pressure cooker for the holding environment; and as anyone who has ever used a pressure cooker knows, some
are stronger than others (domestic versus industrial strength), depending on the strength of the steel and the locking lid.

The term itself was coined to describe the very first holding environment in each of our human experiences: a woman's arms holding a new-
born baby and providing food and safety.[1] The bond between mother and
child is so strong right from the beginning that even when the child spits
up, cries incessantly, and pushes the mother away, she continues to hold
the child. If she is tired out, she will pass the child to someone else to do
the job. Sometimes children are raised in very weak holding environments and are quickly pushed aside and left alone when they fuss. When
that happens, nearly every society has backstop institutions that serve as
holding environments, from extended families to foster families, adoption
services, social service agencies, and the court system. As a last resort,
prisons serve as holding environments, containing individuals and giving
them one last chance to take hold of themselves and behave responsibly.

In doing adaptive work in organizations, you need to create or
strengthen the holding environment to provide safety and structure for
people to surface and discuss the particular values, perspectives, and
creative ideas they have on the challenging situation they all face. As
members of a group work through a conflict, things can get nasty. People

may begin distancing themselves from one another, flying apart as they retreat into their own corners. The harder the adaptive work, the stronger the holding environment must be to contain those divisive forces.

What is required for a holding environment may differ from country to country, from firm to firm, and across boundaries of race and gender. A strong holding environment for a bunch of conflict-loving New Yorkers will be different from one for more deferential Japanese. But there are some common elements that serve to strengthen the bonds of cohesion and offset the tensions as they are surfaced in any culture. Some of these are:

- Shared language

- Shared orienting values and purposes

- History of working together

- Lateral bonds of affection, trust, and camaraderie

- Vertical bonds of trust in authority figures and the authority structure

- At the micro level for a working group, a meeting room with comfortable chairs, a round table, and rules of confidentiality and brainstorming that encourage people to speak their minds

To describe more concretely the components of a strong holding environment, we turn again to the off-site retreat as a literal and metaphorical example.

The purpose of an off-site is to get people out of the office into a different place where they can gain new perspectives and focus on an issue they do not usually deal with during their day-to-day work. Off-sites are often used to work through conflicts. These holding environments aim to generate a level of trust and open discussion not usually present in the workplace.

Many considerations in designing off-sites are routine for any such event, such as workspace layout, administrative support, norms of reporting and confidentiality, a pulse-taking at the beginning, and an accountability mechanism to hold people to decisions and commitments made at the event. But some practices, which we suggest below, are particularly relevant when you are dealing with adaptive work.

Before the Off-site

- *Prepare the senior authority for a different role.* During the off-site, all eyes will be on the senior authority for clues to how seriously to treat the event. Does the senior authority leave the room to answer a cell phone after the meeting begins or nod off as some-one else is talking? If the senior authority keeps delivering orders or answers, it will feel to others that they have not left the office at all. People will soon stop offering their own ideas and opinions, waiting for the boss to speak. So before the retreat even begins, provide coaching as needed to discourage the senior authority from engaging in these and other conversation-stopping behav-iors. We sometimes use the standard that, if someone were to watch a videotape of the off-site, it would be impossible to tell which person was the senior authority in the group.

- *Identify hidden perspectives and conflicts in preparatory inter-views.* Ask some or all of the participants in one-on-one conver-sations what they see as the problem that triggered the off-site. How important do they think this problem is for the organiza-tion? (If they do not agree on the problem or see it as important, that itself becomes an issue for the group.) What are their expec-tations? What key issues are they worried the off-site will ignore? What would success look like?

During the Off-site

- *Establish new processes.* To help people produce a different, less tangible "product" (such as resolution of a conflict) than the more concrete outcomes (sales, strategies, reports) they usually gener-ate at the office, they will need different processes for interacting with one another. New norms send the signal that the retreat has an entirely different goal than the work people normally deal with back at the office. You might ask people to call each other by first names if they do not usually do so at work. Build in time for indi-vidual and collective reflection. Explain that adaptive work is messier than technical work. Legitimize conflict. Ask people to stay in the game when the going gets rough. Hire an outside facilitator or rotate the facilitation among the participants, to help ensure that they do not fall into familiar roles.

- *Watch the initial event.* Pay close attention to what happens first as the event begins. A joke, a casual comment, a request for information, whatever it is may signal something important about the group's mood and the issues that are alive in the room. If someone makes a joke about the senior authority not being at the head of the table, that may suggest that relations with the authority are an issue in the group, and that people would be surprised if the boss didn't jump in and control things when the going got tough.

Select Participants

Just as you select ingredients to throw into a stewpot before you turn up the heat, you need to select carefully the individuals who will take part in a conversation about the conflict you are seeking to orchestrate on the issue you are trying to work through.

Determining which parties to include is a strategic decision: who should play a part in the deliberations, and in what sequence? Including too many parties can overload people's capacity to learn and accommodate one another. However, when you fail to be inclusive, you may risk devising an incomplete solution, a solution to the wrong problem, or, worse, excluded parties that will sabotage the process of sustainable change. At a minimum, if you opt for a smaller group, you must keep track of missing perspectives.

Here are some key questions to consider:

- Who needs to learn what, to make progress on this challenge?

- Does a party represent a constituency whose changes are critical if the larger community is to make progress?

- Does any party's perspective generate so much distress that including it would disrupt the effort to build any kind of coalition?

- Are there parties whose presence is important in the medium or long term but not in the short term, so that they might be excluded initially?

Selection is never an easy process. In the interests of efficiency and order, you may be inclined to minimize the number of people representing a variety of functions or constituencies. But in the interest of furthering adaptive change, you may want to expand your definition of who should be included. Political considerations are relevant. There will be lots of buzz and interpretations back at the office about who was and who was not included.

In *Leadership Without Easy Answers*, we discussed this dilemma and offered a framework for determining how narrowly or widely you should cast your net while selecting participants to work through a conflict.[2]

A conflict that requires immediate resolution suggests that you select fewer stakeholders, in the interest of timeliness. But the more the conflict at hand requires adaptive work to be resolved, the more expansive your definition of whom to include should be. However, the more participants in the conversation, the greater the chances that some of them will be intensely impassioned about the subject, and the more the individual agendas that will be in the room will dominate. Stridency, aggressive advocacy, and individual perspectives and stakes can jeopardize the entire effort by triggering other participants to disconnect, leaving the room or refusing to contribute to the conversation. All of this, of course, can be useful data for identifying deeper conflicts in perspective, but you also may have a hard time reassembling the parties into a working group.

The benefits and costs of exclusion and inclusion fluctuate, and in a tactical sense you have to pace the work in part by sequencing when and which parties are brought into the process. Yet a general bias toward inclusion builds adaptive capacity for the long run. Inclusion stresses that people in the network of relationships respect one another and gives you more options for future crises because you have established a firm relationship with people who have struggled through something difficult together. Inclusion is both a means to accomplish immediate adaptive work and a way to cover future bases.

Regulate the Heat

Humans are temperature sensitive. Think about the many things you do each day to be comfortable: put on a sweater if the room feels cold, turn up the air-conditioning if it is too warm, and take a cold drink to cool off after exercise.

Similarly, people take steps to lower the "heat" in their organizational lives. You might speak soothingly to an irritated coworker to help him calm down, or raise a particularly touchy issue in the hallway with a friend rather than in the meeting because you know he may get distraught and would not want others to see. These skills are valuable in certain circumstances. But they are not as useful for working through conflict related to adaptive change because they are designed to maintain the status quo.

To orchestrate conflict effectively, think of yourself as having your hand on the thermostat and always watching for signals that you need to raise or lower the temperature in the room. Your goal is to keep the temperature—that is, the intensity of the disequilibrium created by discussion of the conflict—high enough to motivate people to arrive at creative next steps and potentially useful solutions, but not so high that it drives them away or makes it impossible for them to function.

This temperature range will differ depending on factors such as the cohesiveness of the group and members' familiarity with adaptive work. A group that is cohesive because members share history and values can stand a much higher level of heat without breaking apart than a newly formed group with members from different parts of the community or organization. One that is less cohesive because members have never before worked together or have profoundly conflicting values may break apart at a high level of heat. Table 11-1 shows examples of

TABLE 11-1

Controlling the temperature

To raise the temperature . . .	To lower the temperature . . .
• Draw attention to the tough questions.	• Address the aspects of the conflict that have the most obvious and technical solutions.
• Give people more responsibility than they're comfortable with.	• Provide structure by breaking the problem into parts and creating time frames, decision rules, and role assignments.
• Bring conflicts to the surface.	
• Tolerate provocative comments.	• Temporarily reclaim responsibility for the tough issues.
• Name and use some of the dynamics in the room at the moment to illustrate some of the issues facing the group—e.g., getting the authority figure to do the work, scapegoating an individual, externalizing the blame, and tossing technical fixes at the situation.	• Employ work avoidance mechanisms such as taking a break, telling a joke or a story, or doing an exercise.
	• Slow down the process of challenging norms and expectations.

actions you can take to raise or lower the heat in an organization or community.

ON THE BALCONY

- Develop your capacity for assessing the temperature. The next time you are in a meeting, sit back and try to track the temperature in the room. After each comment made by any of the participants in the gathering, notice whether the temperature seems to go up or down. Notice when it seems that the overall group is below the level of productive disequilibrium, in the middle of it, or nearing its upper limit of tolerance.

ON THE PRACTICE FIELD

- If you see the group lowering the heat to make things more comfortable rather than dealing with the conflict, try naming the behavior as soon as you notice it. Say something like, "It feels as if we're moving off the tough stuff; can we stay there for a while?" Try naming the issue being avoided: "How can we move forward unless we discuss why we lost the client last week and how people feel about it?" "I think we're all avoiding the reality of Joe having been let go last week. Don't we need to address that and what it represents to us?" "Look, best as I can tell, Jamal and Mary have not spoken since they almost came to blows at the meeting last Friday. Don't we, as a team, need to better understand what that was all about and think about how to move on from here?"

- Try to understand the senior authority's willingness and capacity for raising the heat, by tracking what happens to the room's temperature after the senior authority makes a comment or a decision. Does the temperature remain comfortable? Get distressingly high?

Give the Work Back

For people in authority roles, one of the most difficult aspects of orchestrating conflict is resisting the temptation to take the conflictual elements of the adaptive work off of other people's shoulders and putting it on your own. The pressure to relieve them of that work comes from both them and from you. You have undoubtedly been rewarded for exactly that behavior in the past. People generally get promoted because they are willing to take problems on their own shoulders and come up with solutions. And people both above and below you are expecting, and prefer, that to continue. They want you to make an authoritative decision that "resolves" the conflict.

When she became CEO of Hewlett-Packard (HP), Carly Fiorina saw that the company was facing major adaptive challenges, including its historic dependence on medical technology and challenges to the printer and computer technology end of the business. She came to believe that acquiring Compaq would help solve HP's problems. But it appears that she shouldered a great deal of the decision herself. She may have made a more informed decision and a more widely understood decision if she had orchestrated a debate in the board and among all of HP's key stakeholders about the merits, dangers, and timeline for returns on the investment of the Compaq acquisition as a solution to the challenge. A wider conversation made up of a more diverse array of voices could have generated a shared sense of ownership of the risks and timelines for whatever decision was ultimately made, although she would have risked having to forgo what she thought was the right step. More important, the conflict about the direction the company should take was alive and well in the board and among the stakeholders, and resolving it was their work to do in order to have a united organization on the other side of the decision. By taking so much responsibility for trying to solve HP's problems and becoming the primary advocate of one particular solution, she both relieved them of the work and tied her future to the success of that solution. She made herself the issue. When the acquisition did not work out on the time horizon all had expected, she paid dearly and lost her job.

Giving the work back in organizational life often requires going against the grain of expectations that you're supposed to maintain equilibrium or restore it quickly when people get knocked off balance. When you have authority, people expect you to provide direction, protection, and order, which includes delineating their individual roles and responsibilities. Typically, the more clarity you provide, the more comfortable they are. What they *do not* expect is for you to give them work you have customarily been doing for them. But to build your team's adaptive capacity, you need to push them beyond their comfort zones. "Giving the Work Back in an Advertising and Sales Company" gives an example of the way this worked in one organization.

Giving the Work Back in an Advertising and Sales Company

We worked extensively with a fast-growing advertising and sales organization in New York City. The founder/CEO was brilliant at client presentations, so much so that no one else on the design staff ever spoke up when he was in the room. One key employee was so reticent that clients lacked confidence in his work. The CEO realized that his own competence was hurting the firm's growth by enabling others to avoid stepping into the uncomfortable, unfamiliar, intimidating adaptive waters of leading client presentations. He knew that if he forced them to take on that role, he would court disaster with clients (as they had not yet developed the required skills) and he would be unable to resist interjecting. He would thus further undermine clients' and the subordinates' confidence in their capacity to do the presentations. So first, he raised the heat by telling them that he was no longer going to do this work for them. Second, to help create a holding environment, he hired presentation consultants to facilitate several two-day workshops on client presentations for his entire team, including himself. And third, he committed to holding back when they were making presentations, no matter how much he thought he could help.

The CEO paced the work, giving time for people to take hold of their new responsibilities and develop new competencies. The change took more than a year. Nearly everyone, including some clients, pushed back. He learned to detect when his subordinates would look to him to rescue them in the middle of a presentation. It took every ounce of his courage and self-command to keep sitting on his hands. But eventually his subordinates were driving most of the client presentations, and he was free to focus on those that only he could do.

ON THE BALCONY

- Think back over the past few weeks. When have you volunteered to take adaptive problems off other people's shoulders? Were these people subordinates, peers, or your boss? What were the negative consequences of doing so? What else could you have been doing with that time? What steps might you have taken to give the work back to these individuals?

ON THE PRACTICE FIELD

- The next time you are in charge of a meeting and you sense that others in the room are looking to you to shoulder some aspect of the adaptive work the group is discussing, try what we call the *sit down technique*. Without warning, take a seat at the side of the flip chart, lectern, or other structure that's at the head of the room, or take a seat in the back of the room. Notice how people respond to your sudden abdication of authority. Do some leave the room? Do others rush to the front to take over? Do some people quickly form into more intimate, safe subgroups? Do people struggle to restore order without authorizing anyone new to take any responsibility? After observing for a while, debrief the experience: explain why you abdicated. Then encourage discussion of the problems it creates when people fall into a dependent mode and expect authority figures to do the adaptive work for a team and organization.

CHAPTER 12

Build an Adaptive Culture

FOSTERING AN ADAPTIVE culture will enable your organization or community to meet an ongoing series of adaptive challenges into the future, a future that is almost guaranteed in our day to keep pitching new challenges toward us. Although building adaptive capacity is a medium- and long-term goal, it can only happen by moving on it today and the next. Indeed, every challenge you currently face is another opportunity to both work the immediate problem and institute ways of operating that can become norms for taking on whatever comes next.

In chapter 7, we discussed five distinguishing characteristics of an adaptive culture, based on our experience working with all types of organizations from every corner of the globe.

- Elephants on the table are named.

- Responsibility for the organization is shared.

- Independent judgment is expected.

- Leadership capacity is developed.

- Reflection and continuous learning are institutionalized.

In chapter 7, you assessed how well your organization stacks up against each of these criteria. In the sections that follow, we will explore a few things you can do to improve your organization's rating on each criterion.

Make Naming Elephants the Norm

The capacity for naming elephants in the room, tough issues that no one talks about, is a common and defining characteristic of an organization with extraordinary adaptability. At Toyota, as we've mentioned, anyone on the production line can critique and suggest improvements to the production process. Courageous conversations require far less courage there because critical ideas have become normalized, whereas that is far less the case on other production lines in other companies.

Of course, naming tough issues can be excruciatingly difficult in any organization. "Ignoring the Merger Elephant" gives one example.

What does it take to strengthen an organization's ability to name its elephants? Here are some techniques.

Ignoring the Merger Elephant

A few years ago, we spent some time talking with a global energy company based in South America that was only a year out from a huge merger with a very different firm of almost equal size. Our last meeting with the top team was scheduled for two hours, with the CEO joining us for the last hour.

During the first hour, two members of the team spoke openly and intensely about the unresolved cultural clashes generated by the merger that were preventing the corporation from moving forward. The rest of the team members agreed that cultural differences presented a serious problem. Then the CEO entered. We asked him how he felt the merger issues were going. He said there were no issues left over from the merger. We looked around the table. Heads were looking down. Watching the two most outspoken members, we asked whether anyone wanted to add anything to the CEO's comments. Silence. A few weeks later, we decided to recount this story in our formal proposal to consult to the firm. The resistance was nearly overwhelming.

Model the Behavior

People at the top of an organization are always sending out clues that indicate what behavior is acceptable. And that is nowhere more critical than in naming elephants.

Not long ago, we consulted to a global bank. During an early meeting with the firm's ten-member top team, one of the most junior members of the team made a passing reference by name to a project managed by one of the most senior people in the room. Even though we had done a slew of due diligence interviews, this project had never come up. At a meeting the following day, another member of the team, also one of the most junior, mentioned the project again, once more in an almost off-hand way. Afterward, we discovered that this project was a very large elephant in the room. Many members of the team thought that the project was draining resources at an alarming rate, resources that could be used for critical investments in the firm's future. Moreover, everyone (including the project's sponsor) knew that the project had no chance of delivering as promised. The range of possible outcomes from the project had gone from modest benefit (disproportionately small, given the costs involved) to utter failure. But the sponsor was a candidate to succeed the CEO, who had an aversion to conflict and wanted to believe the sponsor's reassurances that the project would work out fine. But no one on the team was going to name that elephant unless the CEO signaled clearly that he wanted it discussed.

Beginning in childhood, people take their cues from authority. Therefore, when you are the authority, you have to model the simple act of naming the sensitive issues simmering under the surface, because if you do not, the odds are high that no one else will.

Protect Troublemakers

As we have suggested, almost every organization we have worked with has a few troublemakers, those we called dissenters, people who are experienced as "difficult." They are contrarians, often pointing out an entirely different perspective or viewpoint when the momentum seems to be swinging in one direction. They come up with ideas that appear impractical or unrealistic. They make suggestions that others see as off-point. They ask questions that seem tangential. They often claim the moral high ground when most everyone else is just trying to solve the day's problems. But some of the time, they are the only ones asking the questions that need to be asked and raising the issues that no one wants to talk about. Your task is to preserve their willingness to intervene and speak up.

This is not easy. If you're in a position of authority, you will undoubtedly come under pressure to silence troublemakers. But if you want to signal that unpopular thoughts deserve a hearing, you must resist that pressure.

If you are not in a position of authority, then you can help protect troublemakers by making sure they are invited to meetings. And when they do say something that creates disequilibrium, you can choose to be curious: ask them to say more about their idea rather than allow everyone else in the room to ignore them.

Nurture Shared Responsibility for the Organization

To what degree do people feel responsible for the whole organization where you work, as distinguished from their own piece of that whole (such as their team, department, business unit, or division)? Here are some signals suggesting that people feel a shared sense of responsibility for the organization overall:

- Rewards (financial and otherwise) are based at least in part on the performance of the entire organization and not solely on an individual employee's or unit's performance.

- People lend some of their own resources (personnel, time, budget, equipment, office space) to help others in the organization who need it.

- People share new ideas, insights, and lessons across functional and other boundaries in the organization.

- Individuals who advance to positions of authority have worked in a wide range of departments or divisions in the organization.

- People take time to "job shadow," following colleagues around to understand what those in other parts of the organization do all day, to see what kinds of challenges they are dealing with, and to identify practices and norms that could help them in their own part of the company.

Encourage Independent Judgment

In an organization with an adaptive culture, people in authority do what only they can do and make decisions only they can make. Other tasks and decisions are handled by others capable of doing so. Those in authority are constantly asking whether the task or decision they are about to take on could be handled by someone else and, if so, how they will delegate it to that person. This is not about palming off unpleasant chores to underlings. It is about investing in people's independent judgment and resourcefulness, in addition to their technical skills.

Too many people in authority work to make those under them dependent on them. The more dependent the followers, the more indispensable the authority figure feels. Your job in exercising adaptive leadership is to make yourself *dispensable*. The only way you can do that is to constantly give work back to others so you can develop their abilities and calibrate their current and potential talent for skills such as critical thinking and smart decision making. However gratifying it may be in the short term, you don't want followers at all. You want distributed leadership in which everyone, as a citizen of the organization, seizes opportunities to take initiative in mobilizing adaptive work in their locale. In other words, adaptive leadership generates leadership so that people routinely go beyond their job descriptions.

You need to prepare your people to develop a tolerance for the ambiguity that comes with understanding that individuals in positions of authority do not have all the answers and that the easy answers are not necessarily the right ones.

In organizations that encourage independent judgment, people ask before making a decision, "What is the right thing to do to advance the mission of the organization?" rather than, "What would the boss want me to do here?"

ON THE BALCONY

- At what level in your organization do people begin to feel and act as if they are valued more for their judgment than for their technical expertise?

ON THE PRACTICE FIELD

- Most people dislike ambiguity and gravitate toward clarity, pre-dictability, and certainty. And this can manifest itself in a premature push for closure on an adaptive challenge, rushing to a solution before the diagnosis is complete. You can help people strengthen their tolerance for ambiguity by watching for signs of a premature push for closure, for example, complaining about not moving to action, jumping over basic diagnostic questions to focus on solu-tions, or reaching for a work avoidance mechanism (displacing responsibility or diverting attention from the tough issues). The next time you are at a meeting, look for these signs. If you see them, try asking questions such as "What bad things could happen if we did not make this decision today?" "What else might we learn if we waited another day [or week or month]?"

Develop Leadership Capacity

The development of leadership talent is a line manager's job. Although training, coaching, and support from human resources and external sources can be invaluable, nothing can replace the development poten-tial of high-quality day-to-day supervision. Building a leadership pipeline is essential to long-term adaptability because the key bottle-neck to growth is so often the quantity and quality of leadership avail-able in the organization. People learn to lead on the job. Managers who have made a real commitment to individualized leadership develop-ment give their employees a clear sense of their own potential in the organization, review how they are operating and stretching week to week, and help them develop plans for reaching farther.

One way to foster line responsibility for leadership development is to establish a norm of developing succession plans. A manager with a good succession plan will often look for her replacement from the talent close at hand and will be developing that talent.

ON THE BALCONY

- Do you have a plan for your succession?

- Do you and your boss have a clear and shared sense of your potential in the organization and a clear strategy for how you will maximize your chances of getting there?

Institutionalize Reflection and Continuous Learning

Several practices can help you institutionalize reflection and continuous learning in your organization or team. Below we take a look at some of these practices.

Ask Difficult Reflective Questions

To build a more adaptive culture, you might regularly explore questions such as these:

- How is our external environment (including government regulations, competitors' actions, and customers' priorities) changing?

- What internal challenges are mirroring those external changes?

- What are the gaps between where we are (for example, in terms of profit, sustainability, or the diversity of our workforce) and where we want to be?

- How will we know that we are successful?

- What challenge might be just beyond the horizon?

None of these questions is easy to answer. But we believe they are essential if your organization is to thrive amid a constantly changing and challenging world. When people discuss these questions as a normal part of their jobs throughout the organization—whether it is in the board room, staff meetings, performance reviews, or elsewhere—they enhance the enterprise's ability to secure long-term success; deepen commitment from employees, customers, and other stakeholders; and stimulate innovation. Such organizations are much more likely to be around in sixty years than organizations that have ignored these questions. And that is because they have strengthened their people's capacity and will to identify and deal with emerging challenges, no matter how disturbing these may be.

In many organizations, it is extremely difficult to institutionalize time for reflection and continuous learning. For many successful action-oriented, task-driven, outcome-focused people, taking time out to reflect feels like a waste: "There is so much to do and so little time to do it." But in our experience, creating and maintaining time for checking in with people, teasing out the lessons of recent experiences, and sharing those lessons widely in the organization is critical to adaptability in a changing world.

Honor Risk Taking and Experimentation

Another way to foster reflection and continuous learning is not only to run experiments, but also to reward learning from them, particularly when the experiments fail. Experiment widely enough, and you increase the odds of hitting on some great new ideas. For example, at the beginning of Jack Welch's tenure as CEO of General Electric, he did not know that GE Capital would become the company's major engine of profitability. GE Capital was just one of many experiments with new services and managerial processes conducted in Welch's years as CEO.

To survive and grow, economies, societies, and organizations alike depend on an abundance of risk takers: private-sector entrepreneurs who sink their life savings into an invention, people who set out to ease a social problem by creating a nonprofit without secure funding, parents and teachers who devise alternative education platforms, farmers who gamble on new seeds and agricultural technologies, and political activists who make public nuisances of themselves to draw attention to an egregious social inequity.

Running many small risks is less risky than running a few big ones. So encouraging widespread risk taking, particularly with small experiments from which lessons are captured quickly, is in the medium run a safer strategy. But most people do not enjoy taking risks—and for good reason. By definition, risks are dangerous and often fail, and failure is rarely rewarded in organizations and politics. "The Case of the Risk-Averse Retailer" shows one example.

Send the Right Signals to Your People

One way to think about smart risk taking is that people are willing to extract lessons from whatever results or nonresults they produce, getting smarter because they took the risk. Each successive experiment thus becomes informed and smarter because of the previous effort. Try some of the following techniques to signal to your subordinates that it is okay to take smart risks:

- Ask subordinates to think of several small experiments in new ways of doing things that support the organization's mission.

The Case of the Risk-Averse Retailer

At an international retailer, executives and store managers dreamed of seeing the company become number one in its industry and number one in each of its major markets. But they were also under immense pressure to meet quarterly projections. One year, anticipating the big Christmas shopping season, store managers struggled with a dilemma: should they do what they had always done to meet their numbers? Or should they try to make some changes in their stores, such as offering more aggressive customer service and entertainment to see whether the firm's position improved? They knew that experimenting with some changes could help them learn a lot about what might make a real difference going forward. But it could also put their jobs at risk if it meant they could not meet short-term goals. Headquarters, of course, wanted both: "Try your experiments, but not at the expense of current revenues." Not surprisingly, most store managers chose to play it safe because it had worked fairly well before. They shelved their experiments, even though they knew that sticking with the tried and true would not enable them to catch their biggest competitor.

- When you approve an experiment that could generate new knowledge, give it time and resources by clearing something else from the to-do list of those responsible for conducting the experiment and extracting its lessons.

- When people are struggling with an experiment, acknowledge how hard it is to learn from failure and success. Give them resources to figure out the lessons.

- During regular performance reviews, evaluate employees' ability to take smart risks (low-cost, high-learning). Make increases in smart risk taking a goal for the coming year, encouraging some specific experiments that employees could run.

- Take risks yourself, and report your failures as well as your successes to your people.

Reward Smart Risk Taking

How do you reward risk taking? You need to base rewards on criteria other than measurable outcomes, such as how committed people are to experimentation, how many small experiments they have run, and how well they extract lessons from the efforts, their risk assessments, and the mistakes they have made. Otherwise, only successful experiments are rewarded, and people will go underground with the ones that are not, and take fewer risks altogether.

These kinds of reward practices take courage and careful thought: Will you give a raise to or promote someone who conducted an experiment that failed, but who learned and disseminated a valuable lesson from the experience? Will you reward such individuals more than people who scored successes (for example, making their quarterly sales goals) by playing it safe? If you do not reward smart risk taking, you may lose those team members to other organizations where their courage and creativity might be better valued. Indeed, your competitors may be looking for just these folks.

Like turtles, people need to stick their neck out to move forward. One company we know gives a Turtle Award each year to the initiative that generates the most lessons for the organization, even when the initiative bombs.

Foster a Taste for Action

Anyone contemplating a risky experiment may feel compelled to mitigate the risk by spending too much time meticulously planning the experiment. But often, the outcomes, however well planned, are unpredictable because the experiment engages a complex world in a new way. So action is the only way forward. One just has to run the experiment to find out. Often, then, it is better to sidestep analysis paralysis in planning and move forward on extracting lessons from taking action. This goes hand in hand, of course, with the idea of running many small experiments, each of which has less to lose, than a few larger ones.

Run Parallel Experiments

To maximize knowledge gained from risk taking, run parallel experiments. For example, suppose you have an idea for a new marketing strategy that you think will help your firm trounce a powerful new rival. Instead of testing that one strategy through an experiment, try out several different marketing strategies, in different regions or with different target markets where both strategies hold some promise and have some drawbacks. Testing several strategies at the same time generates much more data than experimenting with just one idea at a time. But more important, it also helps you demonstrate that you're committed to ongoing adaptability and that today's plan is always just today's best guess.

ON THE BALCONY

- Look around at your team, and think about those who have been there for more than three years. Think of those who have left. Are more of the risk takers still around, or are they working somewhere else? What does this suggest about your culture's ability to foster smart risk taking in your organization? Are you still around because you're a smart risk taker or risk averse?

PART FOUR

SEE YOURSELF AS A SYSTEM

A S AN OFFICER in the U.S. Army stationed in Iraq, Ray took over a unit charged with eliciting intelligence from Iraqi citizens who might know something about the insurgency seeking to undermine U.S.-led efforts to create a stable, secular, and democratic government. When Ray took command of the unit, he quickly saw that his soldiers often treated villagers roughly to extract information from them, behavior that alienated Iraqis who did not support the insurgency. Ray knew that gaining the Iraqi people's trust and friendship was a high military and political priority. Yet he found himself tolerating his soldiers' harsh treatment of Iraqi civilians, which undermined that aspiration. At the time, he could not get himself to go against the norms that had developed before he took command of the unit, no matter how unsettled he felt about what was going on.

Long after his stint as unit commander was over, still unsettled, he began connecting the events in Iraq to a pattern of decisions he had made in other, very different contexts. He saw that his own deep need for solidarity with his soldiers led him to tolerate questionable behavior. Tracking this tendency far back in his personal history, he connected the pattern to certain needs he had developed from his upbringing in his family.

We tell Ray's story here because we think it represents something everyone wrestles with: understanding the complex, conflicting loyalties within and recognizing which of them are pulling in any particular moment. Ray was pulled by his loyalty to the army's mission and strategy, which explicitly called for winning Iraqi civilians' hearts and minds. Pulling against that was his loyalty to his troops, who saw the tactical advantages of using harsh treatment of civilians to get better information more efficiently, to incur less risk to themselves of getting ambushed and killed. His need for solidarity made him vulnerable to this latter loyalty.

Like Ray, you are not a perfectly clean machine. Like the organization you are trying to lead, you are a complex individual with competing values and interests, preferences and tendencies, aspirations and fears.

Whenever you are trying to lead a group or organization through an adaptive challenge, you may experience conflicts among your various loyalties. That is because you are a system (an individual) within a system (your organization). Within yourself as a system, your interests, your fears, your various loyalties all interact and affect your behaviors and decisions. Understanding the system that is yourself can help you make the personal changes needed for you to lead adaptive change successfully in your organization. Part IV shows you how to move toward this understanding. We will ask you to consider questions such as "What are the complex forces influencing my behavior and choices?" "What role am I playing in this larger organization?" "What purposes am I seeking to serve?" and "What changes do I need to make in myself to lead more effectively?"

Understanding Your Defaults

Like everyone else, you have your own default settings: habits of interpreting and responding to events around you. It is essential to know what those default settings are to gain greater latitude and freedom to respond in new and useful ways.

You can develop greater freedom by understanding three types of default settings within your system:

- **Your loyalties.** Your feelings of obligation toward your colleagues, community, and important figures from your past, feelings that can come into conflict when you are dealing with an adaptive challenge.

- **Your personal tuning.** How your "harp strings are tuned" to respond to challenges and opportunities. Your tuning includes those things that trigger disproportionate responses in you, such as your unmet personal needs, your susceptibility to carrying other people's hopes and expectations, and your level of tolerance for the chaos, conflict, and confusion that accompany adaptive change.

- **Your bandwidth.** Your repertoire of techniques for leading adaptive change and the self-imposed limitation you place on your range of resources by staying in your own comfort zone.

We explore each of these default settings in turn in the next few chapters.

CHAPTER 13

See Yourself as a System

YOU ARE A SYSTEM as complex as the one you are trying to move forward. To understand your personal system, you have to take stock of many different things: your personality, life experiences, cognitive and other skills, and emotional makeup. You also need to appreciate that your behaviors and decisions stem not just from forces within yourself as a system but also from forces acting on you in any given organizational situation. By understanding which roles you play in your organization, you can identify the resources and constraints on your ability to make things happen.

When you combine these situational insights with insights into yourself as a system, you can assess how well (or not well) you are suited to take action on a particular adaptive challenge facing your organization. You can also determine which interventions will most enable you to do what is best for your organization and which personal tendencies will trip you up or cause others to push you aside.

Why not simply use your intuitions based on your experience to lead adaptive change? You have probably done so on several occasions successfully in the past. But our guess is that your intuition has also led you astray at times. That is because while it may serve you well in many situations, your "intuition" is likely to constrain you from seeing certain data, being open to certain interpretations, and making certain interventions that are outside your experience and comfort zone. For

Keeping His Eye on the Ball

Marty's son Max played basketball in high school. In his junior year, Max was the sixth man on the team, the first substitute to come into the game. Then in midseason, because of his good play, he was elevated to a starting role. Of course, Max knew how much that made his parents proud as they rooted from the sidelines. But being among the starting five lasted about three games. Owing to the improved play of the boy he replaced, Max went back to the bench to be, once again, the sixth man.

Of course, Marty was disappointed. But when he asked Max whether he, too, was disappointed at not starting anymore, Max came back with an interesting response: "I'd much rather be the first substitute," he said. "That way I can size up the situation, see what's needed, and come in to play when I know what kind of playing on my part will make a real contribution in this particular game." He kept his eye on the higher objective, considered both his multiple capacities and his role in the system, and did not worry too much about disappointing his dad. Not bad.

---

these reasons, we recommend taking a more disciplined approach to understanding your own system when you step into the fray of leading adaptive change.

The clarity that comes from getting on the balcony to see yourself as a system can give you courage, inspiration, and focus—all vital resources when the distractions, displacements, and conflicting loyalties common in struggling organizations start to crop up. To begin, "Keeping His Eye on the Ball" provides a father's homegrown example of how understanding yourself as a system and your role in the larger system can help with the problem of competing loyalties.

Your Many Identities

The notion of understanding yourself as a system challenges the idea that we each have one "self." Have you ever heard someone say, "Well, that's just who I am—take it or leave it"? Maybe you've said something like that to others at times. However, you are actually made up of several role identities, multiple and not always clear or consistent values, beliefs, ways of being, and ways of doing. Exercising adaptive leadership is about you (an individual system) making interventions in a social system of which you are a part. You have to understand not only the larger system you step into (the subject of part II) but also yourself in its full complexity, multiplicity, and inconsistency. And then you have to think about how the two systems interact.

Seeing this relationship enables you to identify which parts of yourself are most valuable at which moments in the context in which you lead.

Accepting that you are actually multiple "yous," that you have more than one self within you, is critical to exercising adaptive leadership, but it can feel uncomfortable. The system you are in—yourself, friends, family, and colleagues—prefers that you declare who you are, what you stand for, and what you can offer. Then you can march into the world with clarity and confidence about this one "self," and the rest of your environment knows what to expect. This approach to self-definition can unleash useful drive and energy, but it has two drawbacks: First, the resulting feeling of clarity can mask your own complexities and make it difficult to guard against your default responses. Second, a narrow and unambiguous view of yourself can give other people in your organization clues to managing you in ways that keep you where they want you to be (rather than where they need you to be). For example, if you present yourself as conflict averse, managers in your company who oppose an initiative you are advocating may derail you by heightening the conflictual aspects of your plan.

When you understand that you have more than just one identity, you begin seeing possibilities you could not see before. "More Than a 'Cripple'" provides an example.

Who you are probably changes depending on the situation. You do not behave entirely the same way around your spouse, children, friends, and colleagues. And even with one of these groups, you likely do not behave the same way every time you are with them. As a parent, you have to be several very different people, depending on what the situation demands: loving mom, aggressive and protective defender of your child, and stern disciplinarian.

We once worked with the comptroller of an international financial services firm who had to overcome his anxiety about feeling that he was a different person as he moved into different roles in the organization.

More Than a "Cripple"

Ron once worked with a woman who needed crutches to move around. She had lived with the identity of "cripple" her whole life, a role that had left her as well as her brother deeply ashamed. Although she adamantly preferred the term "disabled," the "cripple" identity cast a shadow on her sense of self and in some ways her entire life. But eventually, a considerable amount of structured self-reflection caused her to begin expanding her definition of herself to include qualities that had nothing to do with the "cripple" identity, such as "strong woman," "beautiful woman," "empathetic observer," and "enormously competent." And as she expanded this definition, she began to see her brother's shame as his problem, not hers. And seeing herself in this more complex way gave her the confidence to change careers and imagine a new set of possibilities for herself.

He had started as a technical manager and then became supervisor to people who knew more than he did. Additional new roles included mentoring young people who did not report to him, serving as a confidant to the CEO, and becoming a member of the executive team. Each of these roles called for different aspects of himself to come to the fore in order for him to be effective. And he found that disconcerting.

It would be much easier for you (and for the system in which you're intervening) if you said, "This is who I am" rather than "This is who I am *under these conditions, at this moment in time, given these particular loyalties and values that are most prominent for me now.*" But recognizing the complexities that constitute who you are, not only who you are now but how you are changing over time, gives you more options for leading change effectively in your organization.

People who lead adaptive change most successfully have a diagnostic mind-set about themselves as well as about the situation. That is, they are continually striving to understand what is going on inside, how they are changing over time, and how they as a system interact with their organization as a system.

But maintaining a diagnostic mind-set is not easy. We have met many people, particularly those in senior authority roles, who see themselves as fully defined, crystallized human beings rather than constantly changing parts of a constantly evolving larger system. "Medical or Business Professional?" provides a quick example.

So how do you maintain a diagnostic mind-set regarding yourself as a system? You need to accept that there are different but authentic selves required for you to be effective in each role you play. And you have to remind yourself that you are different today than you were yesterday. You, the roles you play, and the organization of which you are a part evolve and grow as you all interact to tackle challenges.

In the rest of this section, we will provide some ideas and tools to help you unpack your personal identity into its multiple components and use the resulting insights to lead more successfully.

Medical or Business Professional?

Helen, a physician, started a medical practice that grew briskly. She founded the practice to serve patients, without any intention of running a business. And she clung to her definition of herself as a medical professional long after her role had to morph into that of a business professional so she could ensure the practice's survival in the changing landscape of health care. She wanted to believe that she could grow the business and inspire others who worked for her by continuing to think and act solely like a medical professional because, as she told us, "That's who I am." But her practice nearly went bankrupt. It was only after she began to worry about expenses, make hard decisions, and hire people who were committed to do what it took to ensure growth, that she was able to restore the practice to financial health. Each of those steps challenged the narrow sense of her own identity that she had clung to at her peril.

ON THE BALCONY

- Think about how your behaviors, emotions, and decision-making patterns change depending on whom you are with and what situation you are in. How do you feel about these changes? Do they make you feel that you are inauthentic? Normal? Manipulative? Productive?

ON THE PRACTICE FIELD

- With a trusted peer or adviser, discuss the idea that we each act differently around others, depending on the individuals and the situation involved. Ask the other person how he or she shows different "selves" at different times and with different people. Ask whether this ability to adapt has helped or hurt the person's relationships and productivity. Notice whether you are becoming more or less comfortable with the notion that people's selves are multifaceted.

CHAPTER 14

Identify Your Loyalties

To BETTER UNDERSTAND yourself as a system, examine three circles of your loyalties:

- *Colleagues.* Those people with whom you have an immediate professional relationship, such as boss, peers, subordinates, and fellow committee members

- *Community.* Current family members, friends, and groups with whom you identify outside of work in your current social, political, and religious affiliations

- *Ancestors.* People from the past with whom you identify who have shaped how you see the world, such as a revered grandparent, a special teacher, as well as the groups of people who form your gender, religious, ethnic, or national roots.

To identify the factions within each circle of your loyalties, start with your colleagues, move to your community, and end with your ancestors. The process gets increasingly difficult with each category. At times, the loyalties in these categories will pull you in multiple directions.

When Alexander, born from an American Jewish family, decided to marry a Japanese Shinto woman, his community and ancestor loyalties pulled him in two different directions. He could hear the voice of his grandparents urging him to be loyal to their religion and continue the Jewish lineage. At the same time, he could hear the support of his family and friends urging him to be loyal to the love and happiness he

FIGURE 14-1

Depicting your loyalties

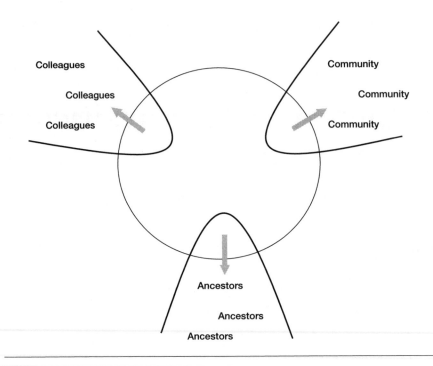

had found. Luckily for Alexander, his Jewish grandmother on her deathbed gave him permission to marry a non-Jew and saved him from a lifetime of tension and guilt between his ancestors and his community. (He still feels guilty occasionally.)

Figure 14-1 shows one way to depict your loyalties. In this diagram, the factions appear the same size and seem to be pulling the person at the center in equally opposite directions.

ON THE BALCONY

- Pick a specific issue where you felt pulled in more than one direction. See whether you can map the loyalties that were pulling you in multiple directions. Create a diagram like the one in figure 14-1, depicting your loyalty groups and the key factions within them.

ON THE PRACTICE FIELD

- Identifying your ancestral loyalties can be hard. Most of the loyalties are hard to name and often unconscious. Rather than being held in place by the unconscious anchors, you have an opportunity to name them so that you can understand them and potentially make new decisions. One of the best ways to surface the ancestral anchors is to interview people with your common ancestry. Ideally, your direct lineage of parents and elders as well as your siblings and cousins are great sources of information. You can also go to members of the same religious or ethnic group. Many people will not think in the language of loyalties and anchors, so you may want to use other language, like "How has your heritage shaped who you are?" "What ideas or values define our family/community?" or "What was it like to be a woman in your grandmother's day?"

Prioritize Your Loyalties

There are multiple players within each of these loyalty categories. And not all loyalties are equal, of course. Some you honor above others when your loyalties come into conflict. You can help identify your primary loyalties in each category by asking yourself some of these questions: To whom do I feel most responsible? Who would react most vigorously if I did something out of the routine? Whom am I trying hardest to please or impress? Who would I most disappoint? Whose support do I most need?

Recognizing how you have prioritized your loyalties is an essential step in exercising adaptive leadership. You will then begin to be able to identify which of those loyalties are holding you, and inhibiting your leadership, rather than you holding them.

One of the best ways to diagnose how you have prioritized your loyalties is to rely less on what you *say* to yourself and others about your loyalties and to begin watching what you *do*. When Marty was a young, ambitious state legislator in Massachusetts, he would routinely rush home from the State House, bring his two young children over to the couch in the living room, read them a book, and then rush out the door to an evening filled with meetings. He told himself all the way to the meeting what a great family man he was. The kids, of course, experienced it all very differently, as did his wife, who had spent the whole day without communicating with anyone above the age of four. Marty never passed up a meeting. If he had been able to get on the balcony and observe himself—watch what he did rather than listen to what he said to himself—he would have had to face a painful truth: he felt more loyal to his political constituents than he did to his wife and children. For Marty, as with many people, succeeding in his career meant making it in the eyes of a host of people in Marty's background that were of defining importance to him.

Go back to the diagram you created for yourself based on figure 14-1. Now redo it, illustrating the various influences a faction has by adjusting the faction's size to represent the strength of its pull on you, the way the circles of expectations partially overlap, and by using arrows to demonstrate the opposing and aligning forces of the factions.

ON THE BALCONY

- Which of your loyalty groups (colleagues, community, ancestors), and which of the factions within each of them, do you believe has the strongest hold on you? For two weeks, keep a log that documents how you are investing your resources. Of these three loyalty groups, which one receives the lion's share of your time, energy, money, attention? Be honest in your log. At the end of the two weeks, what does your log suggest about which loyalty group is really your top priority?

- Zoom in and look more closely at the factions within your colleagues' loyalty group: your boss, peer managers, employees, customers, and clients. Which of these factions do you believe is your topmost priority? Keep another log for two weeks in which you track how you invest your time, energy, attention, money, and so forth in the various factions in your professional setting. What does your log suggest about which faction is really your top professional priority?

ON THE PRACTICE FIELD

- Begin systematically watching what you do rather than listening to what you say about your loyalties. Ask someone to help you identify the gap between your own espoused loyalty priorities and your actual priorities, as revealed by your behavior: how you spend your time, and to whom you devote your time and energy.

- Create a living representation of your loyalties using the following process. Gather a group of trusted friends and advisers. Think of a situation you're struggling with at work. Stand in the center of the room and ask, "To whom am I loyal in this situation?" One by one, have volunteers stand up and represent the different voices you're carrying in your mind: bosses, business units, competitors, customers, mentors, spouses, parents, religious associates, fellow members of your gender or ethnic group, and so forth. Ask each person to stand at a distance from you that represents that group's relative degree of influence on you. Then have all your loyalty group members speak at once about their feelings and thoughts regarding the situation. The resulting sound will give you a taste of the cacophony we all contend with in trying to resolve conflicting loyalties.

Name Your Unspeakable Loyalties

In any organization or community for which you are trying to exercise adaptive leadership, you own a piece of the problem at hand. If you are part of the organizational system, you must be part of the problem. This does not mean that you are responsible for the whole mess. Nor does it imply that you are not doing a lot of good in trying to address the problem. It only suggests that there is an element of the problem, however small, that stems from what you believe and how you behave, from the loyalties that are holding you. For example, if your organization struggles with being more transparent, you may be contributing to the problem by not sharing information widely about salaries because you know that some people will be angry at you, knowing how much money you make. And you may not like people being angry at you.

Typically, the loyalties you have that are getting in the way of the goals you are trying to accomplish are not ones you tell everyone about. They are not on your résumé. We think of them as unspeakable loyalties; they are just as powerful as the people and values you talk about all the time, but not as apparent. Often these unspeakable loyalties come from some need, protection, or insecurity. They are part of being human and can contribute as forcefully as our noble values to the ways we interact with the world.

Identifying your part of the problem, what we call "your piece of the mess," has two key benefits. First, doing so creates the opportunity to fix at least one element of the problem, the one that is more or less under your own control. Second, it models the accountability you are asking others to demonstrate in tackling the adaptive challenge at hand. Thus it may inspire your colleagues to face up to their uncomfortable loyalties and take responsibility for their own part in those problems.

Discovering your piece of the mess is by its very nature an uncomfortable process. You are identifying, and accepting responsibility for, your role in getting in the way of the progress you say you are trying to achieve. The exercises below can help.

ON THE BALCONY

- Think of an adaptive challenge your group or organization is struggling with. Brainstorm three ways in which you may have contributed to the problem. For each response you come up with, consider what changes you might make to fix that piece of the mess.

ON THE PRACTICE FIELD

- The exercise in table 14-1 is modeled after one designed by our Harvard colleagues Robert Kegan and Lisa Lahey in their work on adult learning and resistance to change. We have adapted it here for our purposes. You can read more about the original exercise and their work in their book *How the Way We Talk Can Change the Way We Work*.[1]

TABLE 14-1

Personalize the adaptive challenge

Column 1	Column 2	Column 3	Column 4	Column 5
What things, if they happened more frequently, or less frequently, would help make progress on the adaptive challenge I am working on?	What loyalties or values underlie your column 1 responses? For each response in column 1, complete this sentence: "This response suggests that I am loyal to . . ."	Pick the two loyalties or commitments in column 2 that are *most* important to you. For each of them, answer this question: "What am I doing, or not doing, that is keeping me from more fully honoring this commitment?"	For each behavior you listed in column 3, identify the commitment driving that behavior by completing this sentence: "I may also be loyal to . . ."	Identify what bad outcomes you are protecting yourself from by engaging in the behaviors you listed in column 3. Ask, "If I did not do [column 3 behavior], then [list of horrible things that would happen]."
Example: We were more open with each other at work.	*Example: I am loyal to the value of transparency and to my professional colleagues.*	*Example: I consistently oppose sharing salary information.*	*Example: I may also be loyal to the value of not having people be angry at me and the idea that money is a private matter, both of which my spouse deeply believes in.*	*Example: People would be angry at me, and my spouse would be embarrassed and disappointed in me.*

Notes: The column 2 commitments are the ones you advertise to the rest of the world. The column 4 commitments are the ones you hide, because they get in the way of what you say you want to achieve. By leaving the conflict between the column 2 and column 4 values unresolved, you nurture the status quo. But resolving them would mean either risking the awful outcomes in column 5 or downgrading your noble column 2 aspirations. It is not a happy choice, and it is no wonder that many people steer clear of making it. Try to run a low-risk experiment to treat your column 5 fear as an assumption, not a fact. In our example here, perhaps a low-risk test would be to reveal salary ranges or to reveal the salaries of just senior management.

Consider doing the exercise with two or three others from your group so you can hear one another's responses, help each other clarify reflections, and apply what you have learned to your own situation; but it is probably not a good idea to do the exercise with people to whom you report or people who report to you.

Here's how it works: Together, identify an adaptive challenge with which your group is dealing. Then, each of you take a few minutes to respond to the question in column 1. Discuss together what each of you has written. Then move on to the next column and discuss again, and so forth, until you are finished with all the columns. Then read the notes below the chart.

CHAPTER 15

Know Your Tuning

HOW YOU ARE tuned is another default setting in the system that is yourself. Each person is like a stringed instrument, tuned in a slightly different way from everyone else. As you go through life, your strings resonate with the environment based on your own particular tuning. Your tuning derives from many different things: your childhood experiences, genetic predispositions, cultural background, gender, and loyal identifications with various current and historical groups. Your tuning in your professional life may also be affected temporarily or long term by what is happening in your personal life.

Those strings vibrate continuously, communicating to those around you who you are, what is important to you, where your sensitivities lie, and how you might be vulnerable. When something happens in your environment, your strings may respond more or less strongly, depending on whether the event stimulates a powerful memory or aspiration. Being caught up in the action of everyday events, you may find it difficult to understand just how your strings are being stimulated at any particular moment. But knowing how the environment is pulling your strings and playing you is critical to making responsive rather than reactive moves. "Strings Versus Strings" provides an example.

For many people, the idea that you are always powerfully influenced by your surroundings and history challenges dearly held notions of free will. Yet if you can get on the balcony and observe the forces acting on you, you actually are exercising free will. You have acknowledged the reality that you are embedded in a web of relationships and are

Strings Versus Strings

In one of our leadership development courses, we facilitated a conversation involving an internationally diverse group of about forty men and women. Each participant held a position of significant authority in a public, private, or nonprofit organization. Among them, Miguel was a middle-aged man from Spain and an extremely successful entrepreneur. Maria was a young, ambitious woman from Colombia, also on an entrepreneurial track.

For two days, when either Miguel or Maria spoke, the other would speak, not necessarily in direct response but never in a supportive tone. After we pointed out this pattern, the group tried to understand the dynamic between them. With their cooperation and after an intense and personal conversation, it became clear that Miguel had been reacting to his own frustrating memories of having to contend with the values of a younger generation that differed from his own. In his view, the young "weren't willing to pay their dues," as he had done, or to learn from those with experience, like him. To Maria, he sounded just like her father, who had wanted her to pursue marriage and a family rather than a career.

Miguel's and Maria's particular sets of strings, tuned by markedly different experiences, were resonating dissonantly with each other. To stop this pattern and sort out the problem, we used the human diorama exercise described in the previous chapter and had Miguel and Maria each name the five or six significant voices in their heads that were activated by the other. We then asked members of the group to represent each of these voices and stand behind Miguel or Maria. Finally, we asked Miguel and Maria to talk with one another and, as they did so, to listen to all the voices talking behind them at the same time issuing instructions on the way they should respond. Amid all the noise, no wonder they were stuck, with neither of them free to listen. Once they understood how their different strings were being plucked, they started to laugh, a good sign they were getting some perspective and finding their way up to the balcony. They were able to see how much they had in common and could collaborate during the rest of their time together, moving some issues forward in the group that were of particular concern to both of them.

influenced by those relationships, so you create more freedom for yourself to act with understanding of those influences rather than merely to react unthinkingly to them.

For all persons, particular aspects of their tuning may present both risk and opportunity as they practice leadership. Understanding these aspects of your own tuning enables you to recognize your vulnerabilities and sensitivities and to compensate for them.

For example, suppose you are involved in a dispute and the conflict gets out of hand. Things are rapidly becoming unproductive. To lead effectively, you might need to take action to lower the temperature by taking a break, for example. But if you are predisposed to relish conflict, then you may not even sense that the pressure cooker is about to blow up. To you, the intensifying conflict feels stimulating. But for others in the room, it is so intolerable that many of them are beginning to shut down. If you are aware of how you are tuned to conflict, you will be more likely to watch for signs that it is time to turn down the heat, and actually take the steps needed to do so.

On the other hand, suppose your tuning is such that you have a strong aversion to conflict. This may be true if you grew up in a family that was out of control because of alcoholism or some other illness, or one that was very tightly controlled by very strict parents. In this case, just as the pressure cooker is beginning to reach a temperature conducive to learning and productivity, you might find yourself getting upset and reflexively taking action to cool things off. And you would prematurely halt the learning process.

However much it has worked for you in the past, each aspect of your tuning makes you vulnerable in two ways: First, your responsiveness to that tuning makes you predictable and therefore easily manipulated by people who do not want you to lead change. Second, there is a dark side to each of your strengths.

For example, assume you are highly attuned to the satisfaction and pride you feel at completing tasks successfully. Being "responsible" in this way is a virtue, to be sure. But when you are leading adaptive change, you cannot shoulder all the work yourself. You need to give pieces of it back to the appropriate people, allies who will share the burden, members of the group who should own part of the problem. Someone who does not want to take on a piece of the work may "play" you by praising your responsible nature, which would make you even more reluctant to let go of the work. The dark side of being always responsible is the desire to be thought of as indispensable, that nobody can do it without you. That makes it even harder for you to give pieces of the work to others.

Like individuals, couples, teams, factions, and organizations have their own tuning, too. Sometimes you can see these responses manifest themselves physically. At your next staff meeting, watch and see which cohorts sit up in their seats when the CEO makes certain comments. Which shrink back? What statements and other events cause everyone to resonate so that it almost looks like the wave at a sporting event, moving through the crowd across the stadium? "Tuning In to the Executive Team" offers an example.

Like other default settings, your unique tuning is both a resource and constraint. When you are finely tuned to something that is happening, you see it coming before anyone else does. While others may be naive to it, not understand it, or try to ignore it, you will be sensitive to it and move to respond. Over time, this resonance becomes a skill that can distinguish you from your peers. But you may also see things when they are not there.

Here is an example of tuning as both a resource and a constraint. In that meeting of the top team we just described, the merger had been between a partnership and a publicly held firm. The partnership folks

Tuning in to the Executive Team

We observed a meeting of the executive team at a large multinational corporation with a matrix organization in which the top team contained representatives from different product lines and different geographies. The firm had recently merged two similarly sized organizations based in two different countries. One product line represented a disproportionate share of the firm's revenues but was not growing. As the underlying theme of the conversation shifted, from practices to geographies, from investing in the future to sustaining current markets, from entrepreneurship and autonomy to collegiality and cooperation, different factions in the room would either resonate with the theme by actively participating or sit back in their chairs unmoved.

were particularly animated about the merger and actively helped their new colleagues understand the importance of internal relationship issues, such as sharing information and services, and agreeing on a coordinated and unified strategy for moving forward. The folks from the publicly held firm were more sensitive to the importance of external conditions such as competitive pressures and stock price. It was hard for either party to see that their differing experiences had made them particularly sensitive to the importance of different issues, which each group thought were the keys to success, not just preferences influenced by the tuning from their own organization's culture and experience.

Resonating unwittingly, your reactions may prevent you from seeing the situation more fully and may inhibit you from responding in productive ways. At the newly merged company, the former partners' sensitivity to internal relationship issues made it difficult for them to absorb the importance of also being accountable to thousands of anonymous shareholders.

Further, the more finely tuned your strings become over time, the more you are at risk of seeing the things happening in the environment you are sensitive to, even when they are not there. You may jump to faulty conclusions and become deaf to other explanations of a complex dynamic or set of events. For the partnership legatees, every issue began to look like an internal-relationship issue, and for the publicly held company legatees, every issue was seen through the prism of how it would affect the stock price.

Finally, when others know how you are tuned, they have more power to entice you to partner with them to support their own interests or to derail you from yours. You become seducible. For example, if one of your sensitivities is a discomfort with yelling, all a colleague would have to do is to yell at you to get you to back off from your proposed intervention. If you are vulnerable to others' emotional pain, a colleague could discourage you from launching your intervention by putting on a distressing emotional display.

The improvisational ability to lead adaptively relies on responding to the present situation rather than importing the past into the present and laying it on the current situation like an imperfect template.[1]

This becomes all the more difficult when current circumstances pluck at your strings so sharply that you react impulsively, causing you to make the wrong diagnosis and take the wrong action. These sharp experiences can evoke something in your past or unrelated issues in your current life, and then completely dominate the present moment. To characterize the power these situations have over you, we switch metaphors to discuss "triggers."

Know Your Triggers

Being triggered is a common experience. How often has someone "pushed your buttons" or "hit a nerve"? A brief comment by a coworker, an action from your spouse, just the right small stimulus can set you off and make you crazy, or at least momentarily out of control. Your defense mechanisms kick in, generated by fear and fueled with adrenaline. Your bright, strategic, graceful, attentive self is no longer there, temporarily eclipsed by your more primal, defensive self.

Worse, once you are triggered, you may well trigger others around you. Cacophony ensues. Productivity disintegrates. The more authority you have (whether formal or informal), the more damage you can do to the work at hand. Sometimes such consequences are visible on a large public stage. For example, numerous reports, particularly by Richard Clarke in his book *Against All Enemies*, suggest that President George W. Bush believed that the job his father had begun in Iraq was unfinished business. Triggered by the 9/11 terrorist attacks, Bush jumped to the conclusion that fighting in Iraq and fighting terrorism must be linked.[2]

But triggering plays out on much smaller tableaux as well. For instance, Alexander grew up with his father's mantra "You create your own luck." This has been a useful paradigm for him at times. But sometimes when things are not going well and his anxiety increases, he hears that mantra in his head, and he is triggered as directly as if his father were right there yelling in his ear. He then aggressively tries to "create" his own luck by taking on too much work or trying to fix other people's problems. What he often ends up doing is creating more of a mess.

If you are good at getting on the balcony, you probably notice when others are being triggered. If you are very good at it, you may notice when *you* are triggered as well. Triggering almost always comes with behavioral changes: the person's voice becomes dramatically louder or softer, someone who has said nothing in a meeting suddenly speaks sharply, a normally voluble person withdraws. The person being triggered may also experience physical symptoms such as pounding heart, shallow breathing, and sweating palms.

Recognizing when you are being triggered is the first step at controlling the trigger rather than having it control you and throw you into an unproductive move.

ON THE BALCONY

- Think about a recent incident to which you reacted so strongly that even you were surprised. What stimulated that response? In what respect did the incident connect with something from your past? Why was that past experience so important to you or so unresolved for you? Keep examining the answer until you gain a deeper understanding of your sensitivities. Then make a note so you can begin to anticipate when you are being triggered and can prevent the triggers from undermining you.

ON THE PRACTICE FIELD

- The next time you are in a conversation or a meeting and you feel yourself being triggered, practice taking steps to keep the situation under control. For example, wait until two or three opportunities to intervene pass by rather than seizing on the first opportunity to respond. If you notice that someone else is being triggered, apply some practices to help the person manage the situation, such as simply commenting on the apparently disproportionate response. Notice what happens to you and the other person when these steps are taken. Notice what happens to the conversation or meeting.

Hungers and Carrying Water

From our experience, there are two categories of triggers to which it is important to pay special attention: hungers and carrying other people's water.

Your hungers can make you particularly vulnerable. In *Leadership on the Line*, we wrote about three closely related pairs of normal personal human needs that, if they remain unfulfilled, can become very difficult to manage: (1) power and control, (2) affirmation and importance, and (3) intimacy and delight.[3]

If you find yourself feeling out of control, irrelevant, or unloved, you can fall prey to people who soothe those unmet needs, either innocently or specifically to manipulate you out of leading an adaptive change intervention that they do not support. For example, a peer manager who would lose status as a result of your initiative tells you how important you are, to distract you from pushing the intervention forward.

When these needs remain unmet, people are also at risk of filling them through inappropriate means. Having affairs with colleagues is a well-known example of how people hungry for intimacy and delight satisfy that need; but there are many less dramatic and less destructive examples of people filling these needs in harmful ways, such as undermining their own credibility by insisting on a bigger title or a larger office.

Particularly in the not-for-profit sector but also in public and corporate life, we often encounter people who are burned out or feeling overwhelmed. Many times, a significant element of the burnout is from trying to carry other people's water—other people's hopes, needs, expectations, and fears—trying to do it for them.

From the time we are born, other people load us up with their expectations, their hopes, aspirations, fears, and frustrations. As a young person, you undoubtedly benefited from this, as many of these expectations from parents, teachers, and mentors became sources of wisdom, encouragement, and guidance as you matured and made your way in the world. But when you are an adult, other people's hopes can also take the form of other people's unresolved problems that you unwittingly take on as your own and thereby create enormous vulnerability as you feed their expectations for easy answers. There is no better example of this than watching a U.S. presidential election campaign, where in the search for votes, the candidates welcome being filled up with the hopes and fears of millions of people, only to realize that all those expectations cannot possibly be fulfilled.

Being inclined to carry other people's water can become a major way that you are tuned. For example, if your parents never had much money and were deeply ashamed of their poverty, you may absorb that shame as well and strive to resolve it for your parents by making money you can give to them. But the shame was never yours to begin with; it was your parents'. And you cannot ever resolve it for them. All the money you might give them could never dispel all the ways in which their sense of shame permeates their views of themselves and their ways of seeing and reacting to the world. You may make them proud of you, and far more comfortable, but how that pride compensates for their own wounds is beyond your control. Still, you may keep working the problem in the hopes that you can ease their load. You "carry their water," and they may let you continue to do it.

We often carry other people's water in the workplace, too. For instance, you probably know more than one workaholic who carries the aspirations for pride and material success of an entire family and its ancestors.

Of course, wanting to ease the load for others you care about is an admirable goal. But when you carry *too* much of someone else's water or carry the water of too many other people, you will only end up feeling overwhelmed. That is because solving other people's problems is far less under your control than solving your own. Feel overwhelmed long enough, and you lose your capacity to be productive, whether it is leading adaptive change or managing even the simplest responsibilities in your work, family, or community life. Understanding what is wearing you down is the first step toward relieving yourself of the burden and getting others to carry their own water.

ON THE BALCONY

- The next time you notice that you're feeling overwhelmed, ask yourself, "Whose water am I carrying? Why am I feeling compelled to carry it? What can I do to give this particular issue back to them?" Rather than just picking up another item on your to-do list, break that leap to action by addressing the question of whose work this is and then develop a strategy to give the work back to them at a rate they can absorb.

ON THE PRACTICE FIELD

- Start with the assumption that 25 percent of what you are doing could or should be done by somebody else. Make a list of all the things you need to do in the office over the next two weeks and how much time each should take. Identify a quarter of the things on the list that you are going to hand off to others, and do it. By the end of the day you could have some significant time to devote to what is most important.

CHAPTER 16

Broaden Your Bandwidth

IN ADDITION TO your loyalties and your tuning, your bandwidth—that is, your repertoire of techniques for moving adaptive change forward in your organization—is a key element in the system that is yourself. These techniques span a spectrum, from graceful and inspired rhetoric to in-your-face confrontation. Depending on the situation and people involved, you have to be able to mix and match techniques as needed. That requires a broad bandwidth. As John Wooden, Bobby Knight, and many other great coaches of college and professional sports have suggested, you've got to coach each player differently. Some players are going to require gentle prodding. Others are going to require a lot of hand holding and nursing. And some are going to require a two-by-four.

To broaden your bandwidth, start by diagnosing your current repertoire. What skills are you already very good at doing? What are you not so proficient at doing? Consider the skills you have learned about so far in this book, such as raising the heat, getting on the balcony, or distinguishing the technical from the adaptive aspects of an issue. Knowing your strengths and weaknesses will help you determine whether a particular situation would benefit from your intervention and when it is time to bring in reinforcements. As a simple example, if you are good at keeping people on task, then you probably ought to let someone else lead a brainstorming session to consider a far-ranging set of the next experiments.

Discover Your Tolerances

Exercising adaptive leadership requires that you be willing and competent at stepping into the unknown and stirring things up. Most people prefer stability to chaos, clarity to confusion, and orderliness to conflict. But to practice leadership, you need to accept that you are in the business of generating chaos, confusion, and conflict, for yourself and others around you.

This suggests that building up your tolerance for disorder, ambiguity, and tension are particularly important in leading adaptive change. Your current tolerance constitutes another "string" in how you are tuned. Will you be able to stay in the game, even when you're not sure you are doing the right thing, or doing it the right way? Will you be able to say to yourself, "I don't know whether this is the right way to proceed, but I know we have to try something, and anyway, whatever we do should be treated as an experiment"? If you are a meticulous planner who needs to know ahead of time where you are staying every night on a vacation, an organizer who makes lists and checks off tasks as you complete them, you might have difficulty sitting with the considerable ambiguity that comes with adaptive change.

Similarly, how comfortable are you watching or even helping other people fight (constructively, of course) over deeply held values? Are you skilled at suppressing conflict, at calming things down when tensions begin to erupt, at finding short-term "win-wins" to stave off the formation of factions in your organization or community? If so, you may have difficulty when the tough divisive issues need to be surfaced. (This is particularly true when you are leading from a position of authority because everyone expects you to keep things calm and maintain order.)

Expanding your bandwidth is not easy. It means moving out of your comfort zone into a space where your incompetence may show. But our experience suggests that expanding your bandwidth is at least as much a function of will as of skill. Here are a couple of cases of people who made the effort.

Fred was the charismatic, larger-than-life CEO of a small but very successful professional services firm that had been constructed in his image, with his sensibility, personality, and client network driving rapid growth. Fred loved the role of engaging and wooing clients and creating innovative solutions to their problems. And he equally loved being the go-to person who solved all the firm's internal creative challenges. He knew he did not want to run the firm, so he hired a chief administrative officer (CAO) who took care of all the administrative details. But he also did not want to be the chief personnel officer, a role that every CEO has to assume. He did not like conflict, and he did not enjoy dealing with his employees' personal issues, quirks, and needs, and he was not very good at doing it, either. Trying to do so was beginning to exhaust him and take the fun out of his work. But he was finally convinced that if the firm was to reach his goal of being number one in the market, he was both going to have to get good at managing his people and was going to have to get out of the way so that they could learn to interface with clients. It took him a year to become competent and confident. We remember him telling us how hard it was, when people came into his office to ask him to solve their dispute, to tell them to solve it themselves and let him know what they came up with. It was a big adaptation on his part.

Similarly, Judy, a talented graphic designer, knew that she wanted to have a bigger imprint on publications than she could have by just being another designer in the design department. She was also far more interested in the editorial content than most of her fellow designers. But she also knew that in order to achieve her aspirations for herself and for the design of the publications about which she cared so much, she would have to become a "dreaded manager." Her first stint as a manager had been mixed at best. Her preferred role was to sit over her computer and turn out terrific designs. Turning out terrific subordinates was not in her wheelhouse. It took her longer than it took Fred to train herself to be a manager. But she did so, mostly by force of will and with a number of false starts and midcourse corrections, and went on to become an icon in her industry. The bandwidth that both Fred and Judy needed was not beyond their innate capacity but was way outside their comfort zones.

ON THE BALCONY

- Think about a difficult conversation you had recently. How long did it last? Your response suggests something about your level of tolerance for disequilibrium. For example, if the conversation lasted longer than thirty minutes, you may have a considerable tolerance. If it lasted only three minutes or just seconds, you probably have very little tolerance.

- What do you do when you're feeling overwhelmed by chaos, confusion, or conflict, or when you sense that others are feeling that way? Do you make a joke? End the conversation? Assign the work to someone? Suppress emotion? What do these tactics suggest about your tolerances? If you have low tolerance for chaos, confusion, and conflict, what might you do to build it up?

ON THE PRACTICE FIELD

- When you find yourself in a difficult conversation and looking for an exit, don't take it. See whether you can put off the first chance to get out and can stay in the game until the next exit appears. Then reassess the situation and try again. By slowly building up your bandwidth for conflict and chaos, you will discover either skills you already had or muscles you can now develop. It will be easier to stay in the game on issues you care deeply about and have some stake in as well.

- Ask a colleague to observe you in a meeting and take notes on the various ways you respond to situations of conflict or complexity. Examine the notes afterward to see whether there are patterns. For example, do you tend to rely almost exclusively on either engaging in confrontation or gentle persuasion to get people to make changes you think need to be made? Discuss how you could broaden your repertoire to include more capacity for tension.

CHAPTER 17

Understand
Your Roles

CONTEXT COUNTS. In addition to your own values, priorities, and sensitivities, you embody your organization's values, priorities, and sensitivities. So does every team or group in the organization. Each person and group contains a piece of the larger picture that is the organizational system. Depending on the situation, different elements become activated at different times. This can take the form of alliances coalescing around a problem or a proposed course of action. For example, two people from different departments who have a long history of not getting along may not trust each other at all when negotiating a solution to a problem that affects both of their departments. But if someone who is sitting with them at the bargaining table suddenly collapses from a heart attack, the distrust between them will undoubtedly evaporate as they collaborate in an effort to save someone's life. In the absence of any past or current conflicting stakes between two departments, there is nothing to exacerbate any potential personal distrust between their members. The roles you play and your behavior in those roles depends on the values and context of any given situation.

Likewise, in some situations, you may embody the value of equity— for example, by advocating for equal pay for women employees. But in other situations, you may represent the value of courage and risk taking. Others similarly give human form to other values of the organization. When you and others represent the same value or perspective regarding the challenge at hand, you and they constitute a faction. And a faction can be valuable because leading adaptive change is immeasurably more difficult if you are trying to do it alone. In addition, each person in your faction has relationships, allegiances, and political capital with people in other factions whose support you may need to make progress.

ON THE BALCONY

- Think of all the groups in which you are a member, including your family, your community, your work team, your division, and your organization. What values do you represent for each of those groups? You may well represent contradictory values in different groups. For example, some people embody the value of control in one situation, such as at work, but in their family they represent just taking things as they come (or vice versa). It can be challenging to try to see yourself in terms of the values you represent in a group. But if you look carefully, you can find some clues. For example, if you notice that other people in the group regularly look to you at heated moments to tell a joke, it may suggest that you embody for them the value of depersonalizing the conflict and getting people to take themselves less seriously.

ON THE PRACTICE FIELD

- As your team works on an issue, the individual roles will quickly emerge. Rather than let participants play out their usual roles, name the values and see who else belongs to that faction. Then invite those with opposing values to identify themselves. The goal, then, is to work the issue by engaging the different values and perspectives rather than let the roles just play out.

What Roles Do You Play?

Groups of all kinds (families, teams, departments, factions, companies) create clarity and order by assigning roles to members, usually implic-itly. For example, in your family, perhaps you were assigned the role of mediator when conflicts broke out and people looked to you to solve them; or counselor when any family member needed advice; or nurturer when someone was hurt. In your organization, maybe you were assigned the role of holding people accountable for the bottom line when you were promoted to a vice presidency after being the comptroller. However, you are more than any role assigned to you. And you have some freedom, but not complete freedom, to choose whether and how to play any assigned role.

Sometime it is hard to get out of the role assigned to you. Byron Rushing was an African American Massachusetts state legislator who represented a largely white middle-class district in Boston's South End, with a large gay and lesbian population. But his fellow legislators kept asking him to sponsor low-income housing legislation and to advocate on behalf of disadvantaged people. He had come to the legislature after a career of community activism, and it was easy for them to assign him this role rather than see him as representing middle-class white gays and lesbians. After fighting this assignment for months, Rushing surrendered and chose to play the role well. During the debate on a social welfare proposal, Rushing took the microphone and declared to his colleagues that he realized it was futile to remind them once again of the makeup of his district, and therefore he was throwing in the towel and from that moment forth would accept the role of representing poor people of color.

You can also decide to play more roles than those you have been assigned. Rushing continued to work for the issues of mass transit and gay rights about which his district cared deeply while acceding to the role assigned to him. Perhaps you have experienced this yourself. Maybe in addition to being the hard-nosed manager, you have also been the person to whom everyone looked for the appropriate behavior when a colleague was going through a difficult personal time, or the party animal who would arrange for the entertainment at staff retreats. Indeed, the more roles you can play, the more effective you will be. As with bandwidth, you will have a wider repertoire to draw from in different situations, and you will be less predictable and thus less readily pigeonholed. And the more roles you play, the more factions in which you will be a part, and the more people with whom you will have connections as you try to make progress on tough issues.

Figure 17-1 shows a pie chart representing examples of basic roles a person can play. Think about the roles you play in your own life: spouse, lover, employee, boss, parent, child, friend, taskmaster, forgiver, counselor, counselee, volunteer, member, constituent, peer, competitor, colleague, salesperson. You do not act exactly the same way in these different roles. Yet each of them is authentically you, just not the whole picture of you. The different sizes of the slices of the pie represent the percentage of your time in each of the roles. But you could also make a pie chart where the sizes of the slices represent degrees of satisfaction you get from playing those roles, and can see how the time and the satisfaction match up.

There are many roles you do play, many that you can play but you do not usually play, and plenty of others you could learn. The point here is to give yourself more options in any situation by giving yourself permission to play different roles differently to lead effectively from different places in different contexts.

Whatever role you are playing at any one time, that role does not represent all of who you are, even if it feels that way. You may indeed put your heart and soul into the role, as many people do in the role of parents, for example. But still, the role is not the same as yourself. It is what you're

FIGURE 17-1

Graphic example of a person's basic roles

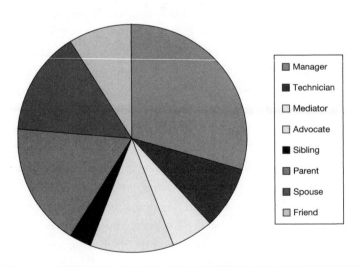

doing at a particular moment in time, hopefully with the purpose of making things better for your family, organization, or community. If that way of playing that role doesn't work—for example, if your conciliatory skills were not what the situation needed and you did not succeed—it is not *you* who did not work. It is simply your performance within that role.

When you think of roles in these terms, you become less vulnerable to taking things personally if your performance in that role does not work out, either in the moment or over time. And that is a good thing. When you take something personally—for instance, if you take it personally and buy into a peer manager's hurtful attack on your competence—all of your attention turns inward. You take your eye off the organizational problem at hand and reduce the chances that it will be addressed. "Personal Attacking in Politics" has lessons to teach those leading change in any organization.

When you make a distinction between the roles you play and yourself, you gain the emotional strength to ignore personal attacks your opponents hope will stymie your initiative. People make attacks personal specifically to divert you from your message. The next time someone tells you that you're "too aggressive" or "uncaring" when you're representing a difficult point of view or change initiative, remind yourself that you (as a person) are not your role (as someone seeking to lead change). Though an attack may feel personal (and be intended as

Personal Attacking in Politics

In the 1972 presidential campaign, Senator Edmund Muskie was running for the Democratic nomination for president and was ahead in the polls against the incumbent, Richard Nixon. Nixon's allies attacked Muskie not by criticizing his positions and perspectives on public policy and the Vietnam War, but by attacking his wife (claiming that she drank and used off-color language). Muskie made the mistake of taking the character assault personally and defending his wife on camera, as the Nixon campaign hoped he would. In doing so, he appeared to shed a tear, which the media blew out of proportion. It is still not certain that he actually did cry. But having drawn his fire and then made him look "unpresidential," Nixon's allies ended Muskie's run for the Oval Office.

personal), it is *not* a statement about your character or your worth as a human being. It is a strategy and an attempt to manipulate you. Try saying something like "I'm sure I could be a better person. Let's get back to the issue before us."

Distinguishing between your roles and yourself also helps you ward off unwarranted flattery, which is often designed (consciously or not) to lull you into inaction. As we have suggested before, when someone tells you that you are indispensable, that you were fabulous in that meeting, listen for a little voice in the back of your head. That voice is a dead giveaway that there is unwarranted flattery afoot. Undue praise is just as powerful a diversion as a personal attack. When you understand that it is about the role you are playing in other people's work and lives (the way your perspective is gratifying to people) and not about you (as a worthy human being), you can stay focused on your message.

If the flattery begins to turn into idealization, that is, people really begin to believe that you are indispensable, you're on a slippery slope. Idealization will tempt even the strongest person. To withstand the dependency, it helps to remember that this is a way people displace responsibility onto someone's shoulders when they feel overwhelmed by the challenge at hand. The implicit message is that you have the magic and they do not. So your task then is to stay focused on developing distributed responsibility for others to come up with new experiments and new solutions. Adaptive leadership generates capacity, not dependency.

ON THE BALCONY

- What roles has your group or organization assigned to you? How has it assigned these roles? Are there other roles that you would like to play instead of, or in addition to, your assigned roles? If so, which of these roles do you already have the capacity to play? Which would you need to learn how to play?

- Draw two pie charts like figure 17-1 for yourself. One pie chart reflects the roles you play in a particular group, or in your life, and the percentage of time you spend on each. The second pie chart reflects your varying satisfaction in those roles. Compare the two pie charts.

ON THE PRACTICE FIELD

- Beyond the role your team has already given you, there may be a role that needs to be played. See whether you can identify what role is missing for the group to make more progress—whether it be advocate, mediator, or project manager—and assign yourself that role. See whether your previous role is necessary, could be handed off, or could be combined with your new role.

- Having done the analysis in the On the Balcony exercise above, look at which of your roles most satisfy you. Try to incorporate switching roles in different contexts to see whether you can derive better outcomes and greater satisfaction with your efforts.

Identify Your Scope of Authority

In every role you play, whether in your professional, personal, or civic life, you have a scope of both formal and informal authority. Your scope of formal authority consists of what your formal authorizers (usually those above you in the hierarchy) have authorized you to do, what they expect you to do, and how they expect you to do it. This scope is probably explicitly laid out in a job description, in rules and regulations, or in organizational bylaws and organization charts. In elective politics, it's laid out in constitution, law, and precedent.

In addition to your formal authorizers, you have informal authorizers. They may be people lateral to and below you on the organization chart, people above you who do not have formal authority over you, and people outside your organization, all of whom look to you in some way to meet their needs and whose support you may need to accomplish your job. Direct reports can have a great deal of informal authority over their supervisor. At the extreme, many managers who are fired get fired by their subordinates. The employees do not have the formal authority to pull the trigger, but they have the power to create the environment and the conditions by, for example, performing just adequately or bad-mouthing their manager to *his* boss, who does have the authority to let him go.

Your scope of informal authority is not spelled out anywhere. And your formal scope of authority probably does not map exactly to this informal authority. If your job description authorizes you to create certain change, your informal authority based on, for example, your personal relationships and your track record may enable you to initiate greater change than that laid out in your job description, or less. Part of what makes knowing your scope of authority difficult is that the limits of your authority are typically opaque and always changing. That is even true for your formal authority, your job description or what you were told at your hiring conference. Have you ever been hired into a job, told what you were supposed to do, and then when you started to do it, run into a brick wall and learned what was in your *real* but unwritten job description? Often, in our experience, people are hired as change agents and quickly come to realize that the person who hired them was part of the problem, but that changing that person was not in the job description.

As you begin to map your own authorizing environment, laying out your various authorizers and their expectations for you, you may see your professional life becoming more complicated if these various groups have conflicting views about your scope of authority. You have probably observed the angst of conflicting expectations when the airline agent to whom you are talking puts you on hold and confers with her boss to negotiate the difference between the accommodation you think you deserve as a loyal customer and the supervisor's mandate to hold the line. When your boss, your subordinates, and your customers have different and irreconcilable expectations of your role and you are then faced with mutually exclusive expectations, you have to either change those expectations or decide which authorizers to disappoint. If you go with some measure of disappointment, you will then have to figure out how to do that without people taking out all their disappointment on you. Figure 17-2 captures this notion of conflicting authorizations.

The wider your scope of informal authority in any of your roles, the better positioned you are to achieve your objectives because there is greater likelihood that those circles in figure 17-2 will overlap. The more they overlap, the more discretion you have without risking the consequences of letting some authorizers down. There are endless pathways to expand your informal authority. As we've suggested in

FIGURE 17-2

Overlapping and mutually exclusive authorizations

Each circle represents individual expectations. Overlaps depict shared expectations.

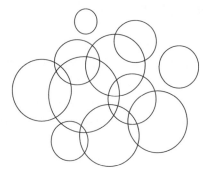

chapter 10, some of the most common are accumulating a track record of success, fostering mutually beneficial relationships, modeling reliability, and exchanging favors and support with others.

Diagnosing your scope of authority helps you discern people's expectations, assess your resources and latitude for authorized action, and answer a host of important practical questions, such as whether you are the best person to intervene in a particular situation, what allies you will need, whether the time is right, which issues to tackle first, where the land mines are likely to be, and which tactics are most likely to succeed. For instance, when Robert Moses built a vast network of parks, bridges, and parkways during his six decades in public office in New York City, he began with a huge project to convert a waterfront on Long Island with a few large private homes into a public beach. The project was hugely popular, of course, except for the handful of families whose homes were taken, and its success increased Moses's informal authority significantly, a resource he badly needed as he shifted his sights into more populated areas closer to the center of the city. Those later projects were difficult politically, but they would have been much more so if he had not had the informal authority from his earlier success to go forward.

The diagnosis of your authorizing environment also reveals ideas for further enhancing your informal authority. For example, if you are authorized to arrange meetings and decide whom to invite, you can use that power to convene a meeting of strategically selected people who can help you tackle problems that might lie outside of your formal scope of authority.

Finally, understanding your scope of authority helps you more easily manage the emotional baggage you may carry when it comes to dealing with authority figures. Many of us carry such baggage. By the time you were twenty-five or thirty years old, you probably had both positive and negative experiences with authority figures: a teacher who opened doors and one who humiliated you, a coach who got the best out of you and one who belittled you, a sponsor who stuck by you when you were not doing so well and one who abandoned you.

Negative experiences with authority figures in the past can leave scars that affect our dealings with those in authority in the present. For example, some people cannot help but rebel against any authority figure they encounter. Others find it impossible to stand up to such figures and assert themselves. Still others decide to avoid being around authority figures completely—for instance, by being self-employed rather than on the staff of a company. The growing edge for many people is to go from dependency and counterdependency to independence and interdependence.

By mapping your scope of authority, you begin to see people in authority not as obstacles or threats but as parts of a larger system in which they carry a mixed load of heavy expectations. Seeing them in all their complexity, perhaps with compassion, enables you to expand your range of options to work and deal with them. Rather than react by rebelling against them, capitulating to them, or avoiding them altogether, you can challenge them, negotiate with them, and leverage their powers in the service of adaptive change.

ON THE BALCONY

- Use table 17-1 to map your authorizers in your professional life. For each authorizer listed in column 1, write down what formal authorization, if any, you have from that person (column 2) and what informal authorization you have (column 3). What are the possible boundaries of their authorization of you—that is, what would you like to do on

TABLE 17-1

Authorization chart

Column 1	Column 2	Column 3	Column 4	Column 5
Authorizer	Formal authorization	Informal authorization	Potential boundary of their authorization of you	Signs of limits to their authorization of you
Boss				
Peers (may be multiple scopes of authority from different factions of peers)				
Subordinates				
Spouse				
Externals (such as customers and suppliers)				
Friends				
Others?				

behalf of what you care about that you think would be beyond the scope of what they would expect of you (column 4)? In column 5, identify when you have met resistance (passive or active) in your role, which may signal some of the boundaries of their authorization.

- List negative experiences you have had with authority figures in the past. How have those experiences affected the way you deal with individuals in positions of authority today? How specifically do you tend to relate to authority figures now: Do you usually rebel against them? Comply with their expectations? Avoid them entirely? What impact has your style of relating to authority figures had on your ability to effect needed change in your organization?

ON THE PRACTICE FIELD

- Pick an authority figure in your organization or community whom you have previously dealt with in an unproductive way (rebelling, capitulating, or avoiding). The next time you interact with this person, practice adopting a new way of relating to her. For example, try challenging the person's assumptions about your role, not in a rebellious way, but respectfully, by engaging in a conversation about, for example, the mixed messages you have been getting, as well as your unproductive prior response.

| CHAPTER 18 |

Articulate Your Purposes

Let yourself be silently drawn to the stronger
pull of what you really love.

—RUMI

TAKING ON ADAPTIVE challenges is difficult and dangerous work. The only reason we can imagine you would want to do this kind of work is to serve purposes that matter to you deeply. Identifying your higher (orienting) purpose—figuring out what is so important to you that you would be willing to put yourself in peril—is a key element in the process of understanding yourself as a system. When you understand your orienting purpose, you can understand and make day-to-day decisions in that larger context, and you can make the tough decisions to subordinate other important purposes to that one. When things get tough, your orienting purpose serves as a reminder to you and to others of the reasons you are seeking to lead change. "Staying Focused on Purpose" presents an example.

Your purposes help you allocate your time. At the end of each day, you can ask yourself, "What did I do today to further my purposes?" Hopefully, you will find it relatively easy on many days to answer this question.

Staying Focused on Purpose

The COO (slated soon to become CEO) of a national engineering firm, an engineer himself, was repeatedly getting caught up in day-to-day crises that took his attention away from the difficult change process he wanted to lead. He enjoyed solving people's problems and fixing things. But he knew if he succumbed to the pressure to spend his time problem solving, the difficult adaptation he believed the firm needed to make would never happen. He needed to remind himself every day of his purpose, which was to change the firm from a traditional engineering firm with a discipline-based organization and several autonomous offices, to a single firm with cross-disciplinary teams and a commitment to be ahead of the pack on collaborating with clients to produce sustainable construction of large engineering projects.

He realized that the best thing he could do for his firm was to maintain some tension among his colleagues and subordinates, reflecting his own sense that they would have to invent the future firm within the broad parameters he articulated, and to be a thorn by constantly reminding people about the gap between their aspirations and the company's current performance. To lead, the COO had to operate in a new and uncomfortable way for him: he had to keep people in a sustained period of disequilibrium rather than let himself get distracted by day-to-day concerns.

He used whatever resources he could assemble to remind himself of his purpose: appointing a senior person in the firm to be in charge of the change and to report to him daily, hiring a coach, and making time for reading and reflection. He tried to keep those day-to-day "fires" in their proper context and guard against being diverted. It was not easy for him because he loved being immersed in day-to-day operations, he handled them well, and his people loved him in that role.

But purposes are not static. Your orienting purpose may change as circumstances change. For example, there may be times when you are willing to put your professional life at risk in order to nurture your personal and family life. At other times, you may decide to make personal relationships less of a priority so you can respond to a professional purpose that seems overriding.

How do you know what your orienting purpose is at a particular point in time? Again, a useful strategy is to watch what you do, rather than listen to what you say. Think about the choices you've made recently, not just big decisions, but also small daily decisions that reveal patterns when seen over time. As a simple example, how often have you repeatedly checked your e-mail and handled business phone calls when you were on vacation, even when you told yourself that the purpose of the trip was to relax and take a break from work? Your behavior reflects your actual purposes. If there is a difference between the purposes you think you have and the purposes that are suggested in your behavior, you may experience an uncomfortable dissonance. If you then stay with the discomfort long enough and think hard about yourself, you can clarify, change, and accept your priorities and live with less internal contradiction. You may then find it useful to write your orienting purpose down in one sentence. Some people find it useful to say it aloud, first to themselves and then to friends and loved ones, or even publicly in meetings or speeches. Others create a symbol or icon that reminds them of their purpose, like a sign, picture, or little statue they keep on their desk; a card with a saying in their wallet; or a mantra, or song, or verse they keep in their head. These symbols can be useful because, in the push and pull of busy lives, it is too easy to forget, or avoid discovering, what your life is about.

Direction can be set at many different levels of abstraction, from the general to the concrete. Being able to move up and down the levels of abstraction enables you to clarify the connection between the daily activities in which you engage and the orienting purposes that guide you. For example, if you find that what you do each day seems to have no link to any higher purpose, you probably want to rethink what you're doing.

But before you even step on the direction ladder, you can simply be purposeful without any specific direction in mind. For example, suppose you are in a meeting about improving sales and the discussion gets mired in details about how many off-site retreats to hold. Clearly, people have lost their compass heading. You can provide a critical corrective and get people back in touch with the purpose of the meeting by simply asking, "What are we trying to do here?" You don't need to have the answer. The question itself is invaluable.

A sense of purpose is even more precious than any specifically defined purpose, because it enables you to step back and examine a particular mission or strategy, objective or task, and ask, "Are we sure this is what we stand for? Is this what we want to do? Is this who we want to be?"

Abstract purposes, such as "ending world poverty" or "being the world's premier accounting firm," provide guidance for evaluating strategies but not for figuring out how best to implement those strategies. There are many ways to pursue the end of world poverty or to become the world's premier accounting firm, but when you begin to express a purpose in more specific terms, it starts to surface conflicts and generate resistance. For instance, with one of our clients, an international accounting firm, tension mounted when the CEO began to give meaning to the mantra, "be the best," by talking about deepening relationships with clients. For the people who wanted to drive growth by further leveraging their technical competence, the purpose suddenly seemed threatening.

In defining direction in your setting, you can move up and down levels of abstraction to test the coherence of your organization, from its orienting values and mission to its daily tasks and operating culture. You can then find your place in it and see if your role makes sense. At the higher levels of abstraction, the folks at the accounting firm talk about "being the world's premier firm" by providing services that are highly valued by clients. Move to a less abstract level, and the purpose becomes more strategically defined: "In light of the changing and challenging business environment, we need to have deeper personal engagement with our clients so the firm can move from a purveyor of products to a provider of trusted counsel on clients' most complex financial challenges." At that level, everyone in the company can begin to assess what they do every day and how well it serves that purpose.

Exercising adaptive leadership is at its heart about giving meaning to your life beyond your own ambition. Having purpose provides the focus for that meaning. But effectuating that meaning, putting it into practice, bringing it to life, requires two difficult diagnostic steps. First, since most people have multiple important purposes, clarifying your priorities among them is essential in giving you the focus this work requires. Clarifying your priorities means subordinating some of your highly valued purposes to others, at least for a while, and that is not an easy thing to do. Second, people make sense out of reality by constructing stories that explain who they are, why things are the way they are, why they happened the way they did, or why they did not happen differently. But once constructed, those stories tend to be treated as facts, not assumptions. Part of the diagnostic work that needs to be done to minimize missteps in exercising leadership is to make explicit, at least to yourself, the stories you are telling yourself, and then to treat them as assumptions that need to be tested, not as truths.

ON THE BALCONY

- Think of people you know who seem most conscious of their higher purposes and most true to them in their day-to-day behaviors and choices. What is it about these people that makes them so aware of and so true to their purposes? What effect do they have on you? What impact do they have on others?

- Write one sentence expressing your overriding sense of purpose. What have you been put on earth to do? What brings you inexpressible joy or a sense of meaning? Keep rewriting the sentence until it connects with you below the neck.

- Think of an intervention you're leading to help your organization address a particular adaptive challenge. Write a sentence that expresses the purpose that's driving you to take on leadership.

ON THE PRACTICE FIELD

- Let your friends and loved ones, and perhaps your colleagues, know the purpose that drives you. By sharing your purpose with others, you are more likely to get the support every person needs to celebrate the good days and stay engaged through the tough days.

Prioritize Your Purposes

You probably have multiple purposes, each of which matters to you. And understandably, you probably want to think that you are honoring all of your purposes, all the time. But like our loyalties, our purposes are not created equal: some of them mean more to us than others at particular times. And prioritizing them can be trying.

But taking real risks on behalf of one of them reveals to you and the world that the others are less important to you, at least at that moment. Marty remembers when his son Max left a terrific job to be with his girlfriend on the West Coast, where no job that he wanted was readily available. And then she left a teaching job that she loved in order to move back to the East Coast with him when he received a fabulous job offer there. Most people have had those defining moments, when the pain of choosing among deeply held purposes means losing something important in the process of gaining something you deem more important.

Purposes can come into conflict in our professional lives, too. For example, you might have had moments when you had to choose between

Conflicting Purposes at an International Law Firm

A successful lawyer, head of a big practice at a major international law firm, was passionate about several different purposes with respect to the firm's future. These included identifying and training the next generation of lawyers to make his department among the best in the world, increasing productivity by rewarding lawyers for collaborative work rather than largely for their own entrepreneurship, and helping his partners see that in a rapidly changing, highly competitive environment, the firm was going to have to overhaul its governance culture and its reward system to survive. These three purposes were interconnected, but pursuing each of them would challenge an array of different, and deeply held, values in the firm. For example, the firm placed a high value on autonomy, which manifested itself in a survival-of-the-fittest culture for associates, a less than nurturing environment, and a lack of cross-selling among departments. By pursuing the three purposes with equal commitment, the lawyer would have risked provoking people to form coalitions against the purposes that threatened their values, putting all three purposes in peril. He decided to make one of them, having the best department in the field, his top priority. It was a difficult choice, but once he made it, he was able to make more progress on that one purpose than he would have made on all three at the same time.

being liked and being respected, both of which were important to you. Whatever choice you made, you paid a price. Marty recalls a difficult moment in his professional life when he was the editor of a weekly alternative newspaper in Boston in the 1970s. The paper's news writers were critical of the actions and plans of a well-known real estate developer, who also happened to be one of Marty's closest friends. They kept writing negative articles about the developer, and Marty's friend kept telling him he had to choose: the paper or their friendship. Both were important to Marty, and having to choose one over the other would be difficult. So he began to edit the articles to soften their negativity. In the end, he damaged his reputation at the paper *and* lost his friendship. Making a choice would have been painful and would have cost him one or the other. But failing to make a choice cost him both. "Conflicting Purposes at an International Law Firm" presents another example.

ON THE BALCONY

- This an exercise we often do with groups. You can follow the activity below either as an individual or with your teams. Given all the possible purposes you could have (professional success, family, spiritual pursuits, stopping global warming, financial success, and so on), do the following analysis.

  - Make a list of the ten purposes to which you feel most connected.

  - Once you have that list, rewrite the ten in the order of most important to least important.

  - Make a line after the top five. In our experience, most people only act on their top few purposes. This is just a general experience, but see what interpretations you can draw from the top half and the bottom half.

  - Next to each of the items, write what you have done on behalf of that item in the last three weeks. Write a *P* next to the ones you have done proactively and an *R* next to the ones you have done reactively.

  - Now, as a last step, write a few things you could do for each purpose that you have been unable or unwilling to do before.

- Look at all the data gathered, and think about what you might be willing to try over the next three weeks.

ON THE PRACTICE FIELD

- Teams and organizations are a mix of various purposes and definitions of success. Rendering the orienting purposes and resulting success criteria explicit is an important activity. Together with your team, generate a list of different orienting purposes for which people are working. From that list, determine which two to four purposes would be the priority and how success would be judged against them. Be careful to acknowledge the other purposes named and those who might experience loss by the choices made.

The Story You Tell Yourself

Stories are the explanations you tell yourself and often to others to show why things happen the way they do and to convey their meaning. For example, the director of a software development project attended a meeting where the initiative on which he had worked for months was suddenly shelved. He told himself later that some of his colleagues abandoned him because they were jealous of the prominence he would have gained if the initiative were implemented successfully. In telling this story, he selected some details that supported his interpretation (one of the initiative's supporters relayed a telling conversation about rivalry she had with another colleague) and he left out other details that did not support his story (that between the time he was asked to develop the concept and the time for the approval, the company had gone through a belt-tightening that made the entire culture more risk averse).

The stories people create help them whittle down and make meaning out of the bewildering array of information coming at them all the time. We find it useful to take the perspective that people don't live in reality—we live in the story we tell ourselves about reality. When you tell your stories to others, such as colleagues, family, and members of your community, the stories also let you explain your actions to these loyalty groups in ways that make you appear sensible, acceptable, or impressive to them, or at least provide a rational explanation for the situation and your role in it.

The stories always bear some relationship to objective reality. They contain some incontrovertible facts. But they are also subjective interpretations, because you have selected the details that go into them (based on your assumptions about the world), left other details out, and then assigned meaning to those details you included. So they are more like interpretations, just one possible version of reality. Because the stories contain a large component of subjectivity, they can get in the way of your leading adaptive change in your organization. They might be off base. They probably are very different from the stories others are telling. They can lead you to overrely on yesterday's "successful" strategy, because you assume that "if it worked for us before, it will work for us again." And they can blind you to potentially valuable change initiatives if you tell yourself that those interventions are inconsistent with your company's values or way of doing things, without really testing that out.

To lead effectively, you have to make your stories explicit and then test their underlying assumptions against reality. What other possible explanations for the current situation might there be? In what ways does your explanation serve some of your needs? How might you test it and then revise the assumption and tell yourself a different story? With enough practice at testing and revising the assumptions underlying your stories, you become open to more interpretations of the dynamics and events around you. You thus open yourself to a wider range of possible courses of action.

Equally important, you create stories that do more than rationalize tough situations. You can tell more powerful and honest stories because they express the values you want to stand for. They point to the loyalties you and others may need to renegotiate to face reality more fully and develop new capacity. And they serve as a compass guiding you toward the actions you need to take to do your own adaptive work.

ON THE BALCONY

- Opening yourself to multiple stories about a particular situation (instead of just telling your usual story) takes practice. Here is one way to get practice: see whether you can come up with ten different interpretations, or stories, to explain why you are in your current job. Do not settle for five, and do not go for all the familiar, noble ones (such as you were the courageous one and everyone else was afraid). Go for ten, each of which has some possibility of telling part of the truth. Include some stories that you would not want to advertise to others. (For instance, "I am in this job because, even though I hate it, I am too afraid to leave and go look for another job.")

ON THE PRACTICE FIELD

- Here's another way to practice telling new kinds of stories. Think about an adaptive challenge your group or organization currently faces and an intervention you would like to make to address that challenge. Practice telling the story of this challenge and your proposed intervention in different ways. Start by articulating the purpose you care about so much that you want to take the risk of leadership. Then explain the assumptions that underlie your decision to make the interventions you are advocating. (For example, if your interventions involve segmenting customers in a whole new way, your assumptions might include "Consumers' preferences are changing in new ways, and our segmentation needs to reflect that.") Now try telling the story from the perspective of others who are involved. What would your boss's version of the story be? Your subordinates' version? Your colleagues' version? The version of someone who thinks your initiative is a bad idea? Identify whom you would disappoint if the story were changed in this way or that. What versions of the story would incur accusations of betrayal from one or more members in your loyalty groups?

- Using the organizing framework of observations, interpretations, and interventions, backtrack the origins of your story. Think about an action you took (intervention). Ask yourself why the action you took was the right one (interpretation). Then examine the data you selected that supported that interpretation (observation). In addition to the data selected, see whether you can identify any other data that you left out that might have been relevant. Now try to build up from there some new stories or interpretations to explain what happened. Would these new stories offer any new potential actions for you to take?

PART FIVE

DEPLOY YOURSELF

ADAPTIVE LEADERSHIP TAKES you out of your daily routine into unknown territory, requiring ways of acting that are outside your repertoire, with no guarantee of your competence or your success. It puts you at risk because you cannot rely on the tried-and-true expertise and know-how you use for tackling technical problems. And as a consequence, you cannot take on an adaptive challenge without making some changes, some adaptations, yourself. Part V is about the types of adaptations you might need to make.

There is a bit of a paradox here. On the one hand, you are trying to lead on behalf of something you believe in that is beyond your individual interest. On the other hand, in order to be most effective in doing so, you need to pay attention to how you manage, use, gratify, and deploy yourself. You need to recognize that you are moving into an unknown space and then act accordingly. It is not self-indulgence; it is smart leadership. The community you are trying to move has an investment in the status quo that will manifest itself in resisting you in ways that may play into your vulnerabilities, not your strengths.

Much of what we have learned from our clients and students about smart ways to deploy yourself is a matter of will more than skill. We doubt that anything here is beyond your capacity. But many of the techniques we suggest may be outside of your own behavioral norms. Being able to do them well when they are necessary will require you to dig a little deeper into your own capacity reservoir than is usually expected in professional or civic life. And your team or organization or community will notice the difference. That in itself is an asset for your leadership, because the people around you will pay attention as they experience you stepping outside your own comfort zone.

Our discussion in part V centers on the emotional elements of leading adaptive change. When you move people, both literally and figuratively, from a familiar place to a place less familiar, you operate on their emotions, on their stomachs and hearts in addition to their heads. To connect with them authentically and powerfully, between the neck and the navel, you must come from that place in yourself as well. Therefore, the next three chapters focus on leading from your own emotional reservoir and the risks and vulnerabilities that come with operating in that territory.

The last two chapters explore ways to protect yourself from the burnout often caused by leading from the heart. For example, we have worked with neighborhood activists from New Orleans who have gone 24/7 to reclaim their city after Hurricane Katrina. They have seemed to us almost uniformly noble, yet exhausted, and as a result, their leadership judgments have suffered. This danger is not the special province of volunteers or people working in the nonprofit sector. We have worked with corporate and political executives under enormous stress whose judgment and health deteriorated in proportion to their degree of burnout. Time and time again, we have seen well-intentioned people doing the right thing, but so caught up in their mission that they forget to notice what is happening to themselves in the process.

In part V, we suggest a series of practices to deploy yourself while leading adaptive change.

- Stay connected to your purposes

- Engage courageously

- Inspire people

- Run experiments

- Thrive

CHAPTER 19

Stay Connected to Your Purposes

THERE IS NO REASON to shoulder the difficult work of leadership if you do not have compelling, higher purposes to serve, whether saving the world, renewing your organization, or helping your community meet long-standing challenges and thrive through tough times. Your purposes provide the inspiration and the direction for your actions. Next, we describe five practices to keep your purposes alive as you lead adaptive change.

Negotiate the Ethics of Leadership and Purpose

A question permeates this book: "In what new ways of thinking and acting are you willing to engage on behalf of what you believe most deeply?" That question in turn raises the corollary: "What will you not do on behalf of what you believe most deeply?" For example, is it ethical to communicate a greater level of confidence in an initiative than you actually have in order to encourage the enthusiasm needed for the effort? How do you calibrate appropriate lines to draw? If you would engage in this level of deception but your colleague would not, does that make her "more ethical" than you or just less effective? We suggest three ways to think about these issues.

First, calculate your intervention's potential damage to others. Many adaptive change efforts create losses, if not casualties, but the extent of the damage wrought raises ethical questions. Just how much damage are you willing to inflict? Few people enjoy causing others pain, even for noble purposes. Yet those who practice adaptive leadership must invite into their lives the discomfort that comes with knowing that their good works are causing distress (or worse) for other people. War is an extreme example. Abraham Lincoln felt an extreme sadness about the casualties he was creating on both sides during the Civil War in the name of saving the union. But that did not deter him.

Second, assess the damage to your self-image and your espoused values. To what extent would leading an adaptive change initiative in certain ways violate your loyalties and long-held values that guide the way you behave and treat people? To lead successfully may demand that you take actions that do not feel right to you (even if you have the capacity for the behavior).

To use a simple example, you probably have the physical capacity to get angry at people, but perhaps you feel it's wrong and intensely dislike doing anything that resembles losing your temper. So you never risk getting angry. Over the years, we have heard numerous stories of people who have been unwilling to step into their own zone of discomfort on behalf of their purposes because it would have required violating their espoused values (such as "be polite," "be honest," or "be quiet"). Of course, context matters in making these choices. For example, most parents would probably be willing to violate certain values (such as "don't steal" or even "don't kill") if doing so were the only way to protect their children.

Marty often has his Harvard Kennedy School students study Robert Moses, the master New York builder of the twentieth century who was responsible for much of the vast network of parks, beaches, and roadways that millions of New Yorkers and visitors enjoy every year. But Moses used quite questionable means to achieve his purposes. Robert Caro's landmark biography of Moses, *The Power Broker*, documents instances when Moses lied, destroyed reputations, and intimidated colleagues to achieve his goals.[1] What makes the Moses case difficult is that he did not gain personally. He worked tirelessly, lived frugally, and died without having accumulated any wealth. It was his purpose that drove his decision to act in questionable ways.

You have probably encountered modern-day Robert Moses types in your own organization, people who are willing to do whatever it takes to achieve their purposes. But we assume that one reason you are reading this book is that you feel some ambivalence about doing what might be necessary to fulfill the higher purposes behind your own efforts. Unfortunately, there is no silver bullet here. We know of no magic formula for determining when the potential value of a tactic that makes you uncomfortable is worth the damage it would cause to others or to your own sense of right and wrong.

Third, keep the question itself alive in all its forms. Do the means justify the ends in this instance? What data am I using to evaluate the consequences? On whom and on what processes of reality testing can I rely to keep me from self-deception and rationalization? How will these short-term decisions generate longer-term consequences? By keeping your heart and mind open to these questions, you increase the odds of taking thoughtful risks and fewer regrettable decisions.

ON THE BALCONY

- Think about times in the past when you might have exercised leadership more successfully had you been willing to push beyond your comfort zone. Consider what that suggests about how you should handle the current adaptive challenge you are trying to address. If you are more the Robert Moses type, think about when you have used tactics that were way outside the norms of your organization or culture to reach your goals. Whether or not you were successful, ask yourself whether those tactics were necessary or whether you used them merely because they were available to you. Again, consider what your insights suggest about the way you might deal with the situation that is now at hand.

- In the worksheet in table 19-1, write across the top a purpose that underlies an adaptive change intervention you are trying to lead. In column 1, list the things you are currently doing to achieve that purpose. In column 3, write actions that could be taken to support your purpose but that are so outrageous (in your opinion) that you feel you would never do them. Now populate column 2 with actions you could take that are bolder than what you are doing now but not

TABLE 19-1

Serving your purpose worksheet

MY PURPOSE:

Column 1	Column 2	Column 3
Things I'm doing now:	*New things I might do:*	*Things I'd never do:*

quite as outrageous as the things you have listed in column 3. Set the worksheet aside for a day or so. Then review the new actions you listed in column 2. Decide whether any of them seem doable to you and whether there are circumstances in which you would be willing to do any of the actions in column 3.

ON THE PRACTICE FIELD

- Name a purpose that is important to you. Now name ten other people from different areas of your life who may share that purpose. Ask them what they have done to fulfill that purpose and what more they would be willing to do.

- Many people are uncomfortable yelling. If you are one of them, practice yelling to help you feel what it is like to adopt a behavior that is unfamiliar yet potentially useful in leading adaptive change. Imagine that you are Cat Woman or Hulk Hogan, the professional wrestler. Try yelling when you are passionate about something or when you are angry. Push this new behavior far enough so you feel the blood rush to your face (even if that means just raising your voice more than you usually do), but not so far that you scratch somebody's face or body-slam your peers.

Keep Purposes Alive

Our purposes often become eclipsed by everyday tasks, crises, and requests from colleagues. When you lose touch with your purposes, you lose your capacity for finding meaning in your life. So it is vital to connect your everyday life with your sense of purpose. You can help maintain this connection through physical reminders and rituals.

- *Physical reminders.* A physical object that you see every day can remind you of the reasons you seek to lead in spite of the difficulties. The more public the physical reminder, the more your friends, family, and associates will hold you accountable for keeping it alive. Here are a few examples we commonly see: (1) a favorite inspirational book kept on a bedside table available for browsing or just as an iconic symbol; (2) a picture of a special hero or mentor on the desk at work; (3) an inspiring saying or paragraph framed and put on a wall where it provides a constant presence; and (4) a keepsake from a treasured departed friend or family member to whom you committed to stay true to certain purposes and priorities. We worked with the stakeholders in a statewide education reform initiative who wore identical T-shirts during their meetings that read, "We do it for the kids." We know an elected official who keeps a card in his wallet with Teddy Roosevelt's famous "Man in the Arena" speech printed on it to keep him focused, purposeful, and courageous when he gets caught up in the day-to-day push and pull of political life. And in our consulting practice, we occasionally give out turtle figures as a reminder that you have to stick your neck out to make progress.

- *Rituals.* Every organization of human beings has rituals, practices repeated over and over again that become part of the cultural DNA; for example, the way people begin staff meetings, socialize new hires, cluster into the same groups at lunch, and gather around the water cooler after a meeting ends. The presence of rituals in everyday organizational life provides an opportunity to use them as prompts to connect to orienting values. For example, newly elected state legislators usually participate in an orientation program that tells them how to file a bill and where to find the bathrooms in the state house, but does nothing to remind them of their most noble reasons for running for office and serving the people. We have been involved in experiments in two states, Washington and Kansas, where sessions on purposes and callings have been part of a program for their newly elected members, connecting a ritual that serves an important if technical and mundane objective to the orienting values of democratic politics as well. We know of more than one organization that formally builds into its regular meetings a time for reflection near the end of meetings to ask whether they have advanced their larger purposes.

These examples illustrate ways to augment existing rituals by adding elements that reinforce purposes. But you can also create new rituals. There was a period in Alexander's life when he was trying to get in better shape (one of several such periods!). He created a ritual whereby every time an ad played on TV trying to sell him a health product, he had to do push-ups. He did more push-ups (he also began watching less TV). Spending time in nature, writing in a journal, having lunch regularly with a mentor or a person who inspires you are all rituals that might help you stay connected to your purposes. And we are familiar with several organizations where reflective off-site retreats on a regular basis were added to the already full plate of scheduled meetings in order to keep purposes alive.

ON THE BALCONY

- When in the past three months did you feel most connected to your larger purposes? Describe the moment—including where you were, the people with you, and what you were doing. What was it about that moment that made you feel so connected? What can you take from that experience and re-create now to serve as symbols or rituals reminding you of your purposes?

- List the objects you could use or the daily or weekly activities you could undertake that would help you connect your everyday life to your purposes.

ON THE PRACTICE FIELD

- Being around people and communities with a strong sense of purpose can inspire you to reflect on your own purposes more frequently. For two weeks, spend some time every day in the company of individuals who regularly connect with their purposes. For example, go to a religious ceremony (not necessarily of your own faith), attend a book reading or lecture, sit in with an elementary school teacher, spend some time in an emergency waiting room, or work in a soup kitchen.

- When you create the agenda for your next meeting, write beside each item how that item can be connected to the higher purposes of the organization.

- Develop a leadership mantra, one sentence that gets to the heart of the purposes that make leading adaptive change worth it to you. Getting it down to one sentence may take a while. ("If I had more time, I would write a shorter letter," said Blaise Pascal.) Once you have come up with the sentence, memorize it, and say it to yourself right after you wake up every morning. Say it to yourself as soon as you get to work, and say it again after you get home at night. Depending on the nature of your working relationships, you may want to share the sentence with others. After doing this for a few weeks, ask yourself and others whether anything has changed.

- Spend five minutes after each lunch thinking about what you would like to achieve in the afternoon.

Negotiate Your Purposes

You have a particular mix of purposes and priorities for your organization, your vision of where you think the enterprise should move. But many purposes are alive and well in the organization, most notably those espoused by different members of the board and other senior authorities. Your purposes may differ from those other purposes. Adaptive leadership often requires reconciling those differences so that multiple purposes do not cancel each other out.

To manage this process, you need to understand others' purposes. That requires putting yourself in their shoes and appreciating their priorities, no matter how different they are from your own sense of what constitutes the right direction. You also have to put your purposes out there and let others chew on them and challenge them. That means accepting that to make progress in the directions you deeply want, you may end up in a different place than your original purposes would have taken you. For example, the vice president for environmental affairs in an automobile company may feel passionately committed to the development and production of green cars, but may have to accede to the competing commitment to short-term profitability needed to keep the company alive.

Many people avoid this process of negotiating purposes entirely. Compromise feels like disloyalty to their purposes and to the individuals who share and support those priorities. They know that by negotiating, they will probably have to give something up and thus disappoint people whose esteem matters greatly to them. Indeed, supporters may cry out, betrayal! So they steer clear of even discussing their purposes with others who have different priorities, and they tell themselves they did it to protect their own integrity. Or they exit the organization and seek out communities of like-minded people where they don't have to advocate for their views and values because everyone shares them already.

It is hard to decide which parts of your purposes are negotiable and which are not. As the father of two young children, Alexander is strongly committed to being a good parent. As occurs with many couples, his wife has different ideas about good parenting, however, and Alexander has struggled at times to determine what part of his view to consider negotiable. Letting go of any of the practices that Alexander considers good parenting makes him feel disloyal to his children and to his own parents, who raised him in the ways he honors.

Another way to negotiate your purposes so that others support them is to translate them into a language that others understand and respond to favorably. Suppose you are committed to reforming the health-care system. Depending on whose support you are trying to enlist, you may want to emphasize different aspects of that larger purpose. When you are talking with fiscal conservatives, you will stress the economic benefits of improving health care. Improving quality and safety will reduce costs by generating greater efficiency. When you are meeting with liberal activists, you will focus on the moral imperative of improving health care. And when you are meeting with health-care providers, you will emphasize reducing the bureaucratic nightmare they have had to endure.

Translating your purposes for others becomes even more critical when you are presenting them to people who oppose them. Take the issue of the lack of funding for post-Katrina renewal in New Orleans. If your job was to get states other than Louisiana to provide funds for New Orleans, you would have a tough task ahead of you. You would not get very far simply by making the moral argument "Giving is the right thing to do." But you might make more progress if you presented your purpose in ways that connected to *their* purposes. Imagine, for example, meeting with a senator from another state who is extremely chauvinistic. You could frame the conversation around national pride: "Americans take care of their own. We cannot afford to have people living in third-world conditions in our own backyard, let alone have the world see that repeatedly on TV."

In addition to negotiating and translating your purposes, you need to make them tangible. That means being specific about their operational implications: objectives, plans, strategy, timelines, and so forth. Rather than presenting some lofty aspiration, many people will need you to give them concrete form so they can get their arms around what you mean. Martin Luther King Jr. had trouble getting people who lived in the northern parts of the United States to actively support the civil rights movement, until he made sure that graphic images of violence inflicted on blacks were broadcast into their living rooms every night on TV. The images gave visual form to the problem that King had committed himself to solving. They brought his purpose to life for northerners. And many people from the North began to take up the cause with political, financial, and personal support.

Important purposes take time. You are not abandoning your purposes when you take an angled step toward them rather than move along a straight line.

ON THE BALCONY

- Think of the different people in your group or organization whose support you need to fulfill your purposes. Using your knowledge of them, what do you think their own purposes are? Are there any areas where your purposes and theirs might overlap, and thus your purposes could be aligned? What are the elements of your purposes you would be willing to sacrifice in the interests of bringing others' along?

ON THE PRACTICE FIELD

- Take your purposes to the streets. Talk with others in your organization about them, and explain in specific terms how you are trying to change things on behalf of those purposes. Give them concreteness. As you talk with each person, notice what images, words, and information seem to resonate and which seem to leave the person cold.

Integrate Your Ambitions and Aspirations

After decades of teaching at Harvard, Marty and Ron have noticed an interesting phenomenon. Students who attend the graduate schools at Harvard devoted to public service (for example, the Kennedy School, the Graduate School of Education, the Harvard School of Public Health, and the Harvard Divinity School) are comfortable talking about their noblest purposes, their aspirations, but they are uncomfortable discussing their ambitions. Lust for power, wealth, prestige, recognition, and fame are all taboo. By contrast, students at the Harvard Business School and many at the Harvard Law School speak readily about their ambitions for fortune and status, but they are often uncomfortable talking about their noble aspirations. They seem worried that discussing these matters openly will make them look like do-gooders who will not be taken seriously in "the real world."

Each of these perspectives is unnecessarily narrow and reflects the culture and values of the institutions where the students receive their professional training. We suggest that you can have both ambitions and aspirations, and you can actively serve both. The best presidents of the United States have been highly ambitious men, skilled in the political artistry required for public leadership. They have also had noble aspirations for doing what was best for their country. Their ambitions and aspirations were integrated, not mutually exclusive.

In the business world, people are just as capable of integrating their ambitions and their aspirations as in politics. Early in his medical career, Ron worked for a year as a physician examining top corporate executives in a medical clinic in New York City. As part of their benefits package, these executives were given a yearly exam, and Ron was one of the six or seven doctors on staff. During his time there, Ron noticed that many CEOs and senior vice presidents, as they reached their late fifties, began to take on more "visionary" or public purposes. They began having aspirations beyond the ambitions that had fueled their ability to build and steward multinational companies. They wanted to channel some of their companies' energy toward these pursuits. It was as if an alarm clock had gone off, reminding them of their mortality. Though they had "made it" in business, they still wanted deeply to leave behind a legacy of meaning somehow more substantial than what they had already accomplished. "Integrating Ambition and Aspiration at Panasonic" shows another example from the realm of consumer electronics.

Of course, at times you will have to make trade-offs between your ambitions and aspirations. For example, at the most everyday level, the aspiration to spend time with your children will occasionally (or frequently) conflict with your ambition to achieve an important goal at work. We all live with the ongoing tension of balancing our ambitions and aspirations. How can you honor both?

We recommend tempering the guilt you may harbor regarding your ambitions and the embarrassment you may feel about your aspirations.

Integrating Ambition and Aspiration at Panasonic

The founder of one of the world's leading companies, Konosuke Matsushita, grew up poor and nearly orphaned. By the age of thirty-eight, he had built one of the most promising companies in Japan, Matsushita Electric Industrial Company, Ltd. (later renowned globally for its Panasonic brand). In 1932, after a brief encounter with a religious group and a two-month period of reflection, at a large gathering of his company's senior executives, Matsushita announced that going forward, the mission of the company would be to "overcome poverty, to relieve society as a whole from misery, and bring it wealth."[2] His colleagues were aghast. Had Matsushita gone mad? But his rationale was simple: the company was in the business of making labor-saving devices and luxury goods available and affordable to ordinary families around the world. By doing so, the company would not only make profits; it would also raise the standard of living for poor people everywhere.

Guilt and embarrassment can sometimes keep you straight, but they can also limit your ability to consider a wider range of options for doing well and good at the same time. Developing the freedom to explore those options requires engaging in the personal challenge of examining and amending the story you tell yourself about who you are and the stories other people tell you about who you ought to be. When we let those stories rule our lives, we can rob ourselves of our full humanity and live smaller lives than we could be living.

ON THE BALCONY

- What are your ambitions? What are your aspirations? In what ways do you make trade-offs between the two? What are your feelings about your ambitions? About your aspirations? What impact do these feelings have on your decisions regarding both?

ON THE PRACTICE FIELD

- Share the ambitions you listed earlier in the reflections with factions in each of your loyalty groups (your colleagues, communities, and ancestors). Start with the factions that would find it easiest to hear your ambitions. Move gradually to the factions that would find it most difficult. With these less receptive factions, try describing your ambitions respectfully but unapologetically. For example, "I want to make enough money to take exciting but comfortable vacations." Now repeat this process, but this time with your list of aspirations.

Avoid Common Traps

Having a sense of purpose is essential to the practice of leadership. Your purposes provide the inspiration and energy you need to survive leadership's choppy ride. But they can also become a constraint if you fall into one or more common traps. The traps are:

- *Going blind and deaf.* The passion and commitment that flow from having noble purposes can also make you blind and deaf.

The more single-minded you become, the more difficult it will be to see and hear contrary data and to notice signals suggesting the need for amendment and midcourse correction. For instance, when Bill and Hillary Clinton proposed massive health-care reform early in Clinton's first term, they were so committed to the righteousness of their cause that they did not read clear signals that a more modest and more experimental proposal might have been possible, whereas the one they submitted had very little chance of being enacted. Similarly, because George W. Bush was so committed to the view that toppling Saddam Hussein was the essence and hard part of regime change, it was months before his administration could deal with the reality that toppling Saddam was only the beginning of the hard work.

- *Becoming a martyr.* People who have a noble purpose to which they are solidly committed are vulnerable to dying unnecessarily for that purpose. In the realm of organizational life, this can take the form of being marginalized or even fired for being too persistent an advocate for a lost cause. There is a tension here, because your purpose is (by definition) something for which you might be willing to risk death, professionally if not literally. Yet the possibility of death can make martyring yourself (for example, by raising the same issue at every top team meeting) seem like a better option than doing the hard, dogged work of garnering small successes punctuated by the inevitable compromises and frustrating setbacks.

- *Appearing self-righteous.* If you are loudly and relentlessly certain you are on the right path, you may come across as self-righteous. And that can trigger resistance in others. Some people may resist you simply because they are contrarians. Others may respond to self-righteousness by reexperiencing what it felt like to live under the thumb of dominating, highly directive parents. And they will revert to adolescent types of resistance to undermine your purposes. We know more than one CEO who has stepped into this trap. In effect, they have repeatedly told their organizations, "We have no choice but to do what I want you to do." They make it impossible for others to feel a sense of ownership of the company's new direction because the chief executive already owns it so completely.

- *Being the self-appointed chief purpose officer.* Reminding people in your group or organization of the collective, larger purpose behind a major intervention is important when you are leading adaptive change. But do not overdo it. Some day-to-day events and decisions are just not related to the group's overarching purpose. Sometimes a cigar is just a cigar, as Freud famously quipped when someone asked him about the meaning of a cigar. And if you try to infuse that purpose into every event, every decision, every meeting, you risk marginalizing yourself as people will get so tired of hearing from you about the purpose that they will just tune you out. And that only undermines your purposes. Rather than appoint yourself the chief purpose officer, remind people of the purpose only when you feel certain that the event or decision at hand truly relates to it.

ON THE BALCONY

- Reflect on your own behavior. To which of the above four traps are you most vulnerable? For example, do you fight against contrary perspectives and data that suggest the need to compromise or take a different direction? If you get discouraged easily, do you risk giving up or martyring yourself when the going gets rough? Are you broadcasting your purposes too loudly, aggressively, and frequently, and triggering resistance as a result? Do you go on and on about your purposes to people, annoying them and prompting them to tune you out?

ON THE PRACTICE FIELD

- Find people who agree with or share your purposes, and ask them to step in and lead your change initiative for a period of time. During that period, observe how they lead the initiative. What tactics prove most successful for them? What traps do they fall into? What lessons can you draw from their experiences and apply to your own leadership effort when you jump back into the fray?

CHAPTER 20

Engage Courageously

A S A YOUNG POLITICIAN, Marty found it fairly difficult to get out of the house each day and ring that first doorbell. He knew rejection awaited him, if not at the first doorbell of the day, then at the next. His distaste for rejection made it tough for him to summon up the courage needed to campaign. There were days when he never made it out of the house.

At least five major constraints can hold you back from summoning courage for the work of leadership:

- Loyalties to people who may not believe you are doing the right thing

- Fear of incompetence

- Uncertainty about taking the right path

- Fear of loss

- Not having the stomach for the hard parts of the journey

We examine each of these constraints in turn below and offer ideas for overcoming them.

Get Past the Past

To lead adaptive change, you have to refashion loyalties; that is, have a conversation both in your heart and in person with people to whom you have loyalty in which you explain to them why the current situation requires you to sift through their expectations of you, honoring many of them but not all. That can be difficult at best, dangerous at worst. Yitzhak Rabin and Anwar Sadat were assassinated by their own people. In the summer of 2000, after negotiations at Camp David over the Middle East peace process, Egyptian president Hosni Mubarak apparently warned Palestinian National Authority President Yasser Arafat that accepting proposals requiring Palestinian refugees to let go of their dream of returning to the homes of their grandparents would lead to his assassination, too.

The Middle East peace negotiation process illustrates the work of refashioning loyalties. To explore options, the negotiators on each side have had to reexamine their loyalties to their constituents, communities, and ancestors. They have had to wrestle with the various voices from the past and present that they had internalized and had become parts of their identity. Many Palestinian refugees dreamed of going home, and many Israeli settlers believed that they had finally come home. Before the negotiators could imagine coming up with a strategy for engaging each of their constituencies and communities, they have had to transcend their own strongly allergic responses to each other when the topics of settlements and the return of refugees have arisen. Breakdowns have been far more frequent than breakthroughs. But sustained engagement has helped at least the primary negotiators to discuss the undiscussable: the transgression and renegotiating of long-held loyalties required in any compromise.

Likewise, in leading adaptive change in your own organization, your loyalties influence the questions you ask, the possibilities you entertain, and the views you are willing to hear. Loyalties powerfully affect, sometimes in unproductive ways, the way you interpret the problem at hand and the actions you decide to take. For example, owing to your loyalties, you may refuse to consider a possible course of action because it would enrage a key group of stakeholders, even if that course of action would be ideal for tackling your organization's challenge. How can you ease the constraint presented by your loyalties? We recommend this process.

Step 1: Watch for Gaps Between Your Words and Actions

What story are you telling about your supposed priorities? Do your actions support that story? In the Middle East, the two sides have made a public commitment to peace, but they have not yet arrived at a sustainable agreement. In your work life, what are you promising to accomplish regarding your purposes? And what are you actually accomplishing?

Step 2: Stay in the Present

When you hear yourself justifying your own current attitude or behavior based on something that happened a long time ago, you are likely having trouble putting the past to rest. For example, in a large professional services firm, a near breakup of the firm twenty years ago over the compensation and reward system is still an emotional reference point for some senior people who resist even placing an evaluation of the current system on the top team's agenda. If you recognize having an allergic reaction such as this, you may be able to identify how the past continues to dominate the present, for you and for others, and then you can help your colleagues name the problem, analyze the differences between yesterday and today, heal some old wounds, and open themselves to a better set of options for tackling today's challenge.

Step 3: Identify the Loyalties You Need to Refashion

Determine the expectations of specific colleagues, community members, and ancestors that you will need to revisit and possibly refashion to create for yourself the latitude to deviate from the past and move forward. In the professional services firm example, the CEO will need to have a conversation with some of the firm's elders, including some of his own mentors, before he can move forward to reform the compensation and reward system.

Step 4: Conduct the Needed Conversations

Go to these individuals and discuss how you need some of their expectations to change. Some of these conversations will be difficult. You will be asking people to tolerate behavior on your part that violates the spoken or unspoken contract that exists between you. And you may be putting a valued friendship or an important alliance at risk. For instance, for the CEO to have those conversations with his mentors would risk disappointing them at least and perhaps alienating them as well.

Sometimes, those conversations will reveal that your assumptions about these loyalty groups and their expectations of you are mostly in your head. Marty remembers such a conversation during his father's last months of life. Marty visited his father one day, determined to renegotiate the unspoken contract that he had to attend synagogue regularly. Marty sensed that if he did not have that conversation before his father died, he would feel obligated to stay loyal to his father by attending services regularly whether or not his heart was in it. "Dad," he began, "there's something I would like to say to you." "Sure," his father responded, "anything." "Dad, I would not have been going to services at all the last few years if it had not been for you." "That's funny," his father said, "because I would not have gone to services at all the last few years if it had not been for *you*." Each had been going to services because he thought the other expected it of him. The conversation generated immense mutual relief and new understanding on both men's parts.

Step 5: Create Rituals for Refashioning Ancestor Loyalties

If the conversation you need to have is with a deceased ancestor or with a faction you can no longer reach, create a ritual that will help you put the unproductive aspects of that loyalty behind you. Throw away the book or the memento that symbolizes that loyalty. Go to the person's grave site and let the person know that you are going to breach aspects of what you understand to be the contract. Apologize, and ask for forgiveness even though you know there will be no verbal response. Write a letter, explaining why you have to do what you have to do.

Ron and his sister took their mother, Betsy, back to Eastern Europe sixty years after she had fled Nazi Germany at the age of twelve. Betsy had little interest at first in going, but she acquiesced because Ron and his sister told her they were still carrying the horrors of the past with them in their own lives. Going in May to the Ukrainian villages she had known in the summers of her youth, Betsy brought life back to life. Stories, jokes, ironies, romance, and characters of all kinds sprang nonstop from Betsy's memory. What had been a black-and-white photograph etched mainly with death turned into color. Amazed, they discovered that their family, even the children, not only died; they also lived.

Wandering in an old abandoned cemetery in a farm field, they discovered Betsy's grandmother's grave; Sarah had evidently died of natural causes just before the war. As Ron communed with her, he asked, "What should I do? How do you want me to honor your life in my life?" And he thought he heard his great-grandmother respond, "Life is a blessing, my son. Just be happy."

Step 6: Focus on What You Are Conserving

Remind yourself that you are remaining true to core principles and values even as you depart from perspectives that are no longer healthy. You are not throwing over all of those loyalties, just the elements of them that are impeding your progress. Even if people are accusing you of betrayal, in time they may come to realize how hard you have tried to honor your loyalty to what is essential and enduring in their perspectives.

ON THE BALCONY

- Write down the names of all those who you consider to be core people in your life. For each, write down what they expect from you. Think about what they would say to themselves about what you represent to them and what they need or want from you. From that list, examine which of those things you want to deliver and which you do not.

ON THE PRACTICE FIELD

- Make next month a clean slate for you. Look at the list of deliverables above, and take up a number of them to give you more freedom to operate next month.

- One way to mitigate the loss of refashioning loyalties is to give a full picture of the loyalties you are committed to and the ones you may disappoint. Have a direct conversation with those around you that may sound something like the following: "Look, I am going to disappoint you in some ways, and I am going to make you proud in others. Here is where I am going to go in a different direction, and here is where I am going to make you really proud."

Lean into Your Incompetence

Leading adaptive change requires you to step beyond your default behaviors into an unknown situation and to learn something new. That means experiencing a period of incompetence. Indeed, if you do not feel that you are operating at the very edge of your talents or even just beyond that edge, then you are probably not attacking an adaptive challenge. Instead, you may be grappling with an issue that is more technical than adaptive, or treating an adaptive challenge as a technical problem.

How do you lean into your own incompetence, so you can put yourself into a state of discovery? Here are two ideas: find structured and challenging learning opportunities, and reframe your truths as assumptions that you can test.

Find Structured and Challenging Learning Opportunities

To diminish the common experience of disorientation and embarrassment as you move past your frontier of competence, find opportunities to try your hand at developing a set of demanding new skills in a structured, safe environment that has nothing to do with the adaptive challenges in your professional or vocational life. Find a low-risk context in which to experience being incompetent. Marty fulfilled a longtime ambition as a former politician and professor when he and his family moved to New York City in 1995; he signed up for acting classes. Nearly twice as old as the next oldest student, amid young, aspiring actors with professional credits already on their résumés, Marty felt pretty awful at the beginning. Yet, for the first time in four decades, he could "wallow in his own incompetence." (He never did get any acting credits, but he learned something about how to better tolerate his own incompetence.)

Almost any environment or experience that throws you off balance will do: spend time at an ashram in India, learn to play golf, take up a musical instrument, go back to school a quarter century after you have last been a student, take a scuba-diving class in the Caribbean, learn a new language, even try out for a role in a community theater production in your hometown. A friend of ours has been making connections between the frustrations of learning to ride a unicycle and the challenges he faces while running a small business.

Seek out challenging new ideas. New ideas exist everywhere, in every bookstore and every place where people are sharing their viewpoints and insights. Look into a discipline other than your own. When you learn about several different disciplines, you can begin to think in terms of metaphors, see how ideas, inventions, and findings in one area of expertise can be applied in another. For example, in this book, we have taken ideas from evolutionary biology about adaptive processes in nature to consider ways in which organizations develop greater adaptability in society. Similarly, we have drawn from music and the performing arts to shed light on ways to handle challenges in your organizational life, such as improvising, listening, and creating a holding environment. A friend of ours uses magic tricks in business consultations to help people see how their assumptions constrain their ability to see a greater range of possibilities.

Reframe Truths as Assumptions

Every day you make sense out of reality by connecting facts together and interpreting those facts to create stories. Suppose you describe what happened on a particular morning as follows: "At 7:00 a.m. I got up. Then I ate a bagel and drank a cup of coffee. I left for the office at 8:15 a.m. and arrived at 9:15 a.m." This straightforward recital of facts involves little interpretation and thus little meaning. Compare it with the following account of the same morning: "At 7:00 a.m. I arose still tired from too little sleep because I had stupidly stayed up too late watching the Red Sox play a night game on the West Coast, but at least they made it worthwhile by pulling out a win in the last inning. Because of that, I was late leaving for the office and forgot to bring the report that I had promised to deliver to my colleague that afternoon."

To create a story about your morning, you choose some facts and leave out others (depending on what strikes you as relevant at the time) and provide some interpretation of the facts you have chosen. The result is an account that has meaning; it suggests that your morning was frustrating, fun, exhausting, and embarrassing, qualities that do not come through in a simple rendering of the facts. You made sense of the facts *you* have chosen to include, not necessarily how *others* might choose which facts to include or how to make sense of those same facts. For example, you might think, "Boy, I really screwed up this time." But a colleague listening to your account might think, "Wow, he's so lucky he got to see the game! His life is much more fun than mine."

In stories you tell about the challenges facing your organization, or about a change initiative you would like to lead, the same process of making meaning unfolds. Because you choose which facts to highlight and include in your story and what those facts mean to you, your story is just one possible "truth" about reality. Other people will construct different stories by selecting different facts about the same challenge or initiative, or by selecting the same facts as you but interpreting them differently. Result? A large number of different "truths."

In our professional services compensation system reform example, there are mutually exclusive views of the values that the current system represents. Starting with the same set of facts, one faction argues that the system rewards practitioner competence, and another faction argues that the system undermines revenues by devaluing collaboration.

Treating stories as truths blinds us to the possibility of alternative versions of reality. That in turn prevents us from connecting with other people where they are, and generating the widest set of options for action. To lean into your incompetence, practice viewing your stories about reality as just that, stories, and treating them as assumptions, not truths. Then test those assumptions, and revise them if your findings suggest that they are not quite on target. The two factions arguing over the compensation system might be able to get together to devise a low-risk test to see which assumption is closer to the mark.

ON THE BALCONY

- When was the last time you risked being incompetent so you could learn something new? When was the last time you resisted doing something because you did not want to feel incompetent or look incompetent to others?

- What new skill have you always wanted to learn? What would it take for you to start acquiring that skill now?

- Describe a problem you are wrestling with in your personal, professional, or civic life. Now describe the problem from the perspective of the other people involved in the problem. What did you learn from this experience? How might you change your story about the problem?

ON THE PRACTICE FIELD

- Think of an adaptive challenge with which your group or organization is struggling. Then spend a few hours away from work talking with people who have expertise in two disciplines, fields of study, or industries that differ from your own area of expertise or industry. Ask them about the latest thinking in their disciplines. Then consider the ways in which those perspectives could shed light on the way your organization is responding to its adaptive challenge.

- Look for opportunities to create metaphors or analogies from these cross-disciplinary experiences that generate new insights for how you might deal with the problem at hand.

    For example, suppose you want to raise the performance of your team members. One day, you decide to attend a lecture given by a pilot for the Blue Angels, the U.S. Navy's flight demonstration squadron. At the lecture, you learn that the Blue Angels' high performance hinges on extensive trust among the pilots. The Angels foster trust by debriefing regularly and making clear commitments to one another. Safety is critical for the Angels. After every demonstration flight, each pilot cites what he did well and what he wishes he had done more safely, and explains what he is going to do differently to be safer on the next flight. Back at the office, you find yourself thinking that regular debriefings might improve your own team. And you develop a new weekly meeting to debrief focused specifically on capturing lessons learned and setting and reviewing commitments.

Fall in Love with Tough Decisions

Exercising adaptive leadership involves making a series of tough decisions. And tough decisions are tough for several reasons. Table 20-1 shows examples.

TABLE 20-1

What makes a tough decision?

Characteristic	Example
It is a close call.	Two potential interventions for tackling a particular adaptive challenge have different (and seemingly equally important) strengths and weaknesses. And you can implement only one of them.
You must choose between the known and the unknown.	You believe things could be better. But you know the current reality, how to navigate it, how to make it work for you, what the rules and rewards are. The other choice, the unknown, is a mystery. It might be better, but it might be worse. So you cannot decide whether to embark on a change initiative.
Doing the right thing would incur significant losses.	The intervention you have in mind for tackling an adaptive challenge will incur losses for you and/or those around you. You are not sure whether those losses will be worth it, or whether you are capable of managing the casualties. For example, you believe you need to divest a business division that's underperforming. But you are worried that the resulting layoff would seriously erode morale in the rest of the organization.
Several of your values are in conflict.	Several values that you believe in strongly are in conflict, and you would need to subordinate one of them to move your change initiative forward. For example, you believe in consensus decision making, but your team is deadlocked on an issue that is critical to the future.

You probably know people who enjoy making tough decisions or at least appear routinely willing to do so. You probably also know people who have trouble deciding anything, from the big (like whether to get married) to the small (such as what food to order from a menu). How do you strengthen your capacity to embrace the tough decisions that come with leading adaptive change? The following tips can help:

- *Accept that you are going to have to make some tough decisions your whole life.* On the other side of any tough decision facing you, there inevitably will be another one. You can choose to be annoyed or anxious about these choices, or you can embrace them. Tough decisions require you to put your heart into them, nourish the possibilities, and then make a commitment to a course of action. It sounds a little like falling in love and making the leap into marriage. That is why we suggest falling in love with tough decisions.

- *Nothing is forever.* Rework your decision. If you are struggling with a decision, then all the options likely have some merit. The odds of making the right decision are close to the odds of making the wrong one. Making no decision is a decision in itself. The only way you are going to get going is to choose. Moreover, the outcome will probably be significantly influenced by factors beyond your control or imagination. And most decisions are iterative: you make a move, take the risk. If things seem to be going well, you continue. If not, you take corrective action.

- *Tough does not necessarily mean important.* Fortunately, few decisions are so important that everything depends on them. Rarely are the stakes as high as people imagine them to be (although sometimes they are, such as in war strategy and medical judgments). Even decisions that seem incredibly fraught at the time will often result in changes only at the margins of your life. In his wonderful book of essays *Rules for Aging*, Roger Rosenblatt begins with this advice: "Whatever you think matters—doesn't. Follow this rule and it will add decades to your life."[1] Try thinking of yourself as just making the next move on the dance floor, and you may actually lighten the weight of the decision and even make better choices.

ON THE BALCONY

- Recall some tough choices you made in the past, such as where to go to school, whether to buy that house, whether to take a particular job, or any other decision that you agonized about at the time. What made those decisions so tough? What process did you use to make the choice? Take heart in knowing that you survived, whatever decision you made. If you feel you made the wrong choice on one or more of those tough decisions, what did you learn from the experience that could be applied in the future? Were there midcourse corrections you could have made that would have resulted in a better outcome?

ON THE PRACTICE FIELD

- Identify a tough decision facing you now. Bite off a piece of it for which the stakes do not feel so high. For example, instead of rolling out a big new strategy, run a pilot project to test the water. Then assess whether you are on the right track, need midcourse correction, or should keep moving in the same direction.

- Try the "inform the gut" tactic.[2] Collect all the information and insights you can from within yourself and from other sources on a tough decision you face. Then immerse yourself in something else entirely for a few days, putting the decision out of your mind. Give the information time to seep from your head to your belly. Think of your head as just a receiver and translator of information. Then go with your gut.

Get Permission to Fail

We assume that you are reading this book because you want to make changes in your organization, community, or family on behalf of something about which you care deeply. You want to succeed. Few people get excited about experiencing failure. More than just not wanting to fail, many people give themselves good reasons why failing is not an option: "I have kids to feed." "The team depends on me." "I don't want to let my parents down."

Sometimes people hold back from leading adaptive change because they just cannot tolerate knowing that they might fail. When Marty was in school, he held himself to a B standard. Bs came easily to him and he knew it. (How he got into Williams College and Harvard Law School remain a mystery to his friends.) To the outside world, a B was a decent grade, far from failing, even though he was not "fulfilling his potential" (according to a slew of teachers and relatives). Holding himself to a B standard protected Marty from failure: if he had aspired to get As, he might not have made it. Lowering his standards enabled him to avoid the risk of failing.

But lowering your standards will not help you lead adaptive change, because leading adaptive change requires an experimental mind-set, involves risk, and brings the real possibility of failure. So you need to give yourself permission to fail. These practices can help:

- *Broaden your definition of success on a particular adaptive change intervention.* Judge your initiative on criteria beyond the binary "it worked" or "it did not work." Thinking experimentally, consider the lessons you gleaned from efforts that did not generate all the outcomes you wanted. Think about the ways you might apply those lessons to your next move.

- *Prepare your constituents.* Manage the expectations of those around you to prepare the ground for possible failure of your effort. Enlist them in giving it a shot and learning from the effort. You will foster a shared sense of ownership and reduce the possibility that they will turn you into a lightning rod for failure or hold you to an unreasonable standard. The language you use is critical to managing your constituents' expectations: instead of saying something like, "You can count on me to pull this off," say, "We are trying something new here," or "We will see what happens if we push the envelope."

- *Conduct small experiments.* Small failures are easier to stomach than large, expensive ones. Conducting relatively low-cost experiments (such as pilot projects) can help you test your idea, fail, and not be destroyed (or destroy your organization) in the process.

ON THE BALCONY

- Think of a change initiative you are considering. In what ways might you give yourself permission to fail at it? For example, could you define milestones of progress in the terms of lessons learned for version 2.0? Is there a way you could test the initiative's chances in a relatively small, safe way?

ON THE PRACTICE FIELD

- Identify the constituents you will need for a change initiative you plan to lead. In describing the initiative to each of them, practice using language that lays the groundwork for experimentation and the possibility of failure.

Build the Stomach for the Journey

Adaptive work generates what can feel like maddening digressions, detours, and pettiness. People often lose sight of what is truly at stake or resort to creative tactics to maintain equilibrium in the short run. All of this can leave you deeply discouraged or burn you out. You may start questioning whether the whole thing is worth it and be tempted to downgrade your aspiration. You may numb yourself to these frustrations. Or you may decide to throw in the towel. It is hard to stay in the game in the face of hopelessness or despair. But to lead change, you need the ability to operate in despair and keep going. And that calls for building the stomach for the journey.

Building resilience is similar to training for a marathon. You need to start somewhere (for example, running a mile or two each day for a few weeks and then gradually working up to the longer distances). In an organizational context, this kind of training can take the form of staying in a tough conversation longer than you normally would, naming an undiscussable problem facing your team, and not changing the subject at the first sarcastic joke designed to move off the uncomfortable topic.

Marathoners in training use benchmarks. You can track your progress if you have clearly defined short-term goals along the way. Targeting a monthly or quarterly goal that feels realistic may help you build stamina for the long haul. Or bringing warring factions together in the same room for even just a few minutes may be good practice for conducting a longer meeting later.

To further build your stomach for the adaptive leadership journey, keep reminding yourself of your purposes. Runners look forward, not down. Staying focused on the goal ahead will help keep you from becoming preoccupied or overwhelmed by the number of steps necessary to get there.

Early in his career, Alexander and a colleague worked with the New York City Department of Health, assessing the patient-care capacity in all forty-seven of the city's public hospitals and health-care centers. They met with resistance at the first few centers they visited.

Uncooperative managers refused to supply the necessary data because they were anxious that they would not come out looking good. After these visits, Alexander and his colleague were exhausted. To stay in the game, the two of them made a decision: after each subsequent visit, they would spend time together reminding themselves of their long-term goals and eating a healthy lunch rather than comfort food to keep their spirits up.

Building a strong stomach requires relentlessness. You probably have a limit to how hard you are willing to push an initiative forward. If opponents of your intervention sense that limit, they will know exactly how hard they have to resist. One of the best practitioners of leadership we know used to say at the beginning of tough meetings when everyone knew this was going to be a difficult conversation, "I am willing to stay in this meeting as long as necessary." As soon as he indicated that he was there for however long it would take, people for whom the issue was not such a high priority would begin to back away rather than stall or sabotage the discussion. He would then be that much closer to getting the needed work done.

Leading adaptive change will almost certainly test the limits of your patience. Even after you have accomplished a lot—for example, increased market share, built more low-income housing, or put your issue on the top team's agenda for the first time—you might well find yourself having trouble celebrating that progress because you know how much more work remains to be done.

Impatience can hurt you in numerous ways. You raise a tough question at a meeting and do not get an immediate response. So you jump right back in and keep pounding on the question. Each time you pound, you send the message that you are the only person responsible for that question. You own it. And the more you pound away, the less willing people are to share ownership of the question themselves. And if they do not feel any ownership of the question, they will have less investment in whatever the resolution turns out to be.

Where are you supposed to find the patience when there is such a long way to go on the issues for which you feel so strongly? You can find patience by tapping into your ability to feel compassion for others involved in the change effort. Compassion comes from understanding other people's dilemmas, being aware of how much you are asking of them. Your awareness of their potential losses will calm you down and give you patience as they travel a journey that may be more difficult for them than it is for you.

ON THE BALCONY

- Recall situations in the past when you experienced great patience. What enabled you to do that? For example, perhaps you were patient as your child learned to catch a ball, or swim, or drive a car, or play the piano, or read, because you could remember how hard it was for you to learn those skills. Or perhaps you believed that most people survive difficult journeys and master needed skills, so you felt a sense of optimism that further fueled your patience.

ON THE PRACTICE FIELD

- Think of an individual or a situation that tends to make you impatient. For instance, perhaps a peer manager's predictable negativity in the face of proposed change instantly raises your hackles whenever you encounter it. Brainstorm practices you can use with this person that will help you develop more patience when he "presses your buttons." Then apply those practices the next time you feel yourself losing your patience around him. For example, ask a question or stare out the window to buy time to get perspective on the way you are being triggered.

CHAPTER 21

Inspire People

DO YOU INSPIRE PEOPLE? The root of the word *inspire* means to take breath in, to fill with spirit. Inspiration is the capacity to move people by reaching in and filling their hearts from deeper sources of meaning.

To lead your organization through adaptive change, you need the ability to inspire. Adaptive challenges involve values, not simply facts or logic. And resolving them engages people's beliefs and loyalties, which lie in their hearts, not their heads.

Inspiration is not an innate capacity reserved for the rare and gifted charismatic individual. To see that everyone already has this capacity, take a walk through the children's unit of a hospital, and the everyday ability of people to inspire will surround you. We believe that with practice, anyone can strengthen this skill and deploy it for leadership.

This chapter explains how to find and use your own voice, because while anyone can develop this skill, the result must be uniquely you. As an inspirational person, you must speak with a unique voice shaped by the purposes that move you, the particular challenges facing your organization and world, and your own style of communication.

The way you connect contributes to your unique voice. But we are not talking about how smooth your voice sounds. Jack Welch inspires, and he stutters. Moses had a speech impediment. What we mean is how well you speak to others' viewpoints, values, and needs. Finding your voice requires doing more than articulating facts and arguments well. You have to translate those facts and arguments into language that reaches into others' hearts.

Some conditions require inspiration: when people have forgotten their purpose, when factions are reaching the limits of their tolerance for each other, when the community is beginning to lose hope, or when a better future is beyond anyone's imagination. At those crucial moments, your inspiration taps hidden reserves of promise that sustain people through times that induce despair. You enable people to envision a future that sustains the best from their past while also holding out new possibilities.

You need to strengthen two skills to master the ability to inspire: listening from the heart and speaking from the heart. After all, you cannot connect deeply with people unless you know what is in their hearts and what is in yours.

Be with Your Audience

In leading adaptive change, you ask people to open their hearts to you and the purposes that you believe you share with them. Demonstrate the same openness to them and their sense of purpose. Don't resent them when you deliver a message that isn't easy for them to hear and their eyes begin to glaze over or they resist. Instead, listen from your heart, take in information beyond what is being said, using as sources of information your own feelings and the nonverbal signals people are giving you.

When you work with a group and begin to experience certain strong emotions, read those emotions as signs that provide a clue to the undercurrents of emotion circulating among others in the group. Your feelings are probably resonating with those of other people. Your anxiety, or euphoria, might well be a rough reflection of theirs.

In addition to hearing your own emotions, listen for signs that there is something else going on in the group beneath what people are saying. Think about what that something else might be. If you are having trouble deciphering it, ask questions to probe beneath the surface of the conversation. "Listening from the Heart in an Automotive Company" shows an example of how this might work in practice.

Listening from the Heart in an Automotive Company

We sat in on a meeting of senior managers at an automobile company in which the managers discussed the merits of a new initiative. On the surface, the conversation seemed analytical and fact based, but there was more negative emotion evident in some people's voices than in others, a slight edge, a little sarcasm.

Afterward, we talked with a vice president and learned that the people questioning the new initiative came from a division that had been on the losing side of several recent disagreements over strategic direction. The engineers in their division had suffered a disproportionate reduction in resources as a result, including positions and financial support for research activities. If the new initiative under discussion were approved, their division would lose even more and the managers would lose credibility with their constituents in the division. These managers could not explicitly talk about their credibility problem, so they focused their comments on the merits and problems of the proposed initiative, albeit with a heightened sense of edgy anxiety.

By noticing that anxiety and teasing out the hidden stakes involved, the executive team was able to develop a strategy that took into account the risks and losses the dissenters and their constituents would have to absorb on their way to developing new engineering capacity for the new initiative. In fact, people in the division began to master new and unfamiliar ways of working in engineering design teams across divisions. By understanding what was fueling the managers' anxiety, the executives promoting the initiative became both more sympathetic and better equipped to support the beleaguered division through its transition.

The art is to listen for the subtext, the song beneath the words, to identify what is really at stake for the others. What is causing the distress you are hearing? What conflicts or contradictions in your group's values or current way of working does this distress represent? What is the history of these contradictions and conflicts? What perspectives do the senior authorities in the group embody, according to the various factions now in conflict? In what ways are the emotions you're sensing mirroring a problem in the larger environment? Leading adaptive change often means distributing gains and losses, and it is the losses that trigger resistance to a change initiative. Losses may take the form of mastering challenging new competencies, disappointing constituents, or even giving up one's status or job. Understanding and acknowledging what those losses will look like is essential for leading adaptive change effectively. Listening from the heart can help you achieve that understanding.

Here are some guidelines for strengthening your ability to listen from the heart.

Listen with Curiosity and Compassion, Beyond Judgment

Listen from your heart with curiosity and compassion, beyond judgment, to understand the sources of people's distress over a proposed initiative. It is not enough to say, "I hear what you are saying," or to repeat it back. Try to "walk in their shoes" to feel something akin to what they are feeling, and then tell them what you have come to understand. At the very least, you have to be able to say with credibility, "I see."

The morning after the 9/11 terrorist attacks, New York City mayor Rudolph Giuliani spoke eloquently and directly to the suffering and fear New Yorkers and all Americans felt that day. As reported in the *New York Times*: "'Today is obviously one of the most difficult days in the history of the city,' he said softly. 'The tragedy that we are undergoing right now is something that we've had nightmares about. My heart goes out to all the innocent victims of this horrible and vicious act of terrorism. And our focus now has to be to save as many lives as possible.'. . . The mayor looked up through his glasses, aware that among the viewers of this live broadcast were the mothers, fathers, spouses, lovers and children of those who labored in the smashed towers. 'The number of casualties,' he said, 'will be more than any of us can bear ultimately.'"[1] During the following weeks, he stood in the streets daily and let city residents know that he felt what they felt. His consistent presence and compassion provided a holding environment for a people in shock and pain. He held his people.

Even though you may not be able literally to feel someone else's suffering or fear, you *can* feel what they are saying in your heart and stomach as well as your head. You can understand what is at stake for them and what is causing their resistance, and that will position you to connect with and move them.

Allow for Silence

Most people we've known who get neutralized in leading adaptive change go down with their mouths open. They get taken out of action because they keep talking beyond the point where key parties are listening. People rarely get taken out because they have spent too much time listening.

How tolerant are you of silence? People differ in how much silence they can stand before they feel compelled to say something. But silence has a purpose. Silence gives people time to absorb what you have just said. When you encounter resistance to a proposed intervention, remind yourself how hard it is for your audience to take in your message because it may be about losses they may have to sustain. Then give them time—five minutes, five days, five weeks, months, or longer—before returning to your message. If you are watching and listening closely, they will send you verbal and nonverbal clues that suggest how much time they need before they are ready to move forward. Resist the urge to take an instant reaction to your message in a meeting as the last word and then feel compelled to provide your last word.

Silence is also useful for holding people's attention, particularly when you are in the authority role. When the dynamics are becoming chaotic in our training workshops, sometimes we stand silently in front of the room at the beginning of a session to focus participants' attention. The chair of a business meeting can often bring people to attention by using silence, for example, when people are first gathering or when the conversation spirals out of hand. Finally, silence can provide *you* time to process what has just happened, to get on the balcony and sort out the political dynamics around the table.

Silence also has content. Silence can contain tension, relief, peace, or curiosity. You can read its content by watching others' body language and eye contact and by simply feeling the mood in the room. Then you can incorporate that data in calibrating your next move.

When leading a large and complex system with multiple parties operating across boundaries, all of whom have a stake in meeting the challenge, but each of whom see it from their own vantage point of interests and loyalties, silence becomes an even more critical resource to read the clues and take the next step. The lag periods change. The clues to decode are more complex. Buying time to listen and taking action experimentally with the next debriefing in mind become critically important orientations for leadership.

When You Are in Authority

Listening from the heart is particularly difficult when you are in a position of authority. Indeed, by the time you rise through the organizational or political system to a higher-level role you have probably been trained to talk more than listen. If you are chairing a working group and you start the meeting by saying, "Here's the adaptive challenge on the table; tell me what you all have to say," people will likely wait for you to speak, perhaps not with silence but by giving superficial answers and waiting to hear your perspective. In our work with top teams, we often sit in on meetings and watch the CEO set the agenda and "invite participation." Typically, the others in the room present a few ideas cautiously, but what they are really trying to do is sense the CEO's position on the issue.

You may feel a lot of pressure to fill that vacuum when there are long silences during a gathering at which you are the authority figure. It is hard to keep sitting with the silence; holding steady is not what the people around you want or expect. You are the one who is supposed to come up with decisive direction, whether you have it or not, and whether or not your answer would help your group tackle the challenge at hand.

ON THE BALCONY

- When people respond to something you say with behaviors that suggest they are in some distress, how do you react? What do you feel? Do you immediately become defensive or dismissive? Do you judge the person, perhaps muttering to yourself something like, "Well, if he cannot step up to the plate on this, we are better off without him"? What steps could you take to set aside a defensive or judgmental reaction and become curious about what the other person is thinking and feeling?

- What do you do when silence descends on a conversation or meeting? Do you respond differently when you are running the meeting than when you are just one of the participants? What are the consequences of your typical behavior?

ON THE PRACTICE FIELD

- Sit facing another person, with your knees just about touching. For five minutes, just look into each other's eyes without saying anything. This may feel like an eternity, but it is helpful for learning to tolerate silence. During the five minutes, notice what is happening inside you. To what are you paying attention? How are you feeling? What are you thinking? At the end of the five minutes, explain your observations to each other.

Speak from the Heart

The ancient Greek philosopher Aristotle described God as the "unmoved mover": Aristotle's deity sets the world in motion and then is often unfazed by human anguish. The modern philosopher Rabbi Abraham Joshua Heschel described God as "the most moved mover": this deity sets the world in motion, then suffers with us. Which image resonates with you more deeply?

In addition to *listening* from the heart (understanding what others are feeling), inspiring people calls for you to *speak* from the heart (expressing what you are feeling). If you care deeply about the challenges facing people, find a way to tell them. You need to be moved yourself at the same time you seek to move others.

Why speak from the heart? It communicates the values at stake, the reasons that make it worthwhile for people to suffer and stay in the game. It sustains them through the ebb and flow of hope and despair that often come when people tackle tough challenges. Your ability to speak from the heart is reflected just as much in the "music" of your voice and your demeanor as it is in the particular words you say. Have you ever been in a meeting where the chairperson kept people from breaking apart or breaking down by maintaining a poised presence and a strong yet calming tone of voice?

Speaking from the heart requires being in touch with your own values, beliefs, and emotions. Yet in your professional life, this may conflict with pressures to be rational—that is, to "be in your head." But when you are leading people through adaptive change, it is their hearts (not their heads) that hold them back. And they will not let you into their hearts if you are not willing to let them into yours.

So when you are leading adaptive change, you need to open up more of yourself than you might usually display in a professional setting. This is often a particularly difficult tightrope for women to walk, since they may worry about being dismissed as "too emotional."

How do you open yourself in this way? Suppose you are about to go into a meeting where you are going to propose a difficult change initiative, and you know you are going to find resistance. Prepare yourself physically and emotionally, by rehearsing what you are going to say, reminding yourself why you are doing what you are doing, and then give yourself a few minutes of silence to clear your head of whatever else is on your mind. Center yourself physically, perhaps by planting your feet to anchor yourself. Once at the meeting, allow yourself to display more emotion about your purposes and your commitment to those purposes than is typical in your organization. Being on the edge of your own comfort zone emotionally may make you feel at risk of being out of control. But putting yourself out there in that way also enables you to engage your listeners' hearts. The following additional suggestions can help.

Hold Yourself and Others Through the Emotion

When you are speaking from the heart, you are allowing yourself to be moved in the service of moving others. But this requires holding yourself and your audience through the emotion. What do we mean by this? Consider the following example: you are giving a toast at your daughter's wedding, and in the middle of it, your eyes well up with tears and your voice breaks. To transform that moment from a simple display of emotion to an inspiration, you need to let yourself be moved while also continuing with your toast. Think of yourself as a pot containing a stew, or a frame containing a painting.

Many people rupture the moment by stopping or holding back and repressing the feeling when they are suddenly overcome with emotion during a presentation. Some even prematurely end the speech and walk offstage or out of the meeting room. The challenge is to allow yourself to be emotional while also seeing your presentation through. By doing this, you let your listeners know that the situation is containable, that *you* can stay with the emotion and that therefore they can, too. You give your audience permission to also be moved by permitting yourself to both feel the emotion and remain poised, even as you might momentarily appear overcome. As we suggested earlier, Rudolph Giuliani illustrated this ability when he spoke so plainly and truly to the tragedy of 9/11. At times, his voice broke with emotion, which, as New Yorkers knew, was uncharacteristic of their tough mayor. Yet he kept speaking despite his emotion. And by so doing, he gave voice to millions of people's experience. That inspired them to find meaning in their despair and sustain hope.

Speak Musically

As infants, we interpret messages from our parents and elder siblings through the tone of their voices and the modulation of sound and silence. One way you can inspire people is to speak musically, attending to a number of aspects of your voice, such as cadence, pitch, volume, and tone.

Consider cadence. When you have something to say that will be difficult for people to hear, pausing gives them time to catch up with you. With short periods of silence, you give people the opportunity to let your message sink in and consider its import. They get the chance to reconnect with the purposes that might make the changes you advocate worth the cost.

Use voice pitch, volume, and tone to speak musically. To communicate with the audience, the orchestra conductor draws on all the instruments, from certain trumpets to sweet violins. Think of your voice in similar terms. Sometimes when you are describing a change effort to people, you will need to use a trumpet to pull people out of the doldrums or communicate the significance of the values that are at stake, using the certainty in your voice to raise the temperature in the room. At other times, such as when tensions are rising to unproductive levels, speaking with the grace of a violin can help lower the temperature and calm people down.

You may tend to use your voice differently when you are in a position of authority than when you are a subordinate or peer. This will be shaped by the culture you live in. In varying ways in different cultures, people in authority tend to speak in a calmer, more dispassionate, and more self-confident way. Moreover, they tend to make statements more than raise questions. Audiences expect this because they look to authority figures to hold them through tough times, sort out problems, and find solutions. And though this way of speaking may be entirely fitting in many circumstances, what should authorities do in adaptive situations when the problem and the solution lie in the hearts, minds, and habits of people spread across the boundaries of an organization or community?

In contrast, when you are not in a position of authority, you may worry that no one is listening to you. Unconsciously, you might turn up the volume, speaking with more urgency or even stridency. Regardless of your degree of authority in any situation, your goal should be to use your voice in a way that makes sense in that situation, to meet the needs of that particular audience, the difficulty at hand, and the vicissitudes of the moment.

When you are the authority figure facing an adaptive situation, you have four basic choices: you can be strong in both your tone and message (the usual default), tentative in both tone and message (rare), tentative in just the tone of your message, or tentative in just the content of your message. We suggest that last one, that you be tentative in only the content of your message. Your challenge is to speak with that authoritative presence people want to see so they can be reassured that what you are asking them to do can be done. But don't just make authoritative pronouncements and assertions, caving in to pressure to reduce the disequilibrium and provide certain answers. Instead, raise questions in a calm, assertive way, authoritatively claiming the challenge and legitimizing the uncertainty inherent in the adaptive process of discovering and implementing new solutions.

When you are leading change without authority, the task is the same, though your challenge will be different. You may find it easy to raise questions without having answers, but resist the urge to become overly strident or urgent (or unduly self-effacing) because you think people are not going to listen to you otherwise. Instead, assume that people *are* going to listen, and imagine that they will be paying attention. People tune out when a speaker starts talking in an overly urgent, anxious tone.

If you are confident that people are going to listen to you, then you will naturally sound confident. And people listen to those who are confident.

Make Each Word Count

In speaking from the heart, make each word count, clearly communicating the one overarching point that you care most about and making one supporting point at a time. However impressive and credible you may sound by making many points at once, people cannot generally absorb rapid-fire arguments.

Making each word count also means understanding and using wisely the different meanings that certain words can have. Value-laden or historically weighted words will touch on many of the sensitivities that need to be engaged if your group hopes to tackle the adaptive challenge at hand, but they can also backfire if you activate these sensitivities unwittingly and don't then follow through artfully. President Bush discovered this shortly after 9/11 when he used the word *crusade* to describe the need to combat terrorism, only to realize quickly that the word dredged up unresolved history and its use played right into the views and strategy of the terrorists themselves. He never publicly used that word again.[2]

Knowing whether you have selected the right word for your intended meaning is a process of trial and error. People tend to choose their words intuitively, based on the meanings a word has for them. But a particular word may have different connotations for different listeners. Discover which words will produce which reactions by saying them and then observing your audience. If you get a strongly negative reaction to a word, it's too easy to say, "They misunderstood me," or "That's not what I intended." In truth, your listeners heard something in your words that resonated with them, even if not with you. Therefore, you might need to use their reactions as a clue that you've unwittingly surfaced important unresolved issues that await resolution and, rather than back off permanently, give proper voice to articulating just those issues. In the example of the word *crusade* used after 9/11, the unresolved history and impact of brutal competition for religious legitimacy and political empire between the Christian and Muslim worlds continues to await proper leadership and resolution.

"King's Heart" provides an example of listening and testing to discover how to make words count.

King's Heart

In 1955, when Martin Luther King Jr. was twenty-six years old, he had just finished his PhD and taken a job as a preacher for a small church in Montgomery, Alabama. He was the new kid on the block in a black community with well-established churches and with highly respected elders among the black clergy. When Rosa Parks set off demonstrations in Montgomery in December that year by refusing to give up her seat to a white person on a bus, many elders in the black community saw her action as too risky. In their calculation, no good could come out of Parks's resistance. But they wanted to support her. So they nominated the newcomer, Martin Luther King Jr., to give the main speech at the first big gathering of people upset about the Parks incident. The elders sat on the sidelines. They thought King was expendable, and if the event did not lead to any collective action, then it would be his credibility on the line, not theirs.

King, however, had spent many years studying oration. He had listened to different kinds of sermons and had learned about the various ways to orchestrate people's emotions. And he had practiced these techniques. On many Sundays, he would listen to a different preacher to understand what made some sermons compelling and others not so. Nevertheless, despite those studies and efforts to practice, when he first arrived in Montgomery, King's speeches had an academic quality that left his audiences unmoved. Indeed, as he was giving his speech that night in December urging the launch of the bus boycott, he had begun to lose his audience. But a turning point came when he came out with the line, "... there comes a time when people get tired of being trampled over by the iron feet of oppression."

When he said that, an immediate and responsive moan went up in the audience. King sensed the energy and knew he had struck a chord. He promptly departed from his prepared and erudite remarks and returned repeatedly to that phrase, "people get tired." He then improvised a string of variations on the word "tired." By the end of that speech, he had forged a powerful emotional connection with black people in Montgomery. And that connection enabled them to embark on a long, hard year of activism that ultimately proved pivotal in the civil rights movement.

ON THE BALCONY

- Videotape yourself giving a speech or leading a team meeting. Watch the tape yourself or with others, and track your tone, volume, emotion, and energy. Try to pinpoint the moments when you seem most engaged and when the audience seems engaged. Identify moments when you and they are not engaged. Brainstorm ways you can improve your ability to speak from the heart.

ON THE PRACTICE FIELD

- Take an acting class or an improvisation workshop. Doing so will enable you to practice experiencing and expressing particular emotions, and sensing and responding to shifts in your audiences' reactions. Let yourself be moved, while still holding your audience as you move them.

CHAPTER 22

Run Experiments

LEADERSHIP IS AN improvisational art. There is no recipe, although some books would like to suggest otherwise by providing five, ten, or twenty do's and don'ts. In the complex, fast-changing world we live in today, any "solution" is just a temporary resting place, a park bench where you can pause and take a breath before getting back into the game.

Everything you do in leading adaptive change is an experiment. Many people, however, choose not to see it that way, feeling and succumbing to the enormous pressure to produce certain results from their actions. Framing everything as an experiment offers you more running room to try new strategies, to ask questions, to discover what's essential, what's expendable, and what innovation can work. In addition, an experimental frame creates permission and therefore some protection when you fail.

When you view leadership as an experiment, you free yourself to see any change initiative as an educated guess, something that you have decided to try but that does not require you to put an immovable stake in the ground. Your intervention is evidence of your commitment to your purposes, but it is not your final word on how to get from here to there. The experimental mind-set opens up the possibility of running several initiatives at the same time to discover which approaches work best. Experiments involve testing hypotheses, looking for contrary data, and making midcourse corrections as you generate new knowledge. Indeed, this was central to Franklin Roosevelt's crisis strategy during his first term in office: multiple overlapping experiments that both reduced panic (because activism spoke even louder than reassuring words) and tested an array of programs to provide economic relief, some of which worked. The lessons learned informed not only his next set of initiatives, but also the economic policy experiments run more than seventy years later by the Obama administration.

When you are at a meeting, practice using an experimental mind-set. Resist chasing after every idea you throw out there, every plan you suggest, or every intervention you make. Do not rush to defend or explain. Present an idea, then stand back and observe what the group does or does not do with it. Avoid harping on your point if you think you have been "misunderstood" or your idea has been criticized or disregarded. Try to understand why your idea went nowhere: was it how you communicated the idea? Your role in the group? Your singing the same song over and over again? And remind yourself that it is not you out there being affirmed or discarded; it is an idea that you put out there for testing.

Another way to adopt an experimental mind-set is to design longer-term experiments, complete with clear objectives, specific timelines, performance measures, systems for collecting data, and structured midcourse evaluations. We work with a financial consulting firm run by actuaries that created just such an elaborate design to experiment with ways of cascading leadership deep into the firm.

Although we suggest you bring an experimental mind-set to work, we are not saying you must always tell everyone that you are running an experiment. Particularly if you are in a senior authority role, people will be looking for answers and clarity. They may be highly uncomfortable with the fact that you are not absolutely certain your initiative will work out well for them, especially if it calls for significant sacrifice on their part. So you may have to calibrate how much of your experimental mind-set you want to share with those you are seeking to lead through adaptive change. You may need to pace the work of distributing the burden of uncertainty. In the fall of 2008, U.S. Treasury Secretary Henry Paulson was clearly running an experiment with the bailout plan to revive the financial sector and prevent a deep recession, tweaking and changing the plan as he collected data to indicate how well it was working; but he found it difficult to stand up and say that it was all an experiment. He felt enormous pressure from Washington professionals and from across the nation to project the confidence that each twist and turn was the right step to take.

If you think people will support an initiative framed as an experiment, call it an experiment. If you think the only way to get people on board is to make them believe your idea will work, you may have to call it a solution, express your confidence in it, but be prepared to explain. You have to manage expectations according to the situation, disabusing people of the certainty they may need at a rate they can absorb. "Navigating a Minefield" offers an example of a situation when expressing confidence in a "solution" may turn out to be the right thing to do.

Here are two rules of thumb as guidelines to determine whether you should frame your intervention as an experiment or a solution:

- *If your organization or community is in a state of emergency and the level of distress has reached overwhelming proportions.* Frame your effort as a *solution* rather than an experiment. But you have to quickly manage the unrealistic expectations you've just reinforced. So as soon as the acute distress abates, start informing people that midcourse corrections will be necessary as results (including possibly unintended outcomes) become apparent. Moreover, use the aftermath of the emergency to help people understand that the acute phase of the crisis was merely a

Navigating a Minefield

In the toughest days of the Korean War, a British battalion was trapped between Chinese and North Korean soldiers coming at them from the north and a minefield to the south. Their commanding officer had been killed. A member of the platoon announced that he "knew how to get out of here" and began to walk through the minefield. As he picked his way through the landscape, the others began to follow. They all survived. When they asked him afterward how he knew how to navigate his way, he admitted that he didn't have the foggiest idea. He acknowledged that they were all very lucky, but also that they would not have followed him unless he appeared to know the way.

symptom of an adaptive challenge. Explain that as the real underlying problem comes into focus, they will need to make additional (and perhaps even more difficult) changes.

- *If your group or organization is not in a state of emergency or overwhelming disequilibrium.* Frame the effort as an *experiment* (for example, a pilot project) from the outset. Except in desperate circumstances, people will be more willing to explore new and untested options when their level of distress is not too high.

Take More Risks

An experimental mind-set will mean taking greater risks than you are used to taking. Suppose that previously you have been willing to take, say, 50–50 risks on behalf of an important purpose. That is, you were just as likely to succeed as to fail. If you changed that ratio to, say, 45–55 risks, where the likelihood of failure was slightly more than the likelihood of success, you would be exercising leadership in situations where you would have held back in the past. Summon up the courage to engage in riskier behavior on behalf of issues you care deeply about. Confront the fear that understandably has been holding you back and test the limits for your tolerance and your concerns about worst-case scenarios. Start wherever you are on the risk-averse spectrum. We do not suggest that you go from 50-50 to 10-90 odds. Just increase your tolerance for a slightly higher level of risk taking than what you have been comfortable with before.

ON THE BALCONY

- List opportunities to exercise leadership that you have recently forgone. Then write down the story you told yourself at the time to explain why you should not take action. If applicable, include in your story the anticipatory dread that stopped you. What kind of fear held you back? Select one of those situations, and consider all that might happen, good and bad, if you were to exercise leadership on it the next time the opportunity arises.

ON THE PRACTICE FIELD

- Break the pattern of how you usually run or participate in your staff meetings. For example, at the start of a meeting, lay out key facts and questions and then fall silent. Let one or two of your colleagues know you are trying something new, and ask them to observe what happens. Debrief with them afterward.

- Start the day in a different way than you usually do: go to the gym, read something inspirational, doodle, make the pancakes that you usually save for the weekend, take a bath instead of a shower, wake up an hour earlier, a half hour later . . . something, anything. See what else happens as a result of taking this small risk with your routine.

- Spend a weekend in an unfamiliar and uncomfortable setting. For example, push your physical boundaries at an Outward Bound workshop, challenge your intolerance of quiet by going on a silent retreat, or defy your reluctance to display your emotions by taking acting lessons. Ride a roller coaster if you have never done so before. You put a myth to rest every time you do something you were sure you could not do. And you strike a blow for turning anticipatory dread "truths" into testable assumptions.

- Look again at the worksheet you filled out in chapter 14, table 14-1.
  This worksheet presents an opportunity for you to experiment by taking more risks. Try this: devise and implement a small experiment to test whether the awful things you imagined would happen if you did not do the column 3 behaviors would actually occur. When Marty first did this exercise (in a different context), his column 3 behaviors included accepting all invitations to go out of town for work. This behavior cut against his expressed desires to spend less time traveling for one-shot engagements, more time at home with family, and more time deepening his relationships with clients. His column 5 fear was that if he turned invitations down, they would stop coming. His consulting practice would shrink, and he would not earn enough money to provide the income he thought he and his family needed to live. So he and his wife devised an experiment. For a year, they put aside a significant sum of money each month in an account they could not access in the short term. They wanted to see whether tightening their

belts would affect the way they lived. After a year, they realized (surprise!) that they hardly noticed the sequestered funds. The experiment liberated Marty to be much more selective in the assignments he accepted and much happier in his work and home life.

Exceed Your Authority

Thoughtfully exceed your authority. The exercise of adaptive leadership is dangerous in part because you always dance on the edge of your scope of authority, at least with respect to some of your authorizers—whether they are your superiors, peers, subordinates, or people outside your organization (see figure 22-1). You push the limits of what others think you ought to be doing. You raise difficult issues that no one wants to discuss, or point out the gaps between people's espoused values and their actual behavior.

The need to go beyond what you are authorized to do, both formally and informally, is what distinguishes adaptive leadership from good management. But it is tricky. Your authorizers may experience you as subversive when you deliberately exceed your authority. But unless you purposefully and carefully dance on the edge of your scope of authority and risk the pushback, you may never move your organization or community forward through adaptive change. As long as your authorizers can keep you in the box they want you to stay in, real, deep

FIGURE 22-1

Going beyond your scope of authority

change will not happen; your authorizers are the architects of the status quo. They want solutions at a minimum cost to them.

Exceeding your scope of authority is difficult in another respect: you can never be certain where the boundary lies. The extent of your authority was probably never articulated in precise terms when you were hired or promoted. Your first sense of encountering a boundary to your authority likely came when you started doing something you thought you were supposed to be doing and someone said, "That's not what you were hired to do."

Sometimes people with the most investment in the status quo will tell you that "you're pushing things too hard" when you are actually well within your scope of authority (point A in the figure). And sometimes people who would like to see you fail (and those who want you to keep shouldering the difficult work for them) will encourage you to keep going when you are so far outside your scope that you are vulnerable to being taken out (point B in the figure). Do not venture all the way out to point B, because it is too easy for others to isolate and neutralize you out there. But you may need to push beyond the boundary at least a bit by challenging norms that inhibit—for example, raising a difficult issue during a meeting or questioning someone else's project. You might need to take action and then ask for forgiveness rather than permission to run the experiment.

The challenge is further complicated because the boundary is not fixed in stone. The only way you know that you are dancing on the edge of your scope of authority is by the degree of resistance you encounter when you make a move. No resistance means that the status quo is holding its own, which in turn suggests that you are not really exercising adaptive leadership. Some resistance suggests that you are on the edge of your scope of authority. And intense resistance indicates that you have moved way beyond the boundary of what people expect you to do.

ON THE BALCONY

- What are you are expected to do in your formal authority role? What informal authorization do you have? That is, what do others in your organization expect from you beyond your formal authority?

- When have you received pushback for moving an idea or initiative forward in your organization? In what ways might advancing that idea have been beyond the scope of your authority?

ON THE PRACTICE FIELD

- Tomorrow, in the office, look for signs of resistance to ideas—whatever form it takes and to whomever it is directed. Try to pursue a new idea or course of action until you get pushback. Resistance often comes packaged in hidden, hard-to-discern ways: a joke, a change of subject, an unusually emotional response. Try to dig deeper into these signals to detect what is really bothering people. Identify which boundary has been approached or breached. Ask yourself what value or interest the resistance was meant to preserve.

Turn Up the Heat

Most people do not aspire to the role of troublemaker. Exercising adaptive leadership more often than you currently do inevitably will expose you to just that charge. That is particularly true when you raise the heat in your organization by focusing people's attention on issues and responsibilities they find troubling and therefore avoid. "What Have You Done with the Real CEO?" provides an example.

At times, turning up the heat is essential for leading adaptive change, even if you are labeled a troublemaker. Adjust the heat in your group or organization and test how far you can push people to stimulate the changes you believe are necessary for progress.

ON THE BALCONY

- What change do you believe would help your organization address an adaptive challenge? With what new behaviors could you experiment that might raise the heat just high enough to get people to focus on the needed change, but not so high that they recoil and retreat?

What Have You Done with the Real CEO?

Frank, the CEO of a global services firm, believed that to adapt to changes in the international marketplace, his company would have to change some of its traditional modes of operating. For a while, the company's culture had been characterized by a high level of autonomy, entrepreneurship, and one-on-one decision making. What Frank had in mind was a more collaborative way of doing business—for example, unit leaders working together to develop joint offerings for clients. When his exhortations to "collaborate more!" got no results, he began modeling (through his own behavior) what he was asking of his managers. For example, he started to raise tough questions at executive team meetings and ask for the opinions of people around the table who had no direct stake in the issue under discussion. He wanted to encourage them to engage with managers in other silos and bring a firmwide perspective to the table.

Whenever Frank displayed these sorts of unfamiliar behaviors, the tension in the room became palpable. At first, he himself felt uncomfortable adjusting his behavior and redefining his role. He had always seen himself (and had been seen by others) as someone particularly skilled at keeping the organizational temperature low. Now he was experimenting with raising the heat, and was gratified to be able to observe changes in the top team's behavior not only toward one another but in their own silos over time.

ON THE PRACTICE FIELD

- Turn the heat up on an issue without making yourself the issue. Work avoidance often manifests itself as turning the messenger into the subject and thereby deflecting attention from the tough issue. Frame your heat-raising interventions as a collective issue. Use disclaimers before your intervention like "I know this is an issue for all of us . . ." "Given the purpose of this meeting . . ." "This team is committed to the values of ___. So how do we address . . ." Watch what techniques help the group focus on the message rather than you.

Name Your Piece of the Mess

Identify your contribution to the difficulty your organization has in doing its adaptive work and acknowledge it to others. Demonstrate that you take responsibility for your piece of the mess, that you are willing to make tough sacrifices, just as you are asking them to do.

For example, a CEO who takes a significant pay cut when asking employees to forgo some benefits they thought were secure is much more likely to have a receptive hearing for his proposed changes. Compare that with what happened at US Airways when it faced bankruptcy in 2004. The new chief executive, Bruce Lakefield, tried to negotiate significant pay cuts with airline staff across the board. But according to his spokesperson, he felt he should not have had to take a cut in his multimillion-dollar package, because his salary was already in the range of what executives at low-fare airlines received. Not surprisingly, resistance to his initiatives stiffened after that explanation.[1] Of course, the recent wave of effort that began in 2008 to restructure and renew the American automobile industry has provided important opportunities for senior executives, politicians, and union officials to regain credibility by taking responsibility for their mistakes.

You send a powerful message that you are in the same game with the people you are trying to move when you name your piece of the mess and make painful sacrifices yourself. You show that you are willing to do something that is hard for you on behalf of something you believe in, just as you are asking them to do. And you vastly boost your chances of winning support for the interventions you are proposing.

ON THE BALCONY

- Think of an adaptive challenge your organization or community is confronting. What is your part in the problem at hand? What are you doing or not doing that is getting in the way? What actions could you take to show others that you accept your role in the challenge and that you are willing to make hard changes yourself?

ON THE PRACTICE FIELD

- The next time you are describing changes you believe people in your organization should make, balance discussion of the good things that will come from those changes with acknowledgment of the painful things. Specify the sacrifices you are ready to make personally. Then actually make them (not just talk about them). Notice whether there seems to be more or less resistance to your proposed changes from others in your organization.

Display Your Own Incompetence

You may have risen in the ranks in part because you can solve people's problems and provide answers. People who give you authority, formal and informal, from whatever direction, do not want you to display your ignorance or incompetence. But no one learns anything by repressing their ignorance or incompetence. And when people in an organization do not push past the frontier of their competence, they do not learn what it will take to resolve the adaptive challenges facing them.

You need to make the first move to foster a culture of learning. You can do this by experimenting with displaying your own incompetence. Acknowledge what you do not know, or explicitly try on a new role where everyone knows you are new to that effort. By doing this, you let people know you are willing to do whatever it takes to master the new skills needed to tackle your organization's thorniest challenges. And you inspire them to adopt the same openness and courage to push the frontier.

ON THE BALCONY

- Think of a change initiative you are seeking to lead. List your competencies and incompetencies related to this intervention. Pick an incompetence about which you feel especially uncomfortable. Brainstorm ways you could display this incompetence at work.

ON THE PRACTICE FIELD

- Play with trying something you are not good at doing the next time you call your team together for a meeting. Be candid about the fact that you are incompetent at this thing you are trying. Say something like, "I'm new at this, but I'm going to have some fun trying it out." You and your team members will be better able to see you as someone who tries new things. If it does not work out, acknowledge that and then try something else for which you are no expert.

CHAPTER 23

Thrive

TAKE CARE OF YOURSELF rather than work to exhaustion. All the predictable consequences of burnout can result from poorly deploying your passionate commitments: bad judgments, losing connections with family, and your health. Take care of yourself not as an indulgence, but to help ensure that the purposes you join have the best chance of being achieved, and that you are still around to enjoy the fruits of your labors. Below, we offer several practices for thriving while leading adaptive change.

Grow Your Personal Support Network

You do not have to go it alone, and you should not. Without moral support and counsel from others, you become vulnerable to your own weaknesses and to opponents who are challenged by your perspective. Resilience comes not only from your inner "shock absorbers," but also from sustaining relationships.

Cultivate a personal support network outside of the system you are trying to change. You can do this in three ways:

- Talk regularly with confidants, people outside the environment in which you are trying to lead adaptive change, who are invested in you, not the issues you are addressing

- Satisfy your hungers outside of work so your opponents cannot use them to take you out of the game

- Anchor yourself in multiple communities

Finding Confidants

Leading adaptive change is a long process. You need confidants who will remind you why you are throwing your energy at an ongoing effort and who bear the emotional weight with you so you do not feel like Sisyphus, pushing the boulder relentlessly up a hill yourself.

Confidants can take the form of close friends, family members, consultants, coaches, or therapists. They help you distinguish your role from yourself and tell you when you are falling into a default mode of operating that will not help advance your purposes. They can also help you overcome some of those hard-to-manage, hard-to-master hungers. For example, a supportive spouse or partner can provide intimacy and delight, friends can make you feel relevant and important, and a good coach can help you learn to gain more control over your life.

If they are going to be most valuable to you, your confidants need to affirm what you are doing well and point out the ways in which your triggers are getting you in trouble. If you are working with a new consultant or a new coach, you may have to tell her which of your hungers put you most at risk.

Of course, it is not so easy to expose your vulnerability, even to a trusted adviser. For example, it would be difficult to say something like, "Listen, I really love being smart, you know. And it is getting me in trouble, because people expect me to always be the one to have the answers. But I'm making mistakes. I'm overselling certainty."

Share your vulnerability with your confidants to get the most useful support from them, difficult as that may be for you. This is essential. You might test the waters by sharing one or two smaller vulnerabilities or uncertainties and then go further.

Satisfying Your Hungers Outside Work

If you satisfy your hungers in your private life, you will not be as likely to act them out in your organization. If you yearn to be liked, for example, you will be more likely to back down from an aggressive opponent, unless you have other reasons to do so. We all have natural hungers for love, intimacy, importance, and affirmation. The stresses of leading tend to amplify these hungers, though in different ways for different people. Knowing your own vulnerability and then taking care of yourself can keep you content and out of trouble. Having family, loved ones, friends, and support systems from your community (from 12-step programs to bicycle clubs) can aid you in staying purposeful and productive on days when you feel like you're walking on a high wire. You need to be prepared to lean on the right people when the going gets tough. With your hungers satisfied and under control, you can focus on the work at hand when you go into the office, rather than look around for other sources of warmth, recognition, or praise.

Anchoring Yourself in Multiple Communities

Leading an adaptive change effort will take everything you are willing to give it, all your time, energy, attention, and care. The environment you are immersed in will not set the boundaries for you. Anchor yourself in a number of communities outside of your organization, such as family life, sports, hobbies, civic organizations, and spiritual communities to keep the effort from consuming you. Getting involved in these communities brings an additional benefit as well: you gain multiple insights and skills that you can bring to the adaptive work of your organization. If you have learned how to inspire and be inspired from your volunteer work in your community, you can draw on that same ability to inspire those in your work environment.

ON THE BALCONY

- List the confidants in your life. Next to each name, write down how they can be most helpful to you as you seek to lead a particular set of interventions at work. Commit to talking regularly with each of them so you can draw on their insights and emotional support.

- For each hunger (affirmation and importance, power and control, intimacy and delight), rate the extent to which that hunger is being fulfilled (1 means somewhat fulfilled; 5 means very fulfilled). Decide what you might do to fulfill that hunger even more. For example, if your relationship with your spouse is providing some intimacy but not enough to give you what you more fully need, could you establish a weekly dinner out to enhance the intimacy between you, plan better and regular holidays, or do projects and workshops together? How might you rekindle the sparks?

- In what community activities could you get involved that might help prevent your leadership work from consuming you? List them, and document steps you could take now to get involved.

ON THE PRACTICE FIELD

- Have several confidants so your partner/spouse or best friend does not have to carry the entire burden of providing you with moral support and advice. But potential confidants rarely show up just because you need them. You have to proactively recruit and train them. Identify two or three people outside your work setting who you think would make good confidants. Ask each to be your confidant to call a few times a year. Tell each one the challenges on which you are working and the kind of support or insights you might need.

- Look again at your On the Balcony list of ideas for having confidants to better fulfill your hungers. Pick the ideas you think would be most effective. Put them into action now.

- During the next two months, get involved in the communities you identified in the above On the Balcony reflection. Notice whether you feel less discouraged, less exhausted, less consumed in your work setting. Look for skills you can transfer from one or more of these outside communities to your leadership efforts in your work setting.

Create a Personal Holding Environment

Your body is essential. You need stamina, and for the practice of leadership, you need to be in close enough touch with your body so that you can read yourself for clues to the emotional undercurrents in the system in which you are taking action. You cannot use yourself as a mirror for the dynamics in the system if you are not in tune with your body. When you are in the midst of a leadership initiative, you are taking on additional stress. Consumed with your purposes, you can easily forget to take care of yourself at the very moment when it is particularly important to do so. We do not need to repeat all the helpful research and advice that is out there in bookstores and healthcare offices about the impact of adequate sleep, regular exercise, and a healthy diet on your performance. But we do want to emphasize that adaptive leadership stresses you as much as adaptive change stresses everyone involved in the system.

You need robust strength to lead. You may not feel the stress in the midst of action as your adrenaline and corticosteroids pump you up, but the impact, however hidden, is happening. During those times, what may seem like expendable luxuries of self-care—like going on regular walks, workouts, or dates—are in fact essential. You owe them to yourself, and to the purposes for which you are trying to lead.

Create Sanctuaries

Do you regularly cordon off some space and time to reflect on what has happened over the past few days and prepare yourself for what lies ahead?

Sanctuaries can be anything that works for you: a couple of hours on a Sunday night to set priorities for the week, a long walk every Friday at lunchtime to clear your head and transition into the weekend, a half hour of meditation every morning, or a house in which to worship with your community on your Sabbath. If you do not create such sanctuaries for yourself, you further risk being consumed by the stresses of leading adaptive change.

A sanctuary provides the opportunity for you to get away from conflict and recalibrate your own internal responses. It enables you to move through your reactive triggers, quiet your hungers, and reflect on events rather than be dominated by them. For example, if you tend to be a provocateur in your organization, you might take this time to ask yourself, "Am I pushing too hard? Am I at risk of grinding people into the ground, including myself? Do I fully appreciate the sacrifices I'm asking people to make?" A sanctuary can help you move up on the balcony to regain your perspective on the role you are playing, and revive your belief that, despite the setbacks, your efforts may indeed bear fruit in the long run.

Sanctuaries not only help you process your professional challenges, they enable you to restore yourself. Perhaps you have a spiritual side, or perhaps you have a poetic or aesthetic sensibility from which you reliably rediscover meaning in your life. Whatever you might call it, keeping that side of yourself alive gives you the means to anchor yourself despite the inevitable frustrations and disappointments that come with the territory of pushing for change.

Sanctuaries are spaces (physical or mental) where you can hear yourself think, recover yourself from your work, and feel the quieter inclinations of your spirit.

ON THE BALCONY

- What changes in your sleep, diet, and exercise habits would generate the biggest, fastest improvements in your mental and physical health? These changes may be as simple as setting your bedtime a half hour earlier than usual, adding one vegetable and one fruit to your daily food intake, or increasing the number of days you exercise to four instead of three.

- Have you created sanctuaries for yourself? If so, what are they? How helpful are they? If you do not currently have sanctuaries (or if the ones you have created are not all that helpful), what steps could you take to improve the situation? Again, think in terms of small, manageable steps. For example, could you carve out ten minutes every morning to meditate before you leave the house for work? Could you take a ten-minute walk after an upsetting meeting or a demanding project, to clear your head and calm yourself?

ON THE PRACTICE FIELD

- Put into practice the small changes you identified in the On the Balcony reflection above. Consider talking with your confidants about which of these changes might be most useful for you. Notice what happens after you have begun implementing those changes. Do you feel more or less tired? What about your ability to focus? What happens to your level of optimism or hopefulness? If the small changes you have implemented generate positive results, step things up a bit by making some more.

Renew Yourself

Our aspiration for you goes beyond your survival, important as that is. We want you to *thrive*. Thriving is much more than survival; thriving means growing and prospering in new and challenging environments.

To thrive you need resilience (shock absorbers to remain steady over the bumps of the journey), robust strength (health and stamina), and renewal. Renewal is an active process of removing the plaque of tough experiences and scars from the journey and returning to the core of your values and being. Renewal requires transformation of the heart and guts as well as the head. That explains why so much of this book focuses on the inside work of leadership, both in how you use yourself and in how you mobilize others.

How do you renew yourself to thrive in a rapidly changing environment? We have three final thoughts.

Have a Balanced Portfolio

Invest your need for meaning in your life in more than one place. Have what the investment advisers call a balanced portfolio. Shakespeare's King Lear learned too late that he needed to find meaning and develop skill in his role as a father as well as his role as a king. Look for meaning in multiple places in both your personal and your professional life. Find it in your community life and in the care you take to exercise your mind and body to keep them both functioning at a high level as you grow older. Find it in the friendships that sustain you at difficult moments and provide a means to share and amplify your life's joys. Narrowing your life's meaning to a single sphere, whether it is your work or home or civic or religious life, makes you vulnerable when there are major shifts in the environment in which you are solely invested.

Find Satisfaction Daily and Locally

Don't get lost in the grandiosity of your dreams. There is tension between the grand visionary expeditions that touch your heart and the tangible small transformations you have the opportunity to make every day. Pay attention to what you are doing to improve the lives of people within your personal reach. You cannot measure the meaning of turning on the lights behind one child's eyes.

It will take more than a lifetime to achieve your highest and most noble aspirations for your community, your organization, and the world. Yet, you can accomplish something in the right direction every day, in the micro-interactions between you and the people who work with you, in the empathy you display for that telephone solicitor who interrupts your dinner but is just trying to make a living and feed a family, in the way you model in front of your children the values you espouse to and for them (for example by commending the cab driver who risks your ire when, just as you are trying to get to the airport quickly, stops to help a confused family that has pulled over to the side of the road and is frantically looking at maps).

From that vantage point, you can see the impact of what you do and be renewed to the present moment and its meaning, and thereby thrive in the locality of your day.

Some years ago, Ron and his family suffered a serious fire in their house. The fire department responded quickly and effectively, controlling the fire and preventing it from destroying everything they owned and from spreading to neighboring houses. As he and Sousan, his wife at the time, stood looking at what had been their home and began to assess their losses, Sousan began to sob uncontrollably. A fireman who had finished his part of the job walked over and tried to console her. She told him that her six-year-old daughter's pet parakeet was still in the house. He asked her its name, what room it was in, and where the cage stood in the room. When he got the information, he turned to the house, still ablaze and full of smoke, and went inside to rescue the parakeet.

Be Coolly Realistic and Unwaveringly Optimistic

Practice both optimism and realism. Some people would have you choose one or the other. Believing in one or both is a choice. By holding on to them both, by being unwaveringly optimistic and coolly realistic at the same time, you keep that optimism from floating off into naïveté and the realism from devolving into cynicism.

We have tried to model being optimistic and realistic in our leadership development work and in this field book. We have been moved time and time again in our work by groups and individuals who are able to retain their optimism in the journey despite frustration and setbacks. How do they keep optimism alive? First, they take time to renew their faith that things do not have to be the way they are. They find ways to be reminded that, though they live in a complex environment with rich histories and pressures, different and better is possible. They do not have to settle. Second, they maintain the self-discipline to reflect on their efforts, when they work out and when they do not, as they engage. They expect to make mistakes and they give themselves permission to keep learning in action. And third, they stay alive to the opportunity to contribute—to add value to the lives of other people— every day. The best of them keep finding ways to give and love right up to their last days when people around them learn from them how to bless one another and say good-bye.

By providing you with practical hands-on tools and techniques we have seen be effective, some complex and some very simple, we have tried in this book to honor the perspiration, discipline, and commitment it takes to live with purpose and possibility. This book has been inspired by our watching others make a difference in this world. We feel privileged and blessed to interact with so many people who risk and practice leadership every day on behalf of causes, products, innovations, injustices, organizations, countries, and communities.

Acts of leadership are sacred, and every one may count. The world would be a better place if we all, including us, practiced leadership a bit more of our time.

NOTES

Chapter 1

1. Ronald A. Heifetz, *Leadership Without Easy Answers* (Cambridge, MA: Belknap Press of Harvard University Press, 1994); and Ronald A. Heifetz and Marty Linsky, *Leadership on the Line: Staying Alive Through the Dangers of Leading* (Boston: Harvard Business School Press, 2002).

Chapter 2

1. Ronald A. Heifetz, *Leadership Without Easy Answers* (Cambridge, MA: Belknap Press of Harvard University Press, 1994); and Ronald A. Heifetz and Marty Linsky, *Leadership on the Line: Staying Alive Through the Dangers of Leading* (Boston: Harvard Business School Press, 2002).

2. Sharon Daloz Parks, *Leadership* Can *Be Taught* (Boston: Harvard Business School Press, 2005); and Dean Williams, *Real Leadership* (San Francisco: Berrett-Koehler, 2005).

3. Richard Foster and Sarah Kaplan, *Creative Destruction: Why Companies That Are Built to Last Underperform the Market—and How to Successfully Transform Them* (New York: Doubleday Business, 2001); Donald L. Laurie, *The Real Work of Leaders* (Cambridge, MA: Perseus, 2000); Gary De Carolis, *A View from the Balcony* (Dallas: Brown Books, 2005); Stacie Goffin and Valora Washington, *Ready or Not* (New York: Teachers College Press, 2007); Shifra Bronznick, Didi Goldenhar, and Marty Linsky, *Leveling the Playing Field* (New York: Advancing Women Professionals and the Jewish Community, 2008); and Kevin G. Ford, *Transforming Church: Bringing Out the Good to Get to Great* (Colorado Springs, CO: David C. Cook, 2008).

4. Bill Russell and Taylor Branch, *Second Wind: The Memoirs of an Opinionated Man* (New York: Random House, 1979).

5. See *The Complete Newspeak Dictionary* from George Orwell's *1984*, http://www.newspeakdictionary.com.

Chapter 3

1. David Brudnoy, *Life Is Not a Rehearsal: A Memoir* (New York: Doubleday, 1997).

Chapter 4

1. John Gardner, "The Tasks of Leadership." *Leadership Papers/2* (Washington DC: Independent Sector, 1986).

Chapter 5

1. Chris Argyris, *Knowledge for Action* (San Francisco: Jossey-Bass, 1993).
2. J. O. Hertzler, "Crises and Dictatorships," *American Sociological Review* 5 (1940): 157–169.

Chapter 6

1. Elliot Richardson, *Reflections of a Radical Moderate* (New York: Pantheon Books, 1996).

Chapter 7

1. See Ronald Heifetz and Donald Laurie, "The Work of Leadership," *Harvard Business Review*, OnPoint edition, December 2001.

Chapter 10

1. Donald H. Rumsfeld, "One Surge Does Not Fit All," *New York Times*, November 22, 2008.
2. Personal communication to Ronald Heifetz by a major in the U.S. Army Special Forces stationed in Iraq.
3. Jan Carlzon, *Moments of Truth* (Cambridge, MA: Ballinger Publishing, 1987).

Chapter 11

1. See, among many others, Donald Winnicott, *The Maturational Process* (New York: International Universities Press, 1965).
2. Ronald A. Heifetz, *Leadership Without Easy Answers* (Cambridge, MA: Belknap Press of Harvard University Press, 1994).

Chapter 14

1. Robert Kegan and Lisa Laskow Lahey, *How the Way We Talk Can Change the Way We Work* (Hoboken, NJ: Wiley, 2000).

Chapter 15

1. See Richard E. Neustadt and Ernest R. May, *Thinking in Time: The Uses of History for Decision-Makers* (New York: Free Press, 1986), 88.

2. Richard A. Clarke, *Against All Enemies: Inside America's War on Terror* (New York: Free Press, 2004).

3. Ronald A. Heifetz and Marty Linsky, *Leadership on the Line: Staying Alive Through the Dangers of Leading* (Boston: Harvard Business School Press, 2002).

Chapter 19

1. Robert A. Caro, *The Power Broker: Robert Moses and the Fall of New York* (New York: Knopf, 1974).

2. From John P. Kotter, *Matsushita Leadership* (NewYork: The Free Press, 1997), 111.

Chapter 20

1. Roger Rosenblatt, *Rules for Aging: Resist Normal Impulses, Live Longer, Attain Perfection* (New York: Harcourt, 2000).

2. Personal communication by Alexander Grashow with Mark Grashow.

Chapter 21

1. Michael Powell, "In 9/11 Chaos, Giuliani Forged a Lasting Image," *New York Times*, September 21, 2007.

2. Ron Suskind, "Faith, Certainty and the Presidency of George W. Bush," *New York Times Magazine*, October 17, 2004; "Powell Slips, 'Crusade' Re-Enters US Lexicon on War," *Agence France Presse*, March 23, 2004.

Chapter 22

1. Micheline Maynard, "US Airways to Cut 10% of Management Jobs," *New York Times*, October 5, 2004.

| GLOSSARY |

The definitions in this glossary have been developed and refined over twenty-five years, primarily by Riley Sinder, Dean Williams, and the authors. They are not definitive statements. They are meant to be useful, first-approximation concepts that serve as a resource for thinking more deeply and broadly about the subject and practice of leadership.

act politically   Incorporate the loyalties and values of the other parties into your mobilization strategy. Assume that no one operates solely as an individual but represents, formally or informally, a set of constituent loyalties, expectations, and pressures.

adaptation   A successful adaptation enables an organism to thrive in a new or challenging environment. The adaptive process is both conservative and progressive in that it enables the living system to take the best from its traditions, identity, and history into the future. See also **thrive**.

adaptive capacity   The resilience of people and the capacity of systems to engage in problem-defining and problem-solving work in the midst of adaptive pressures and the resulting disequilibrium.

adaptive challenge   The gap between the values people stand for (that constitute thriving) and the reality that they face (their current lack of capacity to realize those values in their environment). See also **technical problem**.

adaptive culture   Adaptive cultures engage in at least five practices. They (1) name the elephants in the room, (2) share responsibility for the organization's future, (3) exercise independent judgment, (4) develop leadership capacity, and (5) institutionalize reflection and continuous learning.

adaptive leadership   The activity of mobilizing adaptive work.

adaptive work   Holding people through a sustained period of disequilibrium during which they identify what cultural DNA to conserve and discard, and invent or discover the new cultural DNA that will enable them to thrive anew; i.e., the learning process through which people in a system achieve a successful adaptation. See also **technical work**.

ally   A member of the community in alignment on a particular issue.

ancestor   A family or community member from an earlier generation who shapes a person's identity.

assassination   The killing or neutralizing (through character assassination) of someone who embodies a perspective that another faction in the social system desperately wants to silence.

attention   A critical resource for leadership. To make progress on adaptive challenges, those who lead must be able to hold people's engagement with hard questions through a sustained period of disequilibrium.

authority   Formal or informal power within a system, entrusted by one party to another in exchange for a service. The basic services, or social functions, provided by authorities are: (1) direction; (2) protection; and (3) order. See also **formal authority** and **informal authority**.

bandwidth   The range of capacities within which an individual has gained comfort and skill. See also **repertoire**.

below the neck   The nonintellectual human faculties: emotional, spiritual, instinctive, kinetic.

carrying water   Doing the work of others that they should be doing for themselves.

casualty   A person, competency, or role that is lost as a by-product of adaptive change.

classic error   Treating an adaptive challenge as a technical problem.

confidant   A person invested in the success and happiness of another person, rather than in the other person's perspective or agenda.

courageous conversation   A dialogue designed to resolve competing priorities and beliefs while preserving relationships. See also **orchestrating the conflict**.

dance floor   Where the action is. Where the friction, noise, tension, and systemic activity are occurring. Ultimately, the place where the work gets done.

dancing on the edge of your scope of authority   Taking action near or beyond the formal or informal limits of what you are expected to do.

default   A routine and habitual response to recurring stimuli. See also **tuning**.

deploying yourself   Deliberately managing your roles, skills, and identity.

disequilibrium   The absence of a steady state, typically characterized in a social system by increasing levels of urgency, conflict, dissonance, and tension generated by adaptive challenges.

elephant in the room   A difficult issue that is commonly known to exist in an organization or community but is not discussed openly. See also **naming the elephant in the room**.

engaging above and below the neck   Connecting with all the dimensions of the people you lead. Also, bringing all of yourself to the practice of leadership. *Above the neck* speaks to intellectual faculties, the home of logic and facts; *below the neck* speaks to emotional faculties, the home of values, beliefs, habits of behavior, and patterns of reaction. See also **below the neck**.

experimental mind-set   An attitude that treats any approach to an adaptive issue not as a solution, but as the beginning of an iterative process of testing a hypothesis, observing what happens, learning, making midcourse corrections, and then, if necessary, trying something else.

faction   A group with (1) a shared perspective that has been shaped by tradition, power relationships, loyalties, and interests and (2) its own grammar for analyzing a situation and its own system of internal logic that defines the stakes, terms of problems, and solutions in ways that make sense to its own members.

faction map   A diagram that depicts the groups relevant to an adaptive challenge, and includes the loyalties, values, and losses at risk that keep each faction invested in its position.

finding your voice   The process of discovering how to best use yourself as an instrument to frame issues effectively, shape and tell stories purposefully, and inspire others.

formal authority   Explicit power granted to meet an explicit set of service expectations, such as those in job descriptions or legislative mandates.

getting on the balcony   Taking a distanced view. The mental act of disengaging from the dance floor, the current swirl of activity, in order to observe and gain perspective on yourself and on the larger system. Enables you to see patterns that are not visible from the ground. See also **observation**.

giving the work back   The action of an authority figure in resisting the pressure to take the responsibility for solving problems off of other people's shoulders, and instead mobilizing the responsibility of the primary stakeholders in doing their share of the adaptive work.

holding environment   The cohesive properties of a relationship or social system that serve to keep people engaged with one another in spite of the divisive forces generated by adaptive work. May include, for example, bonds of affiliation and love; agreed-upon rules, procedures, and norms; shared purposes and common values; traditions, language, and rituals; familiarity with adaptive work; and trust in authority. Holding environments give a group identity and contain the conflict, chaos, and confusion often produced when struggling with complex problematic realities. See also **pressure cooker** and **resilience**.

holding steady   Withholding your perspective, not primarily for self-protecting, but to wait for the right moment to act, or act again. Also, remaining steadfast, tolerating the heat and pushback of people who resist dealing with the issue.

hunger   A normal human need that each person seeks to fulfill, such as (1) power and control, (2) affirmation and importance, and (3) intimacy and delight.

illusion of the broken system   Every group of human beings is aligned to achieve the results it currently gets. The current reality is the product of the implicit and explicit decisions of people in the system, at least of the dominant stakeholders. In that sense, no system is broken, although change processes are often driven by the idea that an organization is broken. That view discounts the accumulated functionality for many people of the system's current way of operating.

informal authority   Power granted implicitly to meet a set of service expectations, such as representing cultural norms like civility or being given moral authority to champion the aspirations of a movement.

interpretation   Identifying patterns of behavior that help make sense of a situation. Interpretation is the process of explaining raw data through digestible understandings and narratives. Most situations have multiple possible interpretations.

intervention   Any series of actions or a particular action, including intentional inaction, aimed at mobilizing progress on adaptive challenges.

leadership with authority   Mobilizing people to address an adaptive challenge from a position of authority. The authority role brings with it resources and constraints for exercising leadership.

leadership without authority   Mobilizing people to address an adaptive challenge by taking action beyond the formal and informal expectations that define your scope of power, such as raising unexpected questions upward from the middle of the organization, challenging the expectations of your constituents, or engaging people across boundaries from outside the organization. Lacking authority also brings with it resources and constraints.

leap to action   The default behavior of reacting prematurely to disequilibrium with a habituated set of responses.

lightning rod   A person who is the recipient of a group's anger or frustration, often expressed as a personal attack and typically intended to deflect attention from a disturbing issue and displace responsibility for it to someone else.

living into the disequilibrium   The gradual process of easing people into an uncomfortable state of uncertainty, disorder, conflict, or chaos at a pace and level that does not overwhelm them yet takes them out of their comfort zones and mobilizes them to engage in addressing an adaptive challenge.

naming the elephant in the room   The act of addressing an issue that may be central to making progress on an adaptive challenge but that has been ignored in the interest of maintaining equilibrium. Discussing the undiscussable. See also **elephant in the room**.

observation   Collection of relevant data from a detached perspective and from as many sources as possible. See also **getting on the balcony**.

opposition   Those parties or factions that feel threatened or at risk of loss if your perspective is accepted.

orchestrating the conflict   Designing and leading the process of getting parties with differences to work them through productively, as distinguished from resolving the differences for them. See also **courageous conversation**.

pacing the work   Gauging how much disturbance the social system can withstand and then breaking down a complex challenge into small elements, sequencing them at a rate that people can absorb.

partners   Individuals or factions that are collaborators, including allies and confidants. See also **ally**, **confidant**, and the distinction between the two.

personal leadership work   Learning about and managing yourself to be more effective in mobilizing adaptive work.

pressure cooker   A holding environment strong enough to contain the disequilibrium of adaptive processes. See also **holding environment** and **resilience**.

productive zone of disequilibrium   The optimal range of distress within which the urgency in the system motivates people to engage in adaptive work. If the level is too low, people will be inclined to complacently maintain their current way of working, but if it is too high, people are likely to be overwhelmed and may start to panic or engage in severe forms of work avoidance, like scapegoating or assassination. See also **work avoidance**.

progress   The development of new capacity that enables the social system to thrive in new and challenging environments. The process of social and political learning that leads to improvement in the condition of the group, community, organization, nation, or world. See also **thrive**.

purpose   The overarching sense of direction and contribution that provides meaningful orientation to a set of activities in organizational and political life.

reality testing   The process of comparing data and interpretations of a situation to discern which one, or which new synthesis of competing interpretations, captures the most information and best explains the situation.

regulating the heat   Raising or lowering the distress in the system to stay within the productive zone of disequilibrium.

repertoire   The range of capacities within which an individual has gained comfort and skill. See also **bandwidth**.

resilience   The capacity of individuals and the holding environment to contain disequilibrium over time. See also **holding environment** and **pressure cooker**.

ripeness of an issue   The readiness of a dominant coalition of stakeholders to tackle an issue because of a generalized sense of urgency across stakeholding groups.

ritual   A practice with symbolic import that helps to create a shared sense of community.

role   The set of expectations in a social system that define the services individuals or groups are supposed to provide.

sanctuary   A place or set of practices for personal renewal.

scope of authority   The set of services for which a person is entrusted by others with circumscribed power.

social system   Any collective enterprise (small group, organization, network of organizations, nation, or the world) with shared challenges that has interdependent and therefore interactive dynamics and features.

song beneath the words   The underlying meaning or unspoken subtext in someone's comment, often identified by body language, tone, intensity of voice, and the choice of language.

taking the temperature   Assessing the level of disequilibrium currently in the system.

technical problem   Problems that can be diagnosed and solved, generally within a short time frame, by applying established know-how and procedures. Technical problems are amenable to authoritative expertise and management of routine processes.

technical work   Problem defining and problem solving that effectively mobilizes, coordinates, and applies currently sufficient expertise, processes, and cultural norms.

thrive   To live up to people's highest values. Requires adaptive responses that distinguish what's essential from what's expendable, and innovates so that the social system can bring the best of its past into the future.

tuning   An individual's personal psychology, including the set of loyalties, values, and perspectives that have shaped his worldview and identity, and cause the individual to resonate consciously and unconsciously, productively and unproductively, to external stimuli. See also **default**.

work avoidance   The conscious or unconscious patterns in a social system that distract people's attention or displace responsibility in order to restore social equilibrium at the cost of progress in meeting an adaptive challenge.

abstract purposes, 223, 224
accountability, modeling, 192
acting politically, 133–148. *See also*
    political landscape
  balcony perspective of, 135–136
  connection to opposition,
    138–142, 147
  in establishing holding
    environment, 159
  expanding informal authority,
    133–136
  finding allies, 136–138, 147
  managing senior authorities,
    142–144, 147
  practice field actions for, 136, 146
  protecting dissent, 145–146
  responsibility for casualties,
    144–145, 148
  worksheet, 147–148
action(s), 6
  in adaptive culture, 175
  corrective, tough decisions and, 257
  inaction, 110–111, 150
  micro-interactions, importance
    of, 296
  pressure for (*see* pressure for
    action)
  resisting, diagnosis and, 44–45
  words-action gaps, 248–249
adaptability
  constrained by defaults, 64
  organizational culture and,
    60, 61, 62–63
adaptability survey, 108
adaptive capacity, 10–11

adaptive challenge(s)
  adaptive capacity and, 10–11
  compensation structure, 55
  conflict as aspect of, 114, 115
  cycle of failure in, 71–73
  distinguishing from technical
    problems, 19–23, 118
  of globalization, 21–22
  intensity of disequilibrium in, 30, 31
  personalizing, 192–194
  shifts in interpretation
    and, 114–116
  stake in, 91
  unique characteristics of, 52–53
adaptive challenge archetypes, 77–87
  balcony perspective of, 80, 81,
    82–83, 86
  competing commitments, 80–82
  practice field actions for, 80, 81–82,
    83, 84
  unspeakable issues, 82–84
  values-behavior gap, 78–80
  work avoidance as, 84–87
adaptive challenge diagnosis, 69–87
  archetypes in, 77–87
  balcony perspective of, 72–73, 76,
    77, 80
  diagnostic framework, 74–76
  human elements of, 69–70
  informal authority and, 76–77
  practice field actions for 73, 76,
    77, 80
  reality testing in, 74–75
  technical versus adaptive
    elements, 70–76

adaptive change
  foundations of, 15
  hidden alliances and, 97–100
  leading, 9, 10
  preparing stakeholders for, 94–95
  responsibility for, 161–164
  risk of loss in, 96–97
  role of loss in, 16
  techniques for, 164, 205–208
  time frames for, 16–17
adaptive culture, building, 165–175.
    See also cultural norms;
    organizational culture
  acknowledging disequilibrium,
    146, 166–168
  balcony perspective of, 170
  distinguishing characteristics, 165
  encouraging independent
    judgment, 169–170
  encouraging reflection in, 171–172
  experimentation in, 172–173, 175
  fostering action in, 175
  leadership development in, 170–171
  nurturing shared responsibility,
    168–169
  practice field actions for, 170
  practices of, 171–175
  rewards for risk taking in, 174
  sending correct signals in, 173–174
adaptive leadership. *See also*
    leadership
  dangers of, 26–27
  defined, 14
  experimental mind-set and, 36–37
  finding partners in, 41–42
  full engagement in, 37–38
  literature on, 13
  preparation for, 41–46
  role of purpose in, 1–3, 38–40
  theories of (*see* theoretical
    foundations)
  thriving and, 14–15
  timing in, 27
adaptive leadership process, 32–36
  interpretation, 33–35
  interventions, 35–36
  observation, 32–33

adaptive organizations, 101–108
  adaptability survey, 108
  balcony perspective of, 107
  continuous learning in, 105–108
  independent judgment in, 103–104
  open communication in, 102–103,
    106–107
  practice field actions for, 107–108
  professional development in,
    104–105
  shared responsibilities in, 103
  succession planning in, 105, 171
Against All Enemies (Clarke), 200
allies (alliances)
  finding allies, 127, 136–138, 147
  generating, 98
  hidden alliances, 92, 97–100
  in organizational system, 209
  preparing allies for failure, 259
ambiguity, tolerance for, 169, 206
ambition, 242–244
analysis paralysis, 175
ancestor loyalties, 187, 189, 250–251
antiquated protocols, 53
Arafat, Yasser, 248
Aristotle, 269
articulation of purpose.
    See purpose(s)
aspirations, 242–244
assumptions
  reality testing, 229
  reframing truths as, 253–254
AT&T, 52
attention
  diversion of, 84, 85, 214
  focusing through silence, 267
  practice field actions for, 269
  use of vocal qualities and, 272–273
audience
  allowing for silence, 267–268
  as authority, 268
  balcony perspective of, 275
  holding through emotion, 270–271
  listening, 266–267
  openness to, 264–269
  practice field actions for, 275
  reading emotions of, 264

auditioning ideas, 122
authority
    authorizers' expectations and,
        24–26
    conflicting authorizations, 216–217
    core responsibilities of role, 28
    dependence on, 73–74
    exceeding, in experimentation,
        282–284
    formal versus informal, 25
    identifying scope of, 215–220
    leadership distinguished from,
        23–28
    level of, in interventions, 35
    listening and, 268
    as models of behavior, 167
    reality testing, 75
    reinforcement of defaults, 118
    wide experience of, 168
authority figures
    dispensable, 169–170
    effective use of voice, 272–273
    negative experiences with, 218, 219
authorization chart, 219
authorizers
    as architects of status quo, 282–283
    expectations of, 24–26
    formal and informal, 215
    mapping (balcony perspective),
        218–219
authorizing environment, 216, 217–218
automobile industry, 18–19
avoidance
    of decision making, 81
    handling, 130–131
    work avoidance, 30, 31, 75, 84–87

balanced portfolio, 295
"balcony person," role of, 33
balcony perspective of, 7–8, 49
bandwidth
    broadening, 179, 205–208
    tolerances and, 206–208
behavior(s)
    conversation-stopping, 157
    driven by values, 91–92

individual, systems perspective of,
    119–120
purpose-behavior gap, 223
reinforcement of, 51
triggering and, 200–201
unfamiliar, displaying, 285
values-behavior gap, 78–80
values driving behavior, 91–92
behavior modeling
    accountability, 192
    by authorities, 167
    "naming your piece of the mess,"
        286
    optimism and realism, 297
beliefs, 45–46
benchmarks, 260
big picture, 143
biological adaptations, 15
Blue Angels, 255
body language, observing, 142
broken system, illusion of, 17–19
Bronznick, Shifra, 13
Brudnoy, David, 43
burnout, 202–203, 232
Bush, George W., 200, 245, 273

cadence, in speaking musically, 271
Carlzon, Jan, 144
Caro, Robert, 234
casualties, responsibility for,
    144–145, 148
change
    adaptive (see adaptive change)
    consequences to external
        environment, 143
    evolutionary change, 13–14, 123
    framing as experiment, 277
    personal responsibility for
        casualties of, 144–145, 148
    politics of, 94–96
    resistance to, 96–97, 141,
        265–266, 283
Chavez, César, 93
Clarke, Richard, 200
Clinton, Hillary Rodham, 245
Clinton, William Jefferson, 245

coaching, support for, 107
collaboration, barriers to, 94
colleagues, loyalties to, 187
comfort zones
    collective and individual, 29
    designing interventions and, 36
    expanding tolerances and, 206
    giving work back and, 163
    speaking from the heart and, 270
commitments
    competing, as archetype, 80–82
    to learning, 105–108
communication. *See also* audience;
        language
    adapting style of, 154–155
    open, in adaptive organizations,
        102–103, 106–107
    in refashioning loyalties, 249–250
    speaking from the heart, 269–275
community, 187, 291
Compaq, 162
compassion
    in handling opposition, 141
    listening with, 266–267
    patience-building and, 261–262
compensation system structure, 55,
        103, 168
complexity of values, 92
compromise, 239–242
confidants, 289, 290
conflict(s)
    as aspect of adaptive challenge,
        114, 115
    of beliefs, making choices and,
        45–46
    capacity to tolerate, 150, 154
    conflicting authorizations,
        216–217
    nature of, stakeholders and, 159
    personal tuning and, 197
    of purposes, 226–227
    reality testing, 75
    reduction of, interpretations
        and, 121
    responses to, 150–151
    surfacing value conflicts, 149–150

conflict orchestration, 149–164
    balcony perspective of, 161, 164
    creating holding environment for,
        155–158, 163
    practice field actions for, 161, 164
    regulating heat, 159–161, 163
    responses to conflict, 150–151
    selecting participants, 158–159
    steps in, 152–153
    surfacing value conflicts, 149–150
connection to purposes.
        See purpose(s)
conservation, 23
constraints
    on courage to lead, 247
    defaults as, 64
    intuitions as, 181–182
    loyalties as, 189–190, 192
    personal tuning as, 198
    purpose and, 244–246
content of silence, 267–268
continuous learning, 105–108
conversation-stopping behaviors, 157
core values, 78–79, 251
corporate life, role of purpose in,
        39–40
corrective action, in tough
        decisions, 257
courage. *See also* engagement,
        courage for
    in adaptive leadership, 37, 38
    in orchestrating conflict, 153
    rewarding, 174
Creative Destruction (Foster and
        Kaplan), 13
creativity, 123
cross-functional problem solving, 103
Cuban Missile Crisis, 104
cultural norms. *See also* adaptive
        culture, building; organizational
        culture
    acknowledging disequilibrium,
        166–168
    balcony view of, 59, 60, 61, 63
    beginnings of, 50–51
    establishing new processes, 157–158

importance of, 14
  practice field actions for, 59, 60,
    62, 63
  in system diagnosis, 57–63
culture of learning, 287–288
cycle of failure, 71–73

damage to others, in interventions, 234
"dance floor," 7–8
data gathering on stakeholders,
    91–92, 100
De Carolis, Gary, 13
decision making
  avoidance of, 81
  meetings for, 62
  tough choices (*see* difficult
    decisions)
default(s), 54
  balcony perspective of, 66
  beginnings of, 50–51
  individual, understanding, 178–179
  practice field actions for, 66–67
  recognizing, in system
    diagnosis, 63–67
  reinforced by authority, 118
default interpretations
  functions of, 113–114
  reframing, 118–120
dependence on authority, 73–74
deployment, 231–232
  connection to purpose
    and, 233–246
  engaging courageously, 247–262
  experimentation in, 277–288
  inspiring others, 263–275
  thriving, 289–297
desired outcomes, 91
diagnosis, 47–48
  of adaptive challenge (*see* adaptive
    challenge diagnosis)
  of authorizing environment,
    217–218
  importance of, 7
  of meaning, steps in, 224–225
  of political landscape, 89–100

process of, 6–7
  resisting pressure for action, 44–45
  self-diagnosis, 184
  of strengths and weaknesses, 205
  of system (*see* system diagnosis)
diagnosis grid, 6
diagnostic framework for adaptive
    challenge, 74–76
diagnostic mind-set, 184–185
difficult decisions
  acknowledging stakeholder
    sacrifices, 141–142, 174
  balcony perspective of, 257
  characteristics of, 256
  conflict of purposes and, 227
  embracing, 255–258
  practice field actions for, 258
  responsibility for, 45–46
direction, as responsibility of
    authority, 28
disequilibrium
  acknowledging, 146, 166–168
  balcony perspective of, 207–208
  framing experiments in, 279–280
  modeling behavior for, 167
  naming one's contribution
    to, 286–287
  navigating, 28–31
  practice field actions for, 208
  productive zone of, 29–31
  protecting dissenters during, 167–168
  between purpose and behavior, 223
  ripeness of issue and, 126–127
  temperature regulation and,
    159–161, 163
displacement of responsibility
  through flattery, 214
  in work avoidance, 84, 85–86
dissent
  accepting arguments, 154
  protecting, 145–146, 148
dissenters, protecting, 167–168
distraction, in avoiding
    interventions, 131
distress caused by adaptive
    processes, 29

distributed leadership, 169–170
diversion of attention, 84, 85, 214
diversity, role in organizational
    adaptation, 15–16
Dubinsky, David, 93
Dukakis, Michael, 57
dysfunctional organization,
    myth of, 17–19

early wins, 135
Edison, Thomas, 36–37
effective interventions, 125–132
    analyzing factions, 130
    balcony perspective of, 126
    flexibility in, 125
    manager's role in, 128
    practice field actions for, 132
    resistance to, 130–131
    restraint in, 129–130
    ripeness of issue and, 126–127
    thoughtful framing in, 128–129
elements of adaptive challenge,
    70–76
    cycle of failure, 71–73
    dependence on authority, 73–74
    diagnostic framework and, 74–76
    human elements, 69–70
    identifying, 114, 115
"elephant in the room."
    See disequilibrium
emotions
    of audience, reading, 264
    holding audience through, 270–271
    speaking from the heart, 269–270
    use of language and, 273, 274
empathy. See compassion
engagement, courage for, 247–262.
    See also courage
    building resilience, 260–262
    periods of incompetence, 252–255
    permission to fail, 258–260
    refashioning loyalties, 247–251
    tough decisions, 255–258
environment. See external
    environment

espoused values, violation of,
    234–235
ethical issues, 233–236
evolutionary change, 13–14, 123
examples, sources of, 10
exclusion, in holding
    environment, 159
expectations
    of authorizers, 24–26
    carrying other people's water
        and, 202
    challenging, in adaptive leadership,
        26–27
    conflicting, of roles, 216
    managing according to situation,
        279
    of others, determining, 249
    responsibility for adaptive change
        and, 162–163
experimental mind-set
    importance to adaptive leadership,
        36–37
    permission to fail and, 258–259
    practicing, 278
    risk taking and, 280–282
    of senior authorities, 278–279
experimentation, 277–288
    balcony perspective of, 280,
        283–284, 286, 287
    exceeding authority in, 282–284
    framing, in disequilibrium, 279–280
    honored in adaptive culture,
        172–173, 175
    low-risk, 121–122, 172–173
    naming "your piece of the mess,"
        286–287
    in orchestrating conflict, 153
    parallel experiments, 175
    practice field actions for, 281–282,
        284, 285, 287, 288
    risk taking and, 280–282
    role in organizational adaptation, 15
    running multiple experiments
        simultaneously, 277–278
    small experiments, 259
    turning up heat, 284–285

external environment
  acquiring information from, 117
  authorizing environment,
      216, 217–218
  consequences of change to, 143
  influence on "personal tuning,"
      195, 197
  purposes and, 222
  unproductive interpretations
      and, 116–117
  See also holding environment
external loyalties of stakeholders,
      93–96

factions
  analyzing, in effective
      interventions, 130
  antagonistic, interacting with, 154
  awareness of subfactions, 137
  within circle of loyalties, 187,
      188, 190
  desired outcomes of, 52–53
  interests of, interpretations and, 121
  practice field actions for, 210
  tuning of, 198
  value of, 209–210
failure
  adaptive failures, 18–19
  balcony perspective of, 259
  cycle of failure, 71–73
  permission to fail, 258–260
  practice field actions for, 259–260
fear of loss, 96–97, 141, 265–266
"fight or flight" response to
      conflict, 150
Fiorina, Carly, 162
Fitzgerald, F. Scott, 37
folklore, 57, 58–59
Ford, Gerald, 142
formal authority, 25
  insufficiency of, 52
  openness to ideas and, 145, 146
  reliance on, as response to conflict,
      150–151
  scope of, 215

Foster, Richard, 13
framing. *See also* reframing
  change as experiment, 277
  in designing interventions, 128–129,
      279–280
  framework for adaptive challenge,
      74–76
Franklin, Benjamin, 36–37
Freud, Sigmund, 246
frontline employees, learning from, 106
full engagement. *See also* engagement,
      courage for
  in adaptive leadership, 37–38

Gandhi, Mohandas K., 44
Gardner, John, 52
GE Capital, 172
General Electric Corporation (GE),
      104, 105, 172
Gettysburg Address, 79
Giuliani, Rudolph, 266, 271
globalization, 21–22
Goffin, Stacie, 13
Goldenhar, Didi, 13
Gore, Al, 126
Grashow, Alexander, 93, 94–95, 187–188,
      200, 238, 240, 258, 260–261
Great Depression, 85
Greenpeace, 126
ground rules for conflict, 152
group(s)
  finding allies in large groups,
      136–138
  level of cohesion in, 160
  loyalty groups, 188, 190, 191, 210
  subgroup values, 121
group norms, 57, 61–62
Grove, Andy, 102
guilt, about ambition, 243–244

harmony, role of conflict in, 151
health, importance of, 292–293, 295
Heifetz, Ronald, 45, 184, 242–243, 250,
      258, 296

Heifetz, Sousan, 296
Heschel, (Rabbi) Abraham
    Joshua, 269
Hewlett-Packard (HP), 162
hidden alliances, 92, 97–100
hidden perspectives, 82–84, 157
higher (orienting) purpose, 221, 223
holding environment
    inclusion or exclusion in, 158–159
    in orchestrating conflict,
        155–158, 163
    personal, creating, 292–295
    sanctuaries, 293–294
House (TV program), 47
*How the Way We Talk Can Change
    the Way We Work* (Kegan and
    Lahey), 192
HP (Hewlett-Packard), 162
"human diorama" of loyalties, 191
human needs, managing, 202
hungers
    personal tuning and, 201–202
    satisfying in private life, 290–291
Hurricane Katrina, 232
Hussein, Saddam, 138, 139, 245

ideas
    auditioning, 122
    openness to, 145, 146
identity
    labeling and, 184
    self-definition and, 185
IEC (Israel Emergency Campaign), 65
"I have a dream" speech (King), 79
impatience, dangers of, 261–262
implicit roles, 210–211
improvisational expertise, 2–3
impulsivity, 199–200
inaction, 110–111, 150
inclusion, in holding environment,
    158–159
incompetence, leaning into
    fostering culture of learning,
        287–288
    learning opportunities, 252–253

periods of incompetence, 252–255
    truths as assumptions, 253–254
independent judgment, 103–104,
    169–170
individual, as multiple selves, 182–186
individual, as system, 177–179, 181–186
    articulation of purpose, 221–230
    bandwidth, 179, 205–208
    loyalties, 179, 187–194
    multiple selves, 182–186
    personal tuning, 179, 195–204
    roles, 209–220
    systems perspective of behavior,
        119–120
    understanding individual defaults,
        178–179
individual agendas, managing, 159
individual comfort zone, 29
individualized training, 104–105,
    170–171
informal authority, 25
    expanding, 133–136, 216–218
    finding, in diagnosing adaptive
        challenge, 76–77
    lack of, 134
    scope of, 215–216
information sharing, 62–63, 168
"inform the gut" tactic, 258
inspiring others, 263–275
    finding unique voice, 263–264
    openness to audience and, 264–269
    speaking from the heart, 269–276
Intel, 102
interests, 121, 135
internal contradictions, 75
interpretation(s), 113–123
    in adaptive leadership process,
        33–35
    auditioning ideas, 122
    default, 113–114, 118–120
    effects of loyalties on, 248
    multiple, generating, 120–123
    shifts in, adaptive challenge and,
        114–116
    technical, gravitation toward,
        116–118

interventions
  in adaptive leadership process,
    35–36
  avoiding through distraction, 131
  damaging to others, 234
  effective (*see* effective
    interventions)
  framing, in state of emergency,
    279–280
  mobilizing adaptive work, 109–111
intuitions, as constraint, 181–182
Iraq War, 138–140
isolation, dangers of, 41–42
Israel Emergency Campaign (IEC), 65

"job shadowing" 169
Jones, Reginald, 105
judgment, listening without, 266–267

Kaplan, Sarah, 13
Kegan, Robert, 192
Kennedy, John F., 104
King, Martin Luther, Jr., 44, 79, 128,
  241, 274
Knight, Bobby, 205

labeling, 184
Lahey, Lisa Laskow, 192
Lakefield, Bruce, 286
language
  clear communication, 273–275
  meaning and, 273, 274
  nonverbal cues, 142, 267
  observing body language, 142
  shared, in leading change, 9
  value-laden, 273
large groups, finding allies in, 136–138
Laurie, Donald L., 13
Lawrence, Jeff, 17, 78–80
leadership
  adaptive (*see* adaptive leadership)
  core practices in, 6
  distinguishing from authority,
    23–28

distributed leadership, 169–170
  ethics of, 233–236
  as improvisational art, 277
  "leader" label, 25–26
  life as leadership laboratory, 42–44
  peer leadership consulting, 153
Leadership Can Be Taught (Parks), 13
leadership development, 170–171
leadership mantra, 239
Leadership on the Line (Heifetz and
  Linsky), 2, 9, 13, 202
Leadership Without Easy Answers
  (Heifetz), 9, 13, 19, 159
learning
  commitment to, 105–108
  continuous, in adaptive
    organizations, 105–108
  fostering culture of learning,
    287–288
  from frontline employees, 106
  metaphors in, 253
  from mistakes, 106, 174
learning opportunities
  balcony perspective of, 254–255
  practice field actions for, 255
  taking advantage of, 252–253
Leveling the Playing Field (Bronznick,
  Goldenhar, and Linsky), 13
level of engagement, 91
life (everyday life)
  connecting sense of purpose to,
    236–239
  as leadership laboratory, 42–44
  satisfying hungers in, 290–291
Life Is Not a Rehearsal (Brudnoy), 43
Lincoln, Abraham, 79, 234
Linsky, Marty, 13, 45, 51, 57, 90, 127, 141,
  182, 189–190, 226, 227, 234, 242,
  247, 250, 252, 258, 281–282
Linsky, Max, 182, 226
loss(es)
  fear of, resistance to change and,
    96–97, 141, 265–266
  managing, in orchestrating conflict,
    152–153
  resistance to, 22–23

loss(es) *(continued)*
   risk of (*see* risk of loss)
   role in adaptive change, 16
loyalty(ies)
   of allies, understanding, 137
   ancestor loyalties, 187, 189, 250–251
   balcony perspective of, 182, 185
   beliefs shaped by, 45–46
   as constraints or barriers, 94,
      189–190, 192
   effects on interpretations, 248
   factions within, 187, 188, 190
   identifying, 179, 187–194
   prioritizing, 189–191
   refashioning (*see* refashioning
      loyalties)
   of stakeholders, 92, 93–96
   unspeakable, naming, 191–194
loyalty groups, 188, 190, 191, 210

Mahoney, Miles, 134, 135
Mandela, Nelson, 44
"Man in the Arena" speech
   (T. Roosevelt), 237
manipulation by others
   personal attacks, 213–214
   role of personal tuning in,
      197–198, 199
   self-definition and, 183
marginalization, risk of, 246
martyrdom, avoiding, 245
Matsushita, Konosuke, 243
Matsushita Electric Industrial
   Company, Ltd., 243
McCain, John, 114
meaning
   language selection and, 273, 274
   need for, 295
   steps in diagnosis of, 224–225
   stories used in creating,
      228–230, 254
means-end issue, 235
meetings
   in adaptive organizations, 102
   experimenting with, 281

   managing agendas for, 146
   meeting protocols, 57, 62–63
   off-site (retreats), 106, 156–158
Menuhin, Yehudi, 44
mergers and acquisitions, 21, 22, 166
Merrill Lynch, 55
metaphors
   in learning, 253
   pressure cooker, 29–30, 155
   vegetable stew, 94–95
micro-interactions, 296
Microsoft corporation, 61
Middle East conflict
   default responses, 65
   external loyalties and, 93
   Iraq War, 138–140
   peace negotiation process, 248
mistakes, 106, 174, 199
mixed problems, 19–20
mobilizing system for adaptive work,
   109–111
   acting politically, 133–148
   building adaptive culture, 165–175
   designing interventions, 125–132
   generating interpretations, 113–123
   orchestrating conflict, 149–164
Moments of Truth (Carlzon), 144
momentum, slowing, 110–111
Moses (biblical), 263
Moses, Robert, 217, 234, 235
Mother Teresa of Calcutta, 44
Mubarak, Hosni, 248
multiple experiments,
   simultaneous, 277–278
multiple intelligences, 38
multiple roles. *See* roles
multiple selves, 182–186
Muskie, Edmund, 213

negotiating purposes, 239–242
New York Times, 266
Nixon, Richard, 213
nonemergency situations, 280
nonverbal cues, 142, 267
not-for-profit sector, 53

Obama, Barack, 2, 114, 278
objective reality, in stories, 229
observation, 32–33
    in auditioning ideas, 122
    body language and nonverbal
        cues, 142
    at off-site retreats, 158
off-site meetings (retreats), 106,
    156–158
open communication, 102–103,
    106–107
opportunities
    for contributing, 297
    for learning (*see* learning
        opportunities)
    seeing and grasping, 42–44
opposition
    compassion in handling, 141
    interaction with hostile
        factions, 154
    staying connected to, 138–142, 147
    translating purposes and, 240–241
    unexpected, managing, 138–139
optimism, realism and, 296–297
order (stability), 28
organizational culture, 54. *See also*
        adaptive culture, building;
        cultural norms
    adaptability and, 60, 61, 62–63
    folklore, 58–59
    fostering culture of learning,
        287–288
    group norms, 57, 61–62
    meeting protocols, 62–63
    rituals, 57, 60
organizational system, 209, 218
orienting (higher) purpose, 221, 223
Outward Bound, 281

Panasonic, 243
Parks, Rosa, 274
Parks, Sharon Daloz, 13
partners, finding, 41–42
Pascal, Blaise, 239
past, domination of present, 249

patience, in building resilience,
    261–262
patterns, interpreting, 34
Paulson, Henry, 278–279
peer leadership consulting, 153
personal attack, 213–214
personalization of problems, 8
personal responsibility
    for casualties of change,
        144–145, 148
    for difficult choices, 45–46
personal support network,
        289–292, 295
    community anchors, 291
    confidants, 289, 290
    hungers, satisfying, 290–291
personal tuning, 179, 195–204
    balcony perspective of,
        200–201, 203
    carrying other people's water,
        202–204
    example of, 196
    hungers and, 201–202
    influences on, 195–200
    practice field actions for,
        201, 204
    triggers and, 200–201
perspectives
    articulating, in orchestrating
        conflict, 152
    hidden, 82–84, 157
    systemic, of individual behavior,
        119–120
physical reminders of purpose, 237
pilot projects, 135, 259, 280
Plato, 45
political landscape, 89–100.
        See also acting politically
    balcony perspective of, 99
    hidden alliances, 97–100
    losses at risk, 96–97
    loyalties, 93–96
    practice field actions for, 99–100
    pressure in, 89–90
    values driving behavior, 91–92
politics of change, 94–96

power and influence of
    stakeholders, 91
practices, in leading adaptive
    change, 10
preparation
    for adaptive change, 94–95
    for adaptive leadership, 41–46
    of allies, for failure, 259
    for off-site retreats, 157
    in orchestrating conflict, 152
pressure
    political, 89–90
    on senior authorities, 143, 144
    to silence "troublemakers," 168
"pressure cooker"
    disequilibrium as, 29–30
    as holding environment, 155
pressure for action
    quick solutions, 7–8
    resisting, 44–45
    value of diagnosis and, 47–48
priorities
    clarifying, 224
    espoused versus actual, 191
    prioritizing loyalties, 189–191
    prioritizing purposes, 225–228
private sector, 53
problems
    balcony perspective of, 70–71, 192
    cross-functional problem
        solving, 103
    difficulty in describing, 71
    identifying "your piece of the mess,"
        191–192
    mixed, 19–20
    personalization of, 8
    technical, versus adaptive
        challenges, 19–23, 118
problem-solving defaults. See defaults
productive zone of disequilibrium,
    29–31
product sales model, 21–22
professional development, 104–105
professional services firms, 79
protection, as responsibility of
    authority, 28

purpose(s)
    abstract, 223, 224
    articulation of, 221–230
    avoiding traps, 244–246
    conflicting, 226–227
    connecting with, 128–129, 233–246
    ethics of leadership and, 233–236
    higher (orienting) purpose, 221, 223
    integrating ambition and aspiration,
        242–244
    keeping alive, 236–239
    negotiating, 239–242
    prioritizing, 225–228
    role in adaptive leadership, 38–40
    sense of purpose, 223–224, 236–239
    staying focused on, 222
    stories and, 228–230
    translating for others, 240–241

questions
    in establishing holding
        environment, 158–159
    in naming defaults, 119–120
    reflective, 171–172
    use in interpreting, 116
    what-if questions, 120

Rabin, Yitzhak, 248
Ready or Not (Goffin and
    Washington), 13
realism, optimism and, 296–297
reality testing
    of assumptions in stories, 229
    in designing effective
        interventions, 126
    in diagnosing adaptive challenge,
        74–75
    work avoidance and, 84–85
Real Leadership (Williams), 13
The Real Work of Leaders (Laurie), 13
refashioning loyalties, 247–251
    ancestor loyalties, 250–251
    communicating with others,
        249–250

expectations of others, 249
  focus on core principles, 251
  staying in present, 249
  word-deed gaps and, 248–249
reflection
  encouraging, 105–108, 171–175
  in making interpretations, 34
  in orchestrating conflict, 152–153
  reflective questions, 171–172
  sanctuaries and, 293–294
  self-discipline and, 297
reframing. *See also* framing
  of default interpretations,
    118–120
  in stories, 253–254
  truths, reframing as assumptions,
    253–254
relationship-based model, 21–22
relationships, 24, 135
relentlessness, 261
resilience building, 260–262, 295
resistance
  to action, diagnosis and, 44–45
  to change, 96–97, 141, 265–266, 283
  to effective interventions, 130–131
  to loss, 22–23
resources, 35, 168
responsibility(ies)
  for adaptive change, 161–164
  in adaptive culture, 168–169
  of authority, 28
  displacement of, 84, 85–86, 214
  personal responsibility, 45–46,
    144–145, 148
  shared responsibility, 103, 168–169
restraint, 122, 129–130
retreats, off-site, 106, 156–158
rewards, 168, 174
Richardson, Elliot, 90
ripeness of issue, 121, 126–127
risk aversion, 173
risk of loss
  in adaptive change, 96–97
  low-risk experimentation, 121–122,
    172–173
  making tough decisions, 257

multiple interpretations and, 121
  of stakeholders, 92
risk taking
  experimental mind-set and,
    280–282
  need for risk takers, 172
  rewarding, 174
  signaling approval of, 173–174
rituals
  of organizational culture, 57, 60
  refashioning ancestor loyalties,
    250–251
roles, 209–220
  "balcony person" role, 33
  balcony perspective of, 210, 214
  expanding, effectiveness and,
    211–212
  implicit, 210–211
  implicit roles, 210–215
  informal authority in, 216–217
  of manager in effective
    interventions, 128
  personal attack and, 213–214
  practice field actions for, 215
  scope of authority and, 215–220
  self-definition and, 212–213
  "troublemaker" role, 284–285
Roosevelt, Franklin D., 277–278
Roosevelt, Theodore, 237
Rosenblatt, Roger, 257
Rules for Aging (Rosenblatt), 257
Rumi, 221
Rumsfeld, Donald, 47
Rushing, Byron, 211
Russell, Bill, 33

sabbaticals, 106
sabotage, preempting, 144
Sadat, Anwar, 248
sanctuaries, 293–294
SAS (Scandinavian) Airlines, 143, 144
scapegoating, 85, 86
*Second Wind: The Memoirs of an
  Opinionated Man* (Russell), 33
sectors (industries), 53

self-care, 292–293
self-definition
  individual identity and, 185
  multiple selves, 183
  roles and, 212–213
self-diagnosis, 184
self-discipline, for reflection, 297
self-image, damage to, 234–235
self-renewal, 295–297
  balanced portfolio and, 295
  micro-interactions, 296
  realism and optimism, 296–297
  sanctuaries and, 294
self-righteousness, avoiding, 245
senior authorities
  managing, 142–144, 147
  preparing for off-site retreats, 157
  using experimental mind-set,
    278–279
sense of purpose
  articulation of, 223–224
  connecting to everyday life,
    236–239
sensitive issues, 102–103
Shakespeare, William, 295
shared language, 9
shared responsibility, 103, 168–169
Shinseki, Eric (Gen.), 47
short-term goals, 260
Sierra Club, 126
silence
  as intervention, 129
  responding to, 268–269
  tolerance of, 267–268
single-mindedness, avoiding, 244–245
sit down technique, 164
skill, in adaptive leadership, 37–38
social contract, 24
social system, individual and, 183
Socrates, 45
speaking from the heart, 269–276
  holding through emotion, 270–271
  making each word count, 273–275
  speaking musically, 271–273
stakeholders

acknowledging sacrifices of,
  141–142, 174
analyzing, 91–92, 100
external loyalties of, 92, 93–96
finding allies among, 137
gathering data on, 91–92, 100
nature of conflict and, 159
potential opponents, 140
preparing for adaptive change,
  94–95
state of emergency, 279–280
status quo
  investment in, 282–283
  tenacity of, 49–54
stories
  amending, 244
  backtracking, 230
  balcony perspective of, 229–230
  constructing, 224–225
  in creating meaning, 228–230, 254
  folklore, 57, 58–59
  practice field actions for, 230
  reframing in, 253–254
strategic planning, 107, 126–127
strategy(ies)
  for acting politically, 147–148
  reality testing, 75
  unintended consequences of, 52
stress, self-care for, 292–293
structures, formal, 54
  beginnings of, 50–51
  in system diagnosis, 54–56
subjectivity, in stories, 229
subsystems, 54, 99
subtext, listening for, 264–266
success, definitions of, 50–51, 259
succession planning, 105, 171
support
  for coaching, 107
  personal support network,
    289–292, 295
  for unconnected interests, 135
system(s)
  allies in, 209
  illusion of broken system, 17–19

individual as (*see* individual, as system)

within larger systems, 53

mobilizing (*see* mobilizing system for adaptive work)

organizational system, 209, 218

social system, 183

subsystems, 54, 99

tenacity of, 49–51

system diagnosis, 47–48

adaptive challenge (*see* adaptive challenge diagnosis)

cultural norms, 57–63

defaults, 63–67

political landscape in, 89–100

qualities of adaptive organizations, 101–108

structures, 54–56

tenacity of status quo and, 49–54

systemic issues, 114, 115

systems perspective

individual as system (*see* individual, as system)

of individual behavior, 119–120

talent management, 66

technical challenges

disequilibrium of, 30–31

distinguishing from adaptive challenges, 19–23, 118

technical elements of problems, 70–76

technical interpretations, 116–118

technical solutions, 71–73

techniques for adaptive change

broadening bandwidth, 205–208

sit down technique, 164

"temperature" regulation

in conflict orchestration, 159–161, 163

in experimentation, 284–285

Mother Teresa, 44

terrorist attacks of 9/11, 2, 266, 271

theoretical foundations, 13–40

activities in process, 32–36

broken system illusion, 17–19

experimental mind-set, 36–37

full engagement, 37–38

leadership versus authority, 23–28

productive zone of disequilibrium, 28–31

role of purpose, 38–40

technical problems versus adaptive challenges, 19–23, 118

thinking politically, 133

thoughtful framing, 128–129

thriving, 289–297

adaptive leadership and, 14–15

balcony perspective of, 291–292, 293, 294

personal holding environment, 292–295

personal support network, 289–292, 295

practice field actions for, 292, 294–295

self-renewal, 295–297

time, allocation of, 221–222

time frames for adaptive change, 16–17

timing, in adaptive leadership, 27

tolerance

for ambiguity, 169, 206

broadening bandwidth and, 206–208

for conflict, 150, 154

for disequilibrium, 207–208

for silence, 267–268

Toyota Motor Corporation, 103, 166

training and development, individualized, 104–105, 170–171

Transforming Church: Bringing Out the Good to Get to Great (Ford), 13

traps, purposes as, 244–246

triggers, 200–201

"troublemakers"

protecting, 167–168

taking on role of, 284–285

truths, reframing as assumptions, 253–254

two-by-two diagnosis grid, 6

unproductive interpretation, 116, 117
unspeakable issues, 82–84
unspeakable loyalties, 191–194
U.S. Navy Blue Angels, 255
US Airways, 286

value(s)
    in adaptive leadership, 3
    behavior driven by, 91–92
    communicating, 269
    connecting with, 128–129
    core values, 78–79, 251
    courage and, 38
    damage to, 234–235
    reality testing, 75
    stakeholder values, data on,
        91–92, 100
    of subgroups, 121
value conflicts, surfacing, 149–150
value-laden language, 273
values-behavior gap, 78–80
vegetable stew metaphor, 94–95
Veterans of Foreign Wars
    (VFW), 142

A View from the Balcony
    (De Carolis), 13
voice
    speaking musically, 271–273
    unique, finding and using, 263–264
vulnerability
    of experimenters, 283
    thriving and, 290, 291

Washington, Valora, 13
Welch, Jack, 104, 105, 172, 263
Williams, Dean, 13
win-win solutions, 81
Wooden, John, 205
words-action gaps, 248–249
work avoidance, 84–87
    adaptive challenges and, 30, 31
    reality testing, 75

"your piece of the mess"
    identifying, 191–192
    naming, in experimentation,
        286–287

| ABOUT THE AUTHORS |

Ronald Heifetz is the King Hussein bin Talal Senior Lecturer in Public Leadership and Founding Director of the Center for Public Leadership at Harvard Kennedy School. Recognized for his seminal work on both the practice and teaching of leadership, his research focuses on building adaptive capacity in societies and organizations. He lectures and consults in business, government, and nonprofit sectors around the world.

Heifetz's work is the subject of many articles and the book by Sharon Daloz Parks, *Leadership Can Be Taught.* His groundbreaking book, *Leadership Without Easy Answers,* has been reprinted thirteen times and translated into many languages, and his courses on leadership have been among the most popular at Harvard for twenty-five years.

A graduate of Columbia University, Harvard Medical School, and Harvard Kennedy School, Heifetz is also a physician and cellist; he was privileged to study with Russian virtuoso, Gregor Piatigorsky. His children, David and Ariana, attend Carleton College.

Alexander Grashow came to Cambridge Leadership Associates from The Synergos Institute, where he was the cofounder and director of the Bridging Leadership Program, which designed partnerships in Africa, Asia, Latin America, and the United States for collaborations across sectors. In this capacity, he developed training, research, and communities of practice among international businesses, business schools, and national nonprofits. He has been on the executive education faculty at the Wagner School at New York University and the Harvard Kennedy School.

A graduate of Wesleyan University, where he studied economics and fine arts, and a former Coro Fellow, Alexander is also a serious Japanese printmaker. He cofounded the US/Africa Children's Fellowship, an international nonprofit that ships used school supplies from

American schools to partner schools in Africa and was featured in Bill Clinton's book, *Giving*. Alexander lives with his wife Yasuko and their children, Sakura and Shōgo in Brooklyn, NY, and spends significant time in Japan.

Marty Linsky has been on the Harvard Kennedy School faculty for over twenty-five years, except for three years as Chief Secretary to then-Massachusetts governor Bill Weld. He has been chair of several of Harvard's leadership and management executive programs, here and abroad. Before Harvard, Marty practiced, in both senses of the word, as a politician (Massachusetts state legislator), lawyer (very briefly), and journalist (reporter, editor, and editorial page writer).

Marty is a graduate of Williams College and Harvard Law School. He is married and the father of three children. For relaxation he runs (nine marathons, but no more) and works out daily, enjoys good beer and all Mexican food (a reward for the exercise), and collects baseball cards (25,000 of them). He and his wife, Lynn Staley, live in New York City and hope to spend more time in their dotage in Italy, where they have built a house close to Rome.

Heifetz, Grashow, and Linsky are colleagues and partners at Cambridge Leadership Associates (CLA), www.cambridge-leadership.com, a global leadership development practice. Heifetz and Linsky founded CLA and coauthored the bestselling *Leadership on the Line: Staying Alive through the Dangers of Leading*; Grashow is CLA's Managing Director.

TAKE IT
TO THE NEXT LEVEL

NOW THAT YOU'VE READ *The Practice of Adaptive Leadership,* **it is time to put these ideas into action. To help you get started, Ron Heifetz, Marty Linsky, and Alexander Grashow have created online resources that build on the practices in this book.**

- Take part in webinars that will teach you best practices and emerging techniques.

- Hear directly from the authors—watch their videos and read their blog.

- Measure your adaptive capacity with the Adaptive Leadership Profile survey.

- Sign up for the Leading Adaptively newsletter, filled with tactics from the front lines.

- Gain access to exclusive content just for readers of *The Practice of Adaptive Leadership.*

TO UNLOCK ALL THE POSSIBILITIES, VISIT
www.cambridge-leadership.com

HARVARD **BUSINESS**
Press